Social Decision Making/Social Problem Solving

A Curriculum for Academic, Social, and Emotional Learning

Maurice J. Elias

Linda Bruene Butler

with

Erin M. Bruno

Maureen Reilly Papke

Teresa Farley Shapiro

GRADES 4-5

Research Press • 2612 North Mattis Avenue, Champaign, Illinois 61822
(800) 519-2707 • www.researchpress.com

Composition by Jeff Helgesen
Cover design by Linda Brown, Positive I.D. Graphic Design, Inc.
Printed by Malloy

ISBN 0-87822-513-7
Library of Congress Control Number 2004097765

Contents

Tables

Foreword

Writing this foreword is an honor. I have known Maurice Elias since 1979, when we were both young psychologists who had just moved from Connecticut to New Jersey. Maurice was just joining the faculty at Rutgers University, and I had just started as an educator-clinician at the mental health center of the University of Medicine and Dentistry of New Jersey (UMDNJ). We were two young men from two different institutions with two different missions, but our interests and skills were complementary. Into the mix came Tom Schuyler, a seasoned principal with the Middlesex, New Jersey, Public Schools, another institution with another mission. The synergy worked. The three of us conceived and developed the wonderful project upon which the curriculum in this two-book sequence is based.

I have worked with Linda Bruene Butler since 1980. She relocated from Illinois and soon joined me at the mental health center at UMDNJ to devise approaches to help professionals learn to teach social decision making to children. For many years, we collaborated with a wonderful group of colleagues to provide professional development opportunities for educators across our state and across the country.

In August 2000, I accepted an exciting faculty position at the Robert Wood Johnson Medical School, where I teach behavioral science to family physicians. One of the exciting aspects of my present work is passing on the skills of social decision making to physicians in training. Maurice and Linda, at Rutgers and UMDNJ, respectively, have continued to devote their careers to helping children, their parents, and their teachers develop the techniques to create psychologically healthy lives. It is rare in my experience that two professionals can not only stay the course of a particular content area over the long term but are still energetically inventive in moving the field further. These two books are testimony to Maurice's and Linda's long-term commitment to helping children.

One of the reasons that we need a program like the one detailed in this social decision making and social problem solving program is that parents and guardians have less help than they did before from the village of neighbors and local relatives to pass on the wisdom and culture. As a child in the 1950s and 1960s, I spent most of my time playing outside with other kids. As I remember it, it seemed that there were always some adults around, keeping an eye on things: "Does your mother know what you're doing?" We'd say yes. At times, a neighbor might even say, "Oh? Let's see." With that, we might be escorted off to a parent to check out the truth of what we had said. Remarkably, we would go with this neighbor, out of respect, even though it might have meant trouble for us. And our parents seemed to honor what these sentries of the neighborhood would report to them. It was a cultural arrangement that also made youngsters feel safe and secure. We knew that if there was some trouble we couldn't handle, we would be able to flag down one of these adults to help out.

But things have changed in our and in many other neighborhoods. In the cities and small towns of America today, adults who are fortunate to have jobs are anxious about keeping them. They are exhausted from working harder and for longer hours in order to support their families. Children are not only more isolated from adults but from one another. Kids today can entertain themselves in solitary ways with video, computer, or recorded music, and they have fewer opportunities to practice social skills and develop their emotional intelligence.

Something else changed along the way, too: You are only allowed to parent your own children. Although there may be an increasing number of organized recreational activities for children, structured group activities are very different from the free play with caring adult supervision that previous generations experienced. Today's parents have a much smaller village to rely upon to help raise thoughtful and responsible children. A neighbor who witnesses a child being bullied or a group of kids getting into trouble and wants to intervene would probably hesitate because this person wouldn't feel backed up or trusted by the parents of these children. Into this void steps the Social Decision Making/Social Problem Solving (SDM/SPS) program. Because while the village of some neighborhoods has gotten smaller, the village of the school has opened up.

Teachers have always been sanctioned to pass on the culture of relating in a civilized and caring way, but there are now recognized policies for instruction that go beyond the "hidden curriculum" of informal discussions. There are now formal programs in alcohol and drug abuse prevention, character education, and other topics. The SDM/SPS curriculum allows a school not only to address many problems, but also to influence positive development efforts in a comprehensive way. Children of the present generation have an advantage. There is now a science that did not exist years ago that helps adults know the skills and attitudes important for children to become moral decision makers. It is on this science that the SDM/SPS curriculum is based. There is no need to rely only on our intuition about what will help children. We now know what works.

This particular curriculum distinguishes itself from other programs with similar goals. Almost three decades in development, it offers instruction in the most comprehensive range of skills for teachers, students, and parents. In this curriculum, teachers will find ways to help children develop self-control skills—for example, to self-soothe when faced with stressful situations in the classroom. Teachers will also find ways here of teaching skills such as friendship development. In this program, the eight steps of critical thinking are taught explicitly, without mystery. These steps are woven into a wide variety of both social conflict and academic areas. The program also includes parenting materials that children can take home so their families can follow up with them and promote additional skill development.

Beyond the actual suggested instructional activities, this curriculum also distinguishes itself by attending to the art of teaching as well. Teachers who are new to the program can benefit from the experiences of the many master teachers who have gone before them. Readers will see many ways to teach social decision making that make it exciting and fun for children. The program's consistent, well-organized pedagogy provides an easy and soon-familiar flow and rhythm that repeats itself in engaging ways. The instructional tone of this work is respectful of teachers' professionalism—for example, instructional "topics" rather than prescribed "lessons" are provided. Teachers are therefore encouraged to adapt and tailor the instruction to suit their own style and their students' educational needs and learning pace. This process is parallel to the program's goal to encourage independent and competent thinking on the part of children.

So I invite you to settle back and confidently enjoy this collection of social decision making and social problem solving resources for children. This is a treasury of material developed through careful research, underscored by a pedagogy that invites enthusiasm from all, and refined on the basis of over 25 years in the classroom.

JOHN F. CLABBY, PH.D.

UMDNJ–ROBERT WOOD JOHNSON
MEDICAL SCHOOL

Acknowledgments

As our work enters its third decade, we look back with amazement and gratitude at the hundreds of colleagues who have been instrumental in the development of our work. We cannot possibly mention them all, but we hold them all in our hearts with tremendous gratitude and admiration. Those whose role in getting the SDM/SPS work started deserve special mention. These are Myrna Shure, George Spivack, and Steve Larcen, who generously shared their initial work with Interpersonal Cognitive Problem Solving, and Tom Schuyler, John Clabby, and Charlotte Hett, whose collaboration, vision, commitment, and enthusiasm in the first decade of the work helped it flourish despite many obstacles.

In subsequent years, we have been blessed with being able to work with many talented colleagues who have taught us so much and lent their expertise to our work. Again, there are too many to name, but we want to note several whose ongoing work with us has gone above and beyond any reasonable expectation and whose ideas have come to mesh with our own in ways very hard to disentangle. These include Jacqueline Norris, Phil Brown, Vicki Poedubicky, Judy Lerner, Lois Brown, Frank Fehn, Karen Welland, Bruce Ettinger, Larry Leverett, Joseph Sperlazza, and Robin Stern. Linda would like to give special acknowledgment to Bruce Stout of University of Medicine and Dentistry of New Jersey–University Behavioral Health Care for his continuing mentorship and tangible and logistical support, and Maurice would like to extend the same to Lew Gantwerk of the Graduate School of Applied and Professional Psychology–Center for Applied Psychology.

We also mention with deep appreciation and awe Erin Bruno, Maureen Papke, and Teresa Shapiro, who tangibly assisted us in compiling this volume and who carry the legacy of SDM/SPS work so brilliantly every day. They, along with other longtime SDM/SPS staff members Jeff Kress, Carl Preto, Lisa Blum, Margo Hunter, Mary Ellen Taylor, Ronda Jones, and Deborah Mosley, as well as Steven Tobias and Brian Friedlander, have developed the ideas that appear in our curriculum in the spirit of continuous improvement.

Finally, we thank the remarkable team at Research Press, who believe in our work so deeply and care so much about how it is presented to the world. Ann Wendel, Russ Pence, Karen Steiner, Dennis Wiziecki, Hilary Powers (our capable freelance copyeditor), and an incredibly talented production staff have made it possible to put our best work forward and provide materials to our colleagues in schools about which we are very, very proud. The effort represented in this curriculum will have the ultimate effect of helping children, and that is the point of all of our work.

A personal note from Maurice: I am filled with gratitude for so many people, immediate and extended family, friends, close colleagues, and amazing students, past and present, who have been so supportive of my work. Your contributions, tangible and intangible, have made the best of this work better and have helped keep me refreshed, enthused, and ready to persist and create in the service of improving kids' lives. A special thank-you to cherished friend, source of mirth and chocolate, and collaborator Ed Dunkelblau; the incredible team at the Collaborative for Academic, Social, and Emotional Learning; my parents, Agnes and Sol; my in-laws, Myra and Lou Rosen; and last, and most of all, my wife, Ellen, and daughters, Sara Elizabeth and Samara Alexandra—all three of whom are my best sources of feedback, support, and kvelling.

A personal note from Linda: I would like to thank Dr. John Gottman for his mentoring and making me so aware at an early and foundational stage of my career of the critical importance of a child's social and emotional competency. I also want to thank my amazing circle of family and friends for all of their love and support and for so richly filling the much too little time I have to play. My inner-circle family support group includes my mothers, Joan and Edna; my Aunt Marcy; Kay; Joannetta and Mern; my twin sister, Laura, and sisters Diane, Carrie, Linda Bruene II, Jane, Pat, Jeannie, Jennifer, and Amy; my brothers, John and Bob; and my uncles, Mike and Bud. I could not work or survive without my amazing circle of friends, which includes Nancy, Andrew, Annette, Val, Lois, Lizzie, Howard, Freddie, Donna, Sandra, Riki, Vicky, and Teff. Last of all, thanks to my loving husband, Chris, who continues to capture my respect for his emotional intelligence, and to my most adoring buddy/golden retriever, Josh.

Introduction

Guide to Instructional Design and Implementation Procedures

> For students to enter the community of responsible adults prepared for a diversity of social roles, they must possess critical-thinking and problem-solving skills, as well as interpersonal sensitivity. Their future success in citizenship, parenthood, family life, and the workplace will require them to find appropriate answers to numerous difficult questions, and it is up to the schools to help provide a foundation from which to answer them.
>
> —M. J. Elias & S. E. Tobias, *Social Problem Solving Interventions in the Schools* (New York: Guilford Press, 1996, p. iii)

The Social Decision Making/Social Problem Solving (SDM/SPS) curriculum is an evidence-based approach to building skills that students need for success in school and in life: the skills required for effective work in groups, persistent work on projects, constructive handling of frustration and challenge, and nonviolent conflict resolution. Students learn both how and why to care about classmates and teammates; to feel and show empathy; and to practice perspective taking, emotional regulation and self-control, and participation in democratic institutions, workplaces, and family life. In other words, SDM/SPS teaches essential life skills, skills that were once the province of family life but are, for many children, no longer routinely covered in the course of normal growing up. Much as we can lament that this is the case, we also must do something about it. When we do not, our classrooms are chaotic, our schools suffer, and many of our children emerge from education as social casualties, either unwilling or unable to take productive roles in society and lacking the moral character to put their talents to use for good in the world.

STUDENTS NEED SKILLS, NOT SLOGANS

Students need skills, not slogans, and so SDM/SPS is geared to build skills. Ideally, students will have several years of exposure to the curriculum in elementary and middle school, but even one solid year can have benefits. This Introduction is designed to give you a brief overview of the curriculum, the structure of its activities, and a selection of ways you can use the teaching skills you already have to carry out what is required.

The SDM/SPS curriculum is best thought of as a launching pad. Students cannot learn skills merely from engaging in activities on a topic. The curriculum provides a structure for introducing the skills, ensuring their relevance to students and a connection to their everyday lives, and providing numerous opportunities for practice and feedback. It is through this practice and feedback process that skills come to be internalized—but it takes months, not days. The pedagogy of the SDM/SPS curriculum extends beyond the actual delivery of formal activities in the classroom. Teaching of SDM/SPS skills becomes infused into virtually all aspects of the school day, because there really is no part of the day when having solid life skills and exhibiting good character are irrelevant.

The SDM/SPS curriculum is included in the list of Model and Promising Programs from the U.S. Department of Education's Expert Panel on Safe, Drug Free Schools, and has been designated as a Select Social-Emotional Learning (SELect) program by the Collaborative for Academic, Social, and Emotional Learning. (See the "Safe and Sound" guide to selection and implementation of SEL programs, updated periodically, at the Collaborative's Web site, www.CASEL.org.)

The instructional design is as important as the skills targeted in each topic area. Systematic skill-building procedures are used for all curriculum units.

SYSTEMATIC SKILL-BUILDING TOOLS
FOR SOCIAL DECISION MAKING/SOCIAL PROBLEM SOLVING

The program focuses on teaching self-control and social awareness skills as important tools for decision making.

Format for Each Topic

Activities are organized into Topics rather than lessons. This identifier is preferred because of the emphasis on skill building. Teachers must have the flexibility to stay on a topic for the length of time necessary for a sufficient proportion of the class to grasp the concepts and be ready to move on.

Topics begin with a statement of objectives, followed by materials and preparation needed to carry out the main activities. A number of activities involve materials that are handed out to students, which are collectively referred to as worksheets. Except for a few items readily available at school or in the community, these are included at the end of the first Topic to call for their use, with cross-references from later Topics if they are used more than once. Among the materials are various kinds of assessments and charts to be completed by students and teachers, Problem Diaries, and take-home materials for parents.

The next part of the Topic format is a set of instructional activities that incorporates the following components:

- Introducing the skills and concepts and providing motivation for learning; skills are presented in concrete behavioral components.
- Modeling behavioral components and clarifying the concept by descriptions and behavioral examples of using and not using the skill.
- Providing opportunities for practice of the skill in kid-tested, enjoyable activities, to allow for corrective feedback and reinforcement until skill mastery is approached.
- Labeling the skill with a prompt or cue to establish a shared language that can be used to call for exercise of the skill in future situations, to promote transfer and generalization.
- Assignments for skill practice outside the structured lessons.
- Follow-through activities and planned opportunities for using skill prompts in academic content areas, classroom management, and everyday interpersonal situations at school and in the home and community.
- Suggestions for parents and guardians to extend program learning to the home.

The Reflective Summary

Each set of instructional activities includes a Reflective Summary. The purpose of this summary is to give students a chance to think about what they have learned from the Topic, as well as to allow teachers to see what students are taking away with them. Sometimes the Reflective Summary can show when students have misunderstandings or uncertainty about what they have learned, suggesting the need for additional instructional activities before moving on in the Topic sequence. Here is the procedure:

Ask students to reflect on the question "What did you learn from today's lesson?" You can do this with the whole group, in a Sharing Circle format (described later in this Introduction and in more detail in the first Topic for each grade level), by having students fill out index cards, or by having them respond in other formats if you prefer. We recommend that you have some variety in formats. For example, sometimes you might ask, "What are two or three things you will most remember from today's lesson?" After getting a sense of what the students have learned, reinforce key themes that they mentioned and add perhaps one or two that you would like them to keep in mind. Also discuss any follow-up assignments or take-homes.

Tips for Teachers

After the instructional activities you will find a Tips for Teachers section, with specific, practical suggestions for carrying out the activities most effectively, based on feedback from teachers who have used SDM/SPS in various settings. This section is followed by specific worksheets called for in the Topic for the first time.

SYSTEMATIC SKILL BUILDING FOR SOCIAL-EMOTIONAL DEVELOPMENT

The set of skills that students learn does not change from Grades 2 through 8. They are listed in Table 1. Think of these skills as a sort of alphabet. The basic set of letters does not change, but new combinations of the same basic letters become both possible and necessary as children develop and face new and more complex situations. Ultimately, the goal is for students to use their new social and emotional skills independently in the context of the new, increasingly complex, and ever-changing problems and decisions they will encounter. The activities in this curriculum start from the social and emotional skills your students have learned up to this point and build upon them to help your students learn to make socially competent and successful social decisions.

Readiness Skills

Readiness refers to a climate that must be established and a set of skills that must be learned as prerequisites to thoughtful decision making. To create the climate, students need to think of themselves as being part of a problem-solving team, and the first units of the curricula in Grades 2, 3, 4, and 5 all begin with that focus. To accomplish this, we recommend using a group gathering called a Sharing Circle to begin class discussions and skill-building activities. In the Sharing Circle, students are asked to share their name and answer a question or two, beginning with simple things such as naming a favorite restaurant and moving on, after a certain level of trust is established, to describing feelings about a school or classroom issue. This deceptively simple process allows students to share with one another, to learn to listen to and care about their classmates, to get some "air time," and to foster positive transitions from the pressures of home and the pace and action of lunch and recess during the school day. It is a format for

Table 1   Skills Taught in the SDM/SPS Curriculum: Grades 2–8

SOCIAL COMPETENCE SKILLS

Self-Control

Effective listening
Memory strategies
Following directions
Identifying personal stress triggers
Self-monitoring (stress management)
Self-calming
Assertive communication
Giving constructive criticism
Resisting provocations
Role-play for behavioral rehearsal
Self-evaluation

Social Awareness

Working as part of a team
Expressing oneself in a group
Perspective taking
Choosing and caring for friends
Giving and receiving praise
Asking for and giving help
Conversation skills
Joining a group

DECISION-MAKING AND PROBLEM-SOLVING SKILLS

Feelings awareness (self and others)
Articulating feelings
Problem definition
Realistic goal setting
Flexible and creative thinking/generating alternatives
Consequential thinking:
    short- and long-term
    positive and negative
    for self and others
Decision making
    in service of a goal
    positive choices
Planning
Anticipating obstacles
Behavioral rehearsal
Overcoming setbacks
Utilizing previous experience for future decision making

reflection on the weekend past, the day or week ahead, and the weekend to come.

We also find it essential to have a visible, clear rule structure in the classroom. One format for this is the Classroom Constitution. The constitution allows parallels to academics by introducing the idea that, just as is true for the nation, a classroom functions with a set of rights and a set of rules. Students are involved in making these rules, and the list of rules is posted visibly in the classroom. Typically, when visitors walk in and view the constitution, they sense the pride embodied in the values and priorities of the classroom. The constitution should be phrased in positive terms, although some educators maintain that a couple of clear "Thou shalt not's" are also worthwhile. When problems such as classroom disruption, lack of effort, or poor group work are observed, the constitution is invoked and an improvement plan is created.

Parents are highly supportive of Classroom Constitutions and other visible, explicit rule structures, as these enable clear home-school communication about expected behaviors in school. This is an important point, in that teachers do not want to get into conflicts with students about different values and messages they may be getting from home. The Classroom Constitution or other rules for school are exactly that—expectations for how students will act in school and in school-related situations (for example, on the bus, on school grounds, on the way to and from school, on school trips).

Against the backdrop of a climate that fosters social and emotional learning, specific readiness skills can be built—all of them prerequisites for thoughtful social decision making and problem solving in all aspects of life. In addition to the skills needed to become a problem-solving team, readiness also includes skills in feelings—that is, understanding one's own feelings and those of others, as well as learning how to manage strong emotions in everyday situations. This awareness requires students to focus on the areas of self-control and social awareness. *Self-control* refers to the personal skills necessary for self-regulation and monitoring of emotions and interactive behavior; *social awareness* focuses on the skills and knowledge linked with successful participation in a group. Readiness is the focus of Grade 4 in the units titled "Rules and Tools" and "Emotional Regulation," as well as in the first part of the Grade 5 curriculum.

The Instructional Phase: Building a Social Decision Making Strategy in Grades 4–5

The cornerstone of SDM/SPS, like any life skills, character education, or social-emotional program, is to provide students with a problem-solving and decision-making strategy they can internalize to use in a variety of everyday and challenging situations they encounter. This is the emphasis of the Grades 4 and 5 curricula. It is accomplished through a combination of (a) introducing an overall strategy for guided self-talk, summarized with the mnemonic "FIG TESPN," (b) exploring each element of FIG TESPN as a separate skill, and (c) practicing the FIG TESPN strategy in the context of a variety of hypothetical, age-appropriate, and open-ended choice and conflict situations. As each skill is emphasized and practiced, its link to the chain of skills that forms the overall strategy is strengthened.

The "FIG TESPN" acronym reflects the following skills:

F —Find the feelings

I —Identify the problem

G —Guide yourself with a goal

T —Think of many possible solutions

E —Envision consequences

S —Select the best solution

P —Plan and be prepared for pitfalls

N —Notice what happened (Now what?)

The skill areas can be summarized by stating that when children and adults are using their social problem solving skills, they are engaged in the following activities:

1. Noticing and labeling signs of feelings in themselves and others.

2. Identifying issues or problems and putting them into words.

3. Determining and selecting personal goals.

4. Generating alternative solutions—brainstorming.

5. Envisioning—getting a mental picture of—possible consequences (in the short and long term, to themselves and others).

6. Selecting the solution that best meets their goal.

7. Planning and rehearsing the details of carrying out the solution, making a final check for obstacles, and anticipating what to do if they occur.

8. Noticing what happened and using the information for future decision making and problem solving.

In Grades 4 and 5, the skills of FIG TESPN are taught; in both grades, they are also integrated into a variety of social and academic areas, as outlined in the contents. Grade 5 provides particular emphasis on academic application, which is a part of activities in most Topics as well as in the Supplemental Activities (Topics 27–29). The latter can be introduced any time after the first six or eight weeks of the school year and used repeatedly with changing content. Tables 2 and 3 contain a specific topic-by-topic outline of how SDM/SPS is integrated with and includes a range of academic, standards-linked content areas.

**Table 2   Social Decision Making/Social Problem Solving (SDM/SPS):
Academic and Home Application Activities (Grade 4)**

	TOPICS	Language Arts	Social Studies	Health	Behavior Management	Interpersonal and Personal Real-Life Situations	Community Service Learning	Home	Other
1.	Introduction to Social Decision Making/Social Problem Solving (SDM/SPS) Lessons	X	X		X	X		X	
2.	Respectful Listening	X	X	X	X	X		X	
3.	Strategies for Remembering				X	X		X	Spelling; testing
4.	Role-Playing	X	X	X	X	X			Media
5.	Be Your BEST	X			X	X		X	
6.	BEST Applied: Good Teammate Behaviors				X	X		X	Computer skills
7.	BEST Applied: Giving and Receiving Praise	X			X	X		X	
8.	Packing Your SDM/SPS Toolbox	X		X	X	X		X	Media

#	Lesson							Academic connections
9.	Trigger Situations and Feelings Fingerprints			X	X	X	X	
10.	Keep Calm	X	X	X	X	X	X	Media; art
11.	Practice Keep Calm and Be Your BEST	X	X	X	X	X	X	Giving presentations
12.	Be Your BEST and Trigger Journal	X	X	X	X	X	X	Preferral intervention
13.	More Tools for the Toolbox	X		X	X	X	X	
14.	Introducing FIG TESPN			X	X	X	X	
15.	FIG TESPN: Step 1. *F* = Find the Feelings	X	X	X	X	X	X	Art
16.	FIG TESPN: Step 2. *I* = Identify the Problem	X	X	X	X	X	X	Media; science
17.	FIG TESPN: Step 3. G = Guide Yourself with a Goal	X	X	X	X	X	X	Science; math; physical education

Table 2 (continued)

	TOPICS	Language Arts	Social Studies	Health	Behavior Management	Interpersonal and Personal Real-Life Situations	Community Service Learning	Home	Other
18.	Giving Constructive Criticism	X			X	X		X	
19.	FIG TESPN: Step 4. *T* = Think of Many Possible Solutions	X	X	X	X	X		X	Media; math; science
20.	FIG TESPN: Step 5. *E* = Envision Consequences	X	X	X	X	X		X	
21.	FIG TESPN: Step 6. *S* = Select the Best Solution		X	X	X	X	X	X	
22.	FIG TESPN: Step 7. *P* = Plan and Be Prepared for Pitfalls	X	X	X	X	X	X	X	
23.	FIG TESPN: Step 8. *N* = Notice What Happened (Now What?)				X	X		X	Assessment; goal setting

24.	FIG TESPN: Putting It All Together—Teacher-Led Problem-Solving Practice	X	X	X	X	X			
25.	FIG TESPN: Practicing Problem Solving—Find Your Strengths				X	X		X	
26.	Review SDM/SPS Tools and Celebrate Success				X	X		X	Assessment; goal setting
27.	Solving the Problem of Moving to a New Grade or School				X	X			
28.	Using FIG TESPN to Tame Tough Topics	X						X	Library
29.	Using FIG TESPN to Plan Community Service Activities	X	X				X	X	Art
30.	Using FIG TESPN as a Book Report Guide	X	X					X	

Table 3 Social Decision Making/Social Problem Solving (SDM/SPS): Academic and Home Application Activities (Grade 5)

	TOPICS	Language Arts	Social Studies	Health	Behavior Management	Interpersonal and Personal Real-Life Situations	Community Service Learning	Home	Other
1.	Introduction to Social Decision Making/Social Problem Solving (SDM/SPS) Lessons)	X	X	X	X	X	X		Sharing Circle; group rules; Speaker Power
2.	Introduction to FIG TESPN				X			X	Art
3.	Feelings Identification	X	X			X	X		
4.	Trigger Situations and Physical Signs of Stress		X	X		X			Media
5.	Keep Calm		X	X	X	X			Recess
6.	Identify the Problem	X	X	X	X	X	X	X	Media; science
7.	Trigger Journals			X	X	X			
8.	Guide Yourself with a Goal	X	X	X	X	X	X	X	Science

9.	Understanding Different Points of View	X	X		X	X		X	Sharing Circle
10.	Think of Many Solutions and Envision Consequences	X	X	X	X	X		X	
11.	Practice Thinking of Solutions and Envisioning Consequences	X	X	X	X	X			Science
12.	Your BEST Chance for Success	X	X		X	X			Presentations
13.	Select the Best Solution, Then Plan and Prepare for Pitfalls	X	X	X		X			
14.	Notice What Happened (Now What?)	X	X	X	X	X		X	
15.	Problem Solving: Using All the FIG TESPN Steps					X			

Table 3 (continued)

	TOPICS	Language Arts	Social Studies	Health	Behavior Management	Interpersonal and Personal Real-Life Situations	Community Service Learning	Home	Other
16. & 17.	Using FIG TESPN with Literature	X							Book reports
18.	Using FIG TESPN for Creative Writing	X	X	X					
19.	Using FIG TESPN to Critically Examine Stories and Media Reports	X							Media
20.	Using FIG TESPN to Critically Examine Advertising								
21.	Using FIG TESPN to Solve Problems in Science		X						Science
22.	Using FIG TESPN to Examine History	X	X						

23.	Using FIG TESPN to Think About Fairness and Prejudice	X	X		X	X			
24.	Using FIG TESPN to Make Decisions and Solve Problems in Life		X		X	X			
25.	Using FIG TESPN to Prepare for a Test				X	X			
26.	Review SDM/SPS Skills and Celebrate Our Strengths				X	X	X	X	Assessment
27.	Using FIG TESPN to Change Target Behaviors.					X		X	
28.	Using FIG TESPN in Student Government	X	X			X		X	Student government; art
29.	Using FIG TESPN to Understand and Analyze Current Events	X	X			X	X		

The SDM/SPS–Academics Connection

Integrating SDM/SPS into the academic work of students builds their social-emotional learning (SEL) skills and enriches their academics by linking cognitive, social, and emotional processes. Readiness skills are essential for students to accomplish the following academic and learning tasks, among many others too numerous to list here:

- Understand assignments and test instructions accurately.
- Examine passages of text patiently and extract necessary information across a wide range of academic subject areas.
- Delay gratification long enough to think about difficult choices on exams or to prepare well for those exams.
- Participate in cooperative learning groups.
- Complete homework and short- and long-term projects in an organized way.

Beyond the readiness skills, the critical thinking skills denoted by FIG TESPN are the cornerstone of academic understanding and sustained achievement. This is true both in terms of mastering the intricacies of any subject area and in terms of addressing the numerous everyday decisions that are part of life in school and among peers and family. Consider how well a student would function with deficiencies in any one, two, or three FIG TESPN skills. Imagine if the deficiencies occurred in only two or three school or home situations. Is there any doubt that the student would be at risk for academic difficulty, for substance abuse, and for not functioning as a healthy, productive adult citizen? Hence, applications to academic contexts are a regular feature of SDM/SPS, building a broad array of literacy skills in students. As noted earlier, Tables 2 and 3 outline how each of the Topics in the Grade 4 and 5 curricula link with a range of academic areas.

THE SDM/SPS INSTRUCTIONAL AND PEDAGOGICAL APPROACH

In addition to direct instruction and application of a decision-making process, students also benefit from having external coaching and facilitation of their learning. This process is carried out through a form of pedagogy refined over many years to help teachers systematically guide and coach students to use their SDM/SPS skills in a variety of situations. For this reason, the pedagogy of SDM/SPS is of equal importance to the activities and essential if SDM/SPS is to be implemented effectively and internalized by students.

Gathering: The Sharing Circle

Whether one calls it a Sharing Circle, Morning Meeting, Sharing Time, Advisory Group, Circle Time, or any of a number of related titles, the reality is that students welcome the chance to come together informally to address issues of emotional concern. Students benefit from a buffer between socially challenging parts of their day—preparation for and trip to school, lunch and recess, and dismissal—and applying themselves to serious academic work. For this reason, schools find it useful to have gatherings to start the school day, after lunch and recess, and at the end of the day. Such activities recognize and help to implement three essential SEL principles (from the "Lessons for Life" Video-Inservice Kit for staff members new to SEL, National Center for Innovation and Education, www.communitiesofhope.org):

- *Caring relationships form the foundation of all lasting learning:* Gatherings bring everyone together and make a statement that while agendas are important, relationships come first. They also set a climate in which learning is most likely to be internalized and lasting.

- *Emotions affect how and what we learn:* Academic work cannot proceed when students' emotions are churned up, when they are anxious, fearful, or angry. The group focus during start-of-day gatherings is on providing an opportunity for some expression of concern, or at least using a ritual beginning to give students a chance to get their own emotions regulated a bit. By so doing, they are better prepared for the academic tasks ahead of them. At the end of the day, addressing students' emotions makes it more likely that the day's learning will stick, and good intentions with regard to homework and projects and such will get followed through on.

- *Goal setting and problem solving provide direction and energy to learning:* Gatherings provide a chance to reaffirm common goals, set personal goals, work on issues of general concern, or make the transition into the SDM/SPS activity about to be undertaken. Gatherings also reinforce goals by providing opportunities for testimonials about progress on projects and attempts to use new skills, and for students to get feedback on aspects of SDM/SPS that are proving difficult.

It is this flexible use of gatherings that led the activities in the SDM/SPS curricula to be called Topics rather than lessons. Sometimes the immediate needs of the group, including the need to review what went on in the prior meeting, will make it impossible to complete the day's planned activities. However, because the emphasis on SDM/SPS is in long-term, generalizable skill development, when a choice exists between deep learning and coverage of more topics, the former is preferred.

Caveats: Taking Care with Student Disclosure and Student Hurt

In Sharing Circles or other gatherings, as well as in problem-solving discussions, some students are likely to want to share family or other personal home circumstances with peers. It is important to set up ground rules, from the very beginning, that family matters should not be topics of general discussion. Further, many groups establish a rule that they will not talk about people who are not in the room at the time. That being said, you will also want to be sure to convey to students that they can and should individually approach you, a counselor, school psychologist or social worker, or other school professional whenever they are facing difficult personal or interpersonal problems or circumstances.

These considerations are especially powerful when students are coming to class with a great deal of emotional hurt. Often, they are in need of opportunities to express their strong feelings. And they may try to do so despite warnings that such personal disclosures are not appropriate for the group. Try to be aware of what is happening in the lives of students and offer those who are dealing with difficulties chances to meet with you or another member of the school staff on an individual basis. Your alertness to both quiet and overt signs of distress can make a large difference in the lives of students. The work of the PassageWays Institute is a valuable resource to teachers in addressing these concerns (www.passageways.org).

The Facilitative Approach of Open-Ended Questioning

From the SDM/SPS point of view, the main role of the teacher is neither to solve students' problems nor to make decisions for students. Instead, teachers are facilitators of students' own decision-making and problem-solving skills. (This approach is analogous to the old adage about the relative merits of teaching people to fish and of catching fish for them.) The facilitative approach involves asking questions, rather than telling. However, questions are not all the same. Consider four types of questions:

- *Closed:* "Did you hit him?"
- *Interrogative:* "Why did you hit him?"
- *Multiple choice:* "Did you hit him because he was teasing you or because of something else?"
- *Open-ended:* "What happened?"

Closed questions require a yes or no or other one-word response from students and do not elicit much reflection. "Are you angry?" will elicit much less information than a question phrased in an open-ended manner, say, "What feelings are you having?" Students often do not react well to "why" questions because their insecurity can lead them to feel defensive and blamed. Most students are usually not aware of, or able to articulate, the deep reasons behind their actions; this is especially true of students with behavioral and emotional difficulties.

An honest response to "Why did you hit him?" is something very few students will offer: "Because I lack self-control and have an inconsistent social learning history with regard to getting negative consequences as a result of my violent actions" or "I think it comes from a chaotic home, some poor parental modeling, and an overexposure to movies, TV, and videogames that glorify aggression, with inadequate adult supervision." By contrast, open-ended questions such as "What happened?" are apt to maximize a student's own thinking about the problem. Further, getting students more invested in the problem-solving process leads them to feel more ownership of and responsibility for the solution.

Giving students several choices from which to select certainly still has its uses—for example, with students who need to be brought along as problem solvers, are immature or have cognitive limitations, or are initially resistive or draw blanks to open-ended questions. And at times, teachers will have to tell students the answer in an authoritative way. What SDM/SPS pedagogy recommends is that teachers first try to *ask* open-ended questions, then *suggest* options from which students can choose, and then *tell* students, if necessary. Cognitive choice is good exercise for students' intellects, as well as for their social-emotional skills. SDM/SPS activities accomplish this by structuring the initial questions teachers ask, both verbally and in written formats, to be open-ended.

The Two Question Rule: A Specialized Questioning Approach

The Two Question Rule is a powerful, simple way to stimulate students' thinking. In leading a group discussion, the rule is to *follow up a question with another question*. It reminds the teacher to stay in a questioning mode, and it serves notice to students that the teacher is genuinely interested in hearing details. For example, "How are you feeling?" can be followed up by "What other feelings are you aware of?" "What are you going to say when you go up to the lunch aide?" can be followed up by "How exactly are you going to say it?" In an academic context, "Why do you think the character in the book acted in that way?" can be followed up by "What do you think the character will do next?" Or "What are the ways that the body regulates temperature?" can be followed up by "How do you know that is true?" That last follow-up probe—"How do you know that is true?"—is an especially useful tool for grounding and clarifying students' thinking. Overall, the more students elaborate on their ideas about a problem or issue under consideration, the better understanding teachers have of what students mean and what they are taking from the discussion. The Two Question Rule is valuable for clarifying students' thoughts, feelings, goals, and plans.

Role-Playing, Rehearsal, and Practice

Role-playing provides an opportunity for students to rehearse and practice the responses they would make in actual interpersonal situations. Many students find this activity an enjoyable and valuable supplement to classroom discussions. For teachers, it is an opportunity to give students supervised practice and feedback in reacting to a simulation of everyday events. Four basic steps are involved in a role-play, and these can be explained to students:

- Prepare the script.
- Run through the action.
- Action on the set.
- Review the performance.

Prepare the Script

Select a relevant interpersonal situation and establish the problem and conflict. Choose participants who are willing to accept roles and are likely to handle the roles successfully. Do not place students in roles that reflect their typical situation or approach. Carefully explain the overall situation and the expected actions of each character. Characters should have distinct feelings, motives, and goals in the situation. Where applicable, students should know what alternatives to state and what consequences to expect. There is a clear analogy here with the script of a play.

Run Through the Action

This rehearsal has two aspects. First, have the class discuss the situation and encourage audience participation and constructive suggestions during the run-through process. Be prepared to model, or to have students model, specific examples of any desired behavior that will be the focus of the role-play. Then have the actors discuss among themselves what they will say and do and how they will do it. Have them practice expressions of feelings, verbalize alternatives, or run through any other parts of the overall situation that you feel require emphasis.

Action on the Set

Have the students enact the situation. Teachers are director-coaches and should feel free to help the actors portray their roles as the action is occurring. By actively coaching, you are providing students with feedback and support. This makes role-playing less threatening and confusing for them and also helps move the action along. Discontinue role-playing if a student shows any sign of emotional upset or if the actors (or children in the audience) begin acting in a silly or off-task manner.

Review the Performance

After the performance, have the audience share their views of the thoughts, feelings, and actions expressed by the characters. Students can also be asked how it felt to be involved in, or to watch, the role-play. A valuable way to provide closure is for the teacher to discuss how the role-play could be done differently in the future, emphasizing how the various skills the students are learning fit together.

To help students get started, you can share the four-step outline with them and then proceed by introducing a situation to role-play. Choose a situation such as one of these:

- You have a new student in your class, and you want to make that student feel welcome.
- You are having trouble doing a math problem, and you want to ask the teacher for help.
- You are a new student in the class and want to make friends.

Choose volunteers and brief the role-players on their parts. Have them plan what they will say and possibly let them rehearse by themselves. Many topics will feature role-play as part of skill building and practice for generalization.

Questions About Role-Playing

Teachers new to role-playing often have questions about how it will fit into classroom activity. For example:

- When would I use role-playing?
- What exactly does the audience do during the role-play?
- What if students are reluctant to become involved or are not ready?

When would I use role-playing?

Role-playing is useful to:

- Highlight personal feelings and those of others when involved in a problematic situation.
- Act out a possible solution to a problem and make it more real.
- Compare two or more solutions.
- Teach planning skills.
- Teach reactions to obstacles.
- Help children integrate their various social decision making and social problem solving skills.

What exactly does the audience do during the role-play?

Members of the audience should be assigned specific points to observe. This focus will keep them actively involved in the process so they don't just watch it like something on TV. Here are some of the major categories:

- Verbal or nonverbal behaviors such as BEST: body posture, eye contact, content of speech, and tone of voice. (See Tables 2 and 3 for topics in which BEST is presented.)
- Specific social decision making and social problem solving steps. (Specify which ones to watch for.)

- All social problem solving steps.
- One actor. (Specify which one.)
- All actors.

Of greatest importance is that students learn to give positive feedback before making any critical comments or suggestions. Teachers should be sure that reviews of performances begin on a positive note. Over time, this encourages the class to work as a problem-solving team and to participate in the role-plays.

What if students are reluctant to become involved or are not ready?

By following the procedures outlined earlier, especially running through the action and coaching while the action is occurring, teachers ensure that most students will wish to be involved. It is also important to establish a positive working atmosphere in which students know that teasing or ridicule is not tolerated. Beyond this, teachers should attempt to gradually phase students into more and more direct involvement. Role-playing with puppets is often a good beginning point for a reluctant class. Students also enjoy making the puppets. Observation of a videotaped interaction also helps sharpen students' skills at observing and giving feedback. A student can also be assigned a specific observational task, such as watching for signs of feelings or for verbal behaviors. The student can be asked to report these observations during the review. Finally, reluctant students can play the parts of extras—people in nonspeaking parts, such as bystanders or passers-by. One of the most successful ways to gently encourage participation is to say to a student, "Do it as if you were . . . [a sports figure, actor or actress, cowboy, musician, school principal, or some other role the student will be able to identify with]." Teachers can judge from students' reactions to these gradual steps when they might be ready to move into greater involvement.

USING THE FOUR "R'S" TO AID RETENTION

Forgetting and confusion will inevitably interfere with learning, much as occurs in the context of other school instruction. Therefore, activities are designed to reflect four "R's" that can increase retention: review, repetition, reminders, and reinforcement.

Review

Each meeting should include a review of both group discussion rules and what occurred in the preceding meeting. This helps bring people who missed that session up-to-date and also lets the teacher accurately gauge the group's starting point.

Repetition

Especially with youngsters in lower elementary grades, our recommended procedure is to maximize tolerable repetition. Many students' attention, memory, or depth of understanding is not sufficient to permit one-trial learning. They benefit from repetition through different modalities (speaking, reading words, viewing pictures, pantomiming, singing, and whispering) and from different sources (teacher, group of peers, dyad).

For the most part, teachers do not repeat *all* the lessons from one year to the next. Rather, a developmentally sequenced flow is designed for each grade. However, a key aspect of instruction, we have found, is children's own maturing ways of responding to situations. Therefore, there will be times when similar content is presented from one year to the next, with the goal of helping children deepen and elaborate their repertoire of feelings, thoughts, and actions around that content. It is also the case that students tend to appreciate structure. Therefore, instruction in most topics begins with a Sharing Circle and a review of the previous session. These features are not described in detail in the instructional activities sections because the review segment will be tailored to each unique classroom context.

Reminders

In our view, the elementary school years are best viewed as a skill acquisition period. It is not consistent with developmental or educational expectations to look for significant internalization and generalization of skill concepts based solely on their presentation in the classroom lessons. The more children are reminded by group leaders, classroom teachers, aides, peers, bus drivers, building administrators, counselors, and others to use their new skills, the more likely they are to find them salient and worth remembering and developing further. The most effective reminders are tangible ones, such as posters depicting the skill components (such as keeping calm, having a successful conversation, or going through the steps of making a sound decision). As an example, teachers using our program have made signs showing ways to get help, both in words and in pictures, and have referred students to these signs when they seem in need of help. Posting stories, worksheets, or other products generated from SDM/SPS activities also serves as a tangible reminder of the skills. In addition to the classroom, other good locations include guidance offices, group rooms, the main office, and hallway bulletin boards.

Use of Prompts and Cues

Prompts and cues are defined as special types of reminders composed of verbal requests or directives to use a certain set of skills. The set of skills generally has components that have been taught in formal group meetings, and the total sequence of these components is given a label. (For example, the components of the skill of self-calming are given the label "Keep Calm.") Nearly all the readiness topics contain labels that can be used as prompts or cues. Here are some examples, along with indications of when to use them:

- *Speaker Power:* A sign not to talk out of turn.
- *Listening Position:* A cue to sit up and orient attention appropriately.
- *Keep Calm:* A prompt to use deep breathing and "self-talk" to calm down.
- *Be Your BEST:* A prompt to behave in a polite, socially acceptable way, attending to body position, eye contact, speech, and tone of voice.
- *Problem Diary:* A way of monitoring personal problems and a tool for thinking about them (by writing a diary) and, at times, for planning ways to handle them.
- *Role-Playing:* A set of behaviors to enact a problem-solving situation and to take others' points of view.
- *Teammate Behavior:* A prompt to think about how one relates to others and how to maintain a positive relationship or change an unsatisfying one.
- *Giving and Getting Help:* A prompt to share one's problems and to be willing to help others solve theirs as well.

Examples of situations in which to use prompts include these:

- Two children are arguing over a pencil; you see the situation escalating.

  Prompt: "I would like to see you both use Keep Calm. . . . Now, let's see what happens if you two try to Be Your BEST."

- One child is squirming around while you are reading something to the class.

  Prompt: "I will continue when everyone is in Listening Position."

- A child runs to you, upset about a problem; you are not able to deal with this outburst right now.

  Prompt: "I can see you were really hassled. Please go fill out a Problem Diary and then come back and see me, and we can talk about it."

- One child is being led astray by another, and you are concerned about it.

  Prompt: "Is Billy your friend? What good Teammate Behaviors does he use? What does he do that are not Good Teammate Behaviors? How do you feel when he does these things?"

Testimonials

To capitalize on the known potency of peer modeling as an influence on learning, it is advisable to regularly incorporate testimonials into readiness lessons. Testimonials are opportunities for students to tell about situations in which they used skills that they have been taught. A teacher might say, "Let's go around and have everyone share a time in the past week they used 'Keep Calm' or tell about something that happened to you or something you saw where 'Keep Calm' or 'Be Your BEST' might have been helpful."

The reports of the students sharpen their recognition of suitable times to use the skills, provide examples of how the skills can be used in practice, and, for the teacher or group leader, give an opportunity to provide feedback and encouragement that will help promote further skill use. Testimonials may be conducted as part of the Sharing Circle or as a second activity. Some teachers prefer to elicit testimonials on non-lesson days as a way of extending students' involvement with the material.

Reinforcement

The fourth "R" reflects learning theorists' belief that, in the absence of incentives and feedback, proper skill learning is unlikely to occur. Group leaders and others in the students' environment should be alert to their attempts to use their skills. At such times, the attempt should be reinforced with praise or whatever tangible rewards may be applicable in the setting. The opportunity should also be taken to provide specific feedback about which of the students' behaviors would be worth remembering and repeating on future occasions.

If the students can handle it, it would be beneficial to add constructive feedback about what might be useful to try next time to make achievement of goals more likely.

THE APPLICATION PHASE: INFUSION INTO ACADEMICS AND EVERYDAY INTERPERSONAL INTERACTIONS

A particular area in which the SDM/SPS approach is distinctive is the way in which the skills are integrated into everyday academic and interpersonal contexts in classrooms and schools. A teacher who wants to build students' SDM/SPS skills during language arts, health, social studies, civics, science, art, gym, or music will find well-articulated strategies and activities to help this take place in what we call the application phase.

The application phase of SDM/SPS instruction provides students with ongoing opportunities to apply and practice skills taught in the readiness and instructional domains in real-life situations and within the context of academic content areas. Practice is accomplished through a combination of structured practice activities and lessons and facilitative questioning on the part of adults.

Structured Practice Opportunities

Relevant curriculum materials can be found within many of the Topic areas (see Tables 2 and 3) and are emphasized in Supplemental Activities. They take the form of a wide variety of sample structures, frameworks, and materials for infusing a decision-making approach into instruction in almost any subject area, as well as a method for addressing real-life problems and decisions. These lessons and methods are easily adapted to address specific instructional objectives and are flexible enough to use with a variety of content themes, topics, stories, and situations.

For example, worksheets and procedures from Topics for a decision-making approach to social studies or for analyzing literature can be used, with minor variations, with a wide variety of specific topics addressed in social studies or history or for a variety of authors and works of literature.

The FIG TESPN framework can be used to help students think more deeply about and personalize issues in a way that strongly fosters retention and internalization of knowledge. Brain research has provided many insights into how to create more vivid and sustained learning situations, and these are built into the SDM/SPS approach. Consider a series of FIG TESPN–derived questions focused on the topic of immigration or explorers:

1. How did the people feel about leaving their countries? How might you have felt?

2. What countries were they leaving?

3. What problems were going on that made them want to leave?

4. What problems would leaving bring about?

5. What would have been their goals in leaving or staying?

6. What were their options, and how did they envision the results of each possibility? What do you think you would have done?

7. What plans did they have to make? What kinds of things got in their way at the last minute? How did they overcome these roadblocks? How else might they have tried to deal with their situation and solve their problems?

8. Once they arrived, how did they feel? What problems did they encounter at the beginning? What were their first goals?

To help students find fact-based answers to questions posed and check their own views, further reading and research can be assigned. And there are obvious parallels to be drawn in the context of understanding the current diversity of one's classroom, school, or community. Note that students from Grades 2 through 8 can answer the same basic set of questions, bringing to it knowledge, experiences, concerns, and ideas that reflect their developmental differences.

Consider an application-phase approach to holidays or ethnic and cultural commemorations, such as African American History or Latino Heritage months. After students learn some background, you can use FIG TESPN questioning to help students think—as a whole class, in cooperative learning groups, or individually—about how members of different groups feel about the holiday and how they might celebrate it. First, students begin with the group's celebrating the holiday. Then, to broaden their perspectives, they are asked to take the perspectives of other groups—for example, those who are not African Americans, African Americans who lived before the Civil War, people in the United States from different countries. Students can think about alternative ways to recognize events and the consequences of doing so, and then can plan their own way to recognize the event.

The application of frameworks taught in the curriculum can extend to unanticipated events in the life of the classroom, school, or nation. Although the evidence is only anecdotal, there is reason to believe that schools in which SDM/SPS and related SEL programs already existed were well able to address and respond to the events of September 11, 2001, at the World Trade Center in New York, the Pentagon in Washington, D.C., and a field in rural Pennsylvania. Teachers were prepared to address the social-emotional needs of students while the mental health and crisis teams were still being organized and mobilized. FIG TESPN and related problem-solving strategies were used as tools to help students sort through an incredibly complex and charged set of facts and feelings at appropriate developmental levels. Perhaps most important, the tools of SDM/SPS were found to be instruments not only of reflection but also of action. Students were helped to think through how they would cope with the situation immediately and then what they could do to help. And the problem-solving and decision-making approach continued to be used regularly in the days afterward to continually enhance children's understanding and channel their need for contribution.

Similar applications have been made in the context of bullying and school tragedies, as well as in planning positive schoolwide events.

Encouraging Students to Be Thoughtful Decision Makers and Problem Solvers

The SDM/SPS approach is built on promoting generalization and application, and for this, confidence building is essential. Foremost, teachers, counselors, other implementers, and parents are encouraged to communicate with students in a manner that stimulates students' own thinking. Through the use of open-ended questions and dialogue that facilitates students' higher order thinking skills ("What are all the ways that you can think of to handle that problem with

Lee?"), adults keep the channels of communication open. They let students know that they *can* solve their own problems and that their ideas are worthwhile. Moreover, students see adults around them listening to them and caring about and respecting what they say. In this situation, students feel a sense of empowerment. In addition, they are learning skills they can use every day. They are prompted, coached, and guided to practice the skills, and are given feedback aimed at helping them increase their effectiveness. Success is an important source of confidence, but so is praise for effort and progress that gives students the expectation that they are on a pathway to success. This is an important message for self-doubting students, who may be prone to see even a 90 percent full glass as 10 percent empty.

Because SDM/SPS is grounded in the social world of students—even when applied to academic areas—students who otherwise seem disaffected, unengaged, or at high risk feel included. Many teachers find that social decision making activities lead to increases in students' involvement in cooperative learning activities. Thus it is more than the content of social decision making that is important in skill building. The instructional principles built into every activity that follows from the social decision making tradition are designed to enhance a range of social and life skills and build self-confidence by helping students recognize that they are valued members of something that is worthwhile. Whether it is being used in a classroom, group, club, advisory, counseling, or clinical context, or in after-school programs, the SDM/SPS approach helps students (and adults) become part of a cooperative problem-solving and decision-making team. It is the powerful combination of direct instruction and external support that has led to significant and lasting student skill gains using the SDM/SPS curriculum.

Modeling

Instruction is important, but seeing adults use problem-solving skills is much more effective than just telling students to problem solve on their own. As students hear adults try to use SDM/SPS skills, they realize that it is normal to have negative feelings, that adults do not always have the perfect solution right at their fingertips, and that adults turn to problem solving when they face difficult situations or choices. Teachers need to find ways of modeling aspects of the program. When introducing a skill, teachers can discuss times they used the particular skill in their own lives. When a conflict takes place, teachers can talk about how they are calming themselves down and using the skills in the curriculum to address the situation. And when staff members interact with one another in the presence of students, it is important to take a positive, respectful, problem-solving approach, even during disagreements.

GETTING STARTED: PREPARE YOUR STUDENTS, THEIR PARENTS AND GUARDIANS, AND YOUR COLLEAGUES

The first Topic in the curriculum at each grade level is an introduction to SDM/SPS and the way activities will be structured. It is essential to set a regular meeting time because students will come to look forward to this part of the school routine. In addition, as students develop more experience with the SDM/SPS pedagogy, and as they build their skills, they will be able to save a discussion of problems, conflicts, or other interpersonal issues for the regular SDM/SPS meeting time.

SDM/SPS is built on having a set of classroom rules and procedures, ideally developed with students' input. If there is no order and organization in the classroom, it will be difficult to carry out SDM/SPS or any academic or social development activities. Hence, time is taken in the beginning to establish a climate of mutual respect and teamwork. These procedures are outlined in the first few Topics at each grade level. At the end of this Introduction is a sample letter that can be modified and sent to parents on school letterhead or via e-mail to introduce them to the SDM/SPS curriculum and explain any details you would like them to know as you begin.

Also essential is communication of SDM/SPS to parents and guardians. At the beginning of the year, send an e-mail note, letter, or other communication to parents and guardians, letting them know what you are about to begin and when and how it will take place.

At the end of this Introduction is a sample letter that can be modified and sent to parents on school letterhead or via e-mail to introduce them to the SDM/SPS curriculum and explain any details you would like them to know as you begin.

The curriculum incorporates other communications to the home. These take the following forms:

- Pages to send home that help parents and guardians reinforce skills taught in class
- Activities that students can do with their families
- Suggestions to parents and guardians of ways that they can build their children's SDM/SPS skills by making some small changes in their home routines

Also strongly recommended is a paperback book for parents and guardians that supports all of the skills instruction in this curriculum: *Emotionally Intelligent Parenting: How to Raise a Self-Disciplined, Responsible, Socially Skilled Child*, by Elias, Tobias, and Friedlander (2000).

Finally, be sure your colleagues know what you are doing. Let teachers of special subjects and student support services personnel know what you are covering and how they might be able to use the prompts and cues the students are learning. Find time to share about the activities during grade-level and general faculty meetings. Begin to create a conversation about character in your school so that it becomes as clear to others as it is to you that school is not just about preparing students for tests in school, but also about preparing them for the tests of life.

QUESTIONS AND ANSWERS: EVERYTHING YOU ALWAYS WANTED TO KNOW ABOUT SDM/SPS

Those working with SDM/SPS—including teachers, other educators, parents, school board members, and community partners—often have questions about the curriculum and the overall approach. The "big question" concerns how SDM/SPS relates to other forms of character education and to emotional intelligence. That question will be addressed first; a list of other frequently asked questions and their answers will follow.

Relationship to Other Forms of Character Education

SDM/SPS is considered a primary example of a social-emotional learning (SEL) curriculum, that is, a curriculum that builds students' social, emotional, cognitive, and academic capacities in an integrated manner. This curriculum, developed over three decades, is also linked to many other related curricula. For example, SDM/SPS is recognized by the Character Education Partnership as a model program. It is also considered a Promising Program for prevention of violence and substance abuse by the U.S. Department of Education's Expert Panel on Safe and Drug Free Schools, and a winner of the Lela Rowland Prevention Award by the National Mental Health Association as an outstanding program. As noted earlier, SDM/SPS is recognized for excellence by the National Association of School Psychologists and the Collaborative for Academic, Social, and Emotional Learning (www.CASEL.org). Even a cursory look at the FIG TESPN skills (described in the section titled "The Instructional Phase: Building a Social Decision Making Strategy in Grades 4–5" earlier in this Introduction) makes clear that students cannot have skill deficits and expect to achieve meaningful academic and social success, sound character, and the ability to engage in nonviolent conflict resolution and to resist pressures to become involved in substance abuse.

SDM/SPS is most directly related to the Interpersonal Cognitive Problem Solving (ICPS—"I Can Problem Solve") approach developed by Spivack and Shure in the early 1970s and described as it relates to preschool through intermediate grades in three books by Shure (2000, 2001a, 2001b). SDM/SPS is completely compatible with and an excellent follow-up to the ICPS curricula. SDM/SPS principles can be found in other empirically based social-emotional learning curricula, such as Lions-Quest, Second Step, Open Circle, PATHS, and TRIBES.

Relationship to Emotional Intelligence

In 1995, Daniel Goleman published his book *Emotional Intelligence*. In it, he summarized years of work done in schools, hospitals, workplaces, and families showing that intellectual abilities alone were not sufficient to account for life success. The skills of emotional intelligence—referred to in most schools as social-emotional learning—are needed for our success as students and as workers, as citizens, and as parents. SDM/SPS is one of six programs that formed the conceptual and empirical basis behind Daniel Goleman's work.

What are the skills of emotional intelligence? Goleman defines five overlapping areas:

- *Self-awareness:* Recognition of one's emotions, possessing an adequate emotional vocabulary, understanding the reasons for feeling as one does in different situations
- *Self-regulation of emotion:* Capacity to verbalize and cope positively with anxiety, depression, and anger and to control impulses toward aggressive, self-destructive, antisocial behavior
- *Self-monitoring and performance:* Short-term and long-term goal setting, focus on tasks at hand; mobilization of positive motivation, hope, and optimism; and ability to work toward one's optimal performance states
- *Empathy and perspective taking:* Listening skills; sensitivity to others' feelings; and understanding of others' points of view, feelings, and perspectives
- *Social skills in handling relationships:* Assertiveness; the ability to express emotions effectively and to show sensitivity to social cues; skills and strategies for working in groups; leadership; social decision making strategies; and the ability to respond constructively to interpersonal obstacles

Emotional Intelligence/SEL and SDM/SPS are entirely compatible. The steps of FIG TESPN are part of social skills for handling relationships; the first step, of course, is part of self-awareness. The readiness skills are interspersed throughout all aspects of emotional intelligence. What was not present in Goleman's work, including the sections on education, was a detailed discussion of implementation. This curriculum operationalizes what is necessary to bring emotional intelligence to every elementary school and classroom.

Effectiveness of the SDM/SPS Curriculum

Evaluation data on SDM/SPS, gathered over the last three decades, strongly support the effectiveness of the curriculum with regard to teachers' ability to facilitate students' social decision making and social problem solving. The evaluations also show students' improved social decision making and social problem solving skills; increased prosocial behavior in school and better ability to cope with stressors; and retention of positive effects, as indicated in a high school follow-up. A summary of the evaluation data is provided in Appendix A.

Educators are likely to have specific requirements for assessing the effectiveness of the SDM/SPS program as provided in their own educational environments. However, we include in Appendix B two instruments that we have found helpful in evaluating the Grades 4–5 curriculum at the individual program level. The first is a curriculum feedback form designed to obtain educators' opinions of specific SDM/SPS lesson material. The second, the Profile of Social Decision Making/Social Problem Solving Strengths, may serve as a pretest and posttest to provide information about students' skill learning as a result of program participation.

Other Frequently Asked Questions

Looking at the SDM/SPS program for the first time, many teachers share the following concerns:

- How does SDM/SPS integrate into classroom lesson plans and curricula?
- How does SDM/SPS use multiple methods of delivery to make its points?
- How does SDM/SPS promote engaging and experiential learning?
- How does SDM/SPS encourage higher level thinking skills that spur moral development?
- How does SDM/SPS provide opportunities for moral action?
- How does SDM/SPS reach students in a developmentally appropriate manner?
- How does SDM/SPS apply to diverse student populations and cultural backgrounds?
- How does SDM/SPS appeal to diverse learning styles?
- How does SDM/SPS support cooperative learning?
- How does SDM/SPS address decision-making skills in the context of high-risk activities?
- How does SDM/SPS encourage positive core values?
- How does SDM/SPS enhance social skills?
- How does SDM/SPS promote a caring school climate?
- How does SDM/SPS complement extracurricular activities?
- How does SDM/SPS include parents and family members?
- How does SDM/SPS encourage school-business partnerships?
- How does SDM/SPS address the effects of mass media?
- How does SDM/SPS link with academic achievement?

How does SDM/SPS integrate into classroom lesson plans and curricula?

SDM/SPS can be readily infused into most existing academic content areas and is aligned with core curriculum standards in such areas as health, language arts, and social studies. Rather than changing lesson content, SDM/SPS uses a pedagogy in which teachers develop an approach that is active in facilitating students' use of sound problem-solving and decision-making strategies and social and emotional competencies.

SDM/SPS is designed to become a strategic part of the teaching process, influencing behavior, academic learning, and social and emotional life in the school setting. Behavioral and cognitive-emotional skills taught have a broad-based range of applications that can extend to community and home situations as well. The formal curriculum activities are most effectively conducted in a regular, consistent time period, usually at least once per week. Because SDM/SPS provides a foundation of prosocial, critical thinking and life skills learning for all students, it is often a useful structure for organizing existing character education, prevention, social skills, and related school programs.

How does SDM/SPS use multiple methods of delivery to make its points?

Teachers using SDM/SPS with their students make use of multiple methods to teach the skills, including direct instruction, worksheets, group discussions, role-playing and rehearsal, and videos and literature as stimuli for discussion.

Ideally, teacher training sessions will be available to prepare teachers to lead these classes, based primarily on small-group experiential activities. Video clips of master teachers in the classroom and live modeling of teacher skills can help to inform participants prior to role-play practice and performance feedback activities. Lecture components include program history and overview. Print and media are used to support the training, and field testing of new skills is processed in follow-up consultation. (See www.2umdnj.edu/SPSweb for additional information.)

How does SDM/SPS promote engaging and experiential learning?

Through application and generalization activities and supplemental topics, students apply SDM/SPS skills to curriculum content and real-life situations. They learn to see literature and historical events through the eyes of the protagonists and to understand the feelings involved. Many activities involve cooperative learning groups and movement on the part of students. Students are encouraged to use skills in brainstorming and planning to develop creative methods for presenting material (for example, learning about caring for the environment or reducing vandalism through a community-based project). Further, the final step of the FIG TESPN decision-making framework —Notice what happened (Now what?)—is a blueprint for learning the skill of self-reflection and exercising the ability to learn from personal experience.

How does SDM/SPS encourage higher level thinking skills that spur moral development?

A primary goal of this approach is to help students develop the ability to think clearly, even under stress. By providing a combination of direct instruction and multiple and varied opportunities to practice a strategy for thinking through a problem, decision, or life conflict, the program helps students internalize this ability. Although the skills are essential for processing understanding in academic areas, the focus of much of the instruction and practice is on everyday moral and interpersonal choices that students face. These skills are the cornerstone of self-reflection, which is a central aspect of emotional intelligence, moral development, and moral action.

How does SDM/SPS provide opportunities for moral action?

The SDM/SPS approach requires students to develop plans for action and evaluate the results of what they have done. This requirement results in a range of life applications in wide and diverse areas of moral action. For example, educators are trained to help students whose behaviors result in a disciplinary action or have hurt another person to develop a personal plan for restitution.

Educators implementing the SDM/SPS approach have also developed a diverse variety of school and community service projects that promote moral action. These applications include the following:

- Classroom (students solving interpersonal conflicts within the classroom).
- School, community, or peer mediation applications to promote moral action on the playground and in the school bus, cafeteria, and other less structured school community situations.
- Community service projects. (Examples include a project that resulted in the recycling of plastics, inspired by student presentations to a town council, and a "Community Sharing Circle," involving students from public and private schools within a township that led the recreation department and the mayor's office to develop a three-year plan to reduce vandalism in the community.)

The SDM/SPS approach focuses on providing students with a foundation for moral action. They learn basic skills that are then applied to endless and ongoing opportunities to stop and reflect on choices made and the impact these choices have on oneself, on others, and on the community.

How does SDM/SPS reach students in a developmentally appropriate manner?

SDM/SPS uses a developmentally sensitive scope and sequence of skills to provide students with social-emotional competencies they can use at once. The program is built on foundations of research and practice from the fields of child development, child clinical psychology, the cognitive sciences, brain and emotion research, educational practice, and primary prevention. Professional psychologists developed the curriculum, which was then field-tested and revised by teachers working within the school systems over a period of three decades. SDM/SPS is used, and has been adapted for use, with all students (general and special education) in elementary and middle schools, regardless of ability level, ethnic group, and socioeconomic status.

How does SDM/SPS apply to diverse student populations and cultural backgrounds?

Many of the SDM/SPS skills are also key components of promoting a multicultural perspective in students. Instruction in SDM/SPS includes learning to care about and respect one's classmates (regardless of issues of difference), to listen and learn from one another, and to comfortably share diverse opinions and backgrounds. Activities are included to build group cohesion, acceptance of differences, and the ability to understand different points of view. In this way, respect for diversity moves beyond knowledge acquisition and into the realm of systematic skill building to develop students' ability to perform successfully according to established classroom norms and expectations.

How does SDM/SPS appeal to diverse learning styles?

An awareness of diverse learning styles was a part of the original goals for program design and is built into the activities, pedagogy, and Tips for Teachers. Because of the nature of the content, almost all areas of instruction lend themselves to the use of varied modes of content delivery and application across the modalities of the multiple intelligences.

Curriculum-based activities include the use of a wide range of instructional methods to ensure that students who favor imaginative, analytic, commonsense, and dynamic learning styles are all addressed. Instruction includes these methods:

- Visual displays
- Mnemonic devices for remembering skills and concepts
- Hands-on activities
- Storytelling
- Role-play and real-life practice
- Live modeling
- Reflective discussions to highlight the purpose of a lesson after experiential activities
- Activities that allow students to teach others
- Multimodal formats for presentation of projects and other learning

Much of the curriculum consists of innovations developed by teachers to match students' different learning styles and needs.

How does SDM/SPS support cooperative learning?

The SDM/SPS model supports cooperative learning in two ways. First, the initial phase of the curriculum is focused on helping students treat their classmates as a problem-solving team. By learning and practicing these skills in a controlled situation, students become better prepared to be productive and to behave acceptably in a cooperative learning group. Second, both skill-building lessons and the ongoing infused application of these skills are conducted by using a wide range of cooperative learning methods, such as pair shares, small-group brainstorming, problem solving, and role-playing activities.

How does SDM/SPS address decision-making skills in the context of high-risk activities?

Traditional prevention programs tend to be organized around a single problem area, such as substance abuse, handgun violence, or risky teenage sex. SDM/SPS serves as a research-validated framework for prevention programs that are not limited to specific problems but rather are more unifying in their prevention messages. This unifying framework teaches students to become more socially aware and socially skilled decision makers in both routine and high-risk problem situations.

How does SDM/SPS encourage positive core values?

A number of positive core value areas are encouraged and supported by the SDM/SPS curriculum. The program focuses on building skills that will enable a person to be a caring, compassionate, responsible, and respectful friend and classmate, thus preparing students to become positive and productive citizens. Students are taught to be reflective, nonimpulsive, and responsible decision makers and problem solvers who consider the way in which their actions will affect both themselves and others. The basis of the curriculum at each grade level is teamwork, operationalized by activities that build the skills that underlie this value, such as self-control, listening, respectful communication, giving and receiving help and authentic praise, working cooperatively and fairly in small groups, and understanding and respecting others' different points of view.

How does SDM/SPS enhance social skills?

The purpose of the SDM/SPS program is to develop the social and decision-making skills children need to cope with stress, make sound choices, avoid self-destructive behaviors, and resolve conflicts peacefully. These are the goals of the program:

1. Develop children's self-control and social awareness skills (including monitoring and regulating stress and emotions, group cooperation, and the ability to develop positive peer relationships).

2. Improve students' decision-making, problem-solving, and conflict resolution and mediation skills.

3. Increase students' academic and interpersonal self-efficacy by providing them with a problem-solving framework and social-emotional competencies upon which they can rely in stressful situations.

4. Enhance positive social behaviors and healthy life choices.

How does SDM/SPS promote a caring school climate?

The SDM/SPS curriculum has many activities and strategies for building class cohesion and transforming classrooms into problem-solving teams. Moreover, when SDM/SPS becomes part of schoolwide procedures, changes occur in the way problems and discipline are handled in the school. The focus shifts to setting positive behavioral norms and to dealing with violations as problems to be solved. Students develop and make agreements to follow a new plan for action in the future.

How does SDM/SPS complement extracurricular activities?

Ideally, SDM/SPS becomes an integral part of the overall school climate and easily complements the school's extracurricular activities. Coaches of both school- and township-sponsored athletic programs have been trained to reinforce the SDM/SPS skills that the children are learning in their classroom-based program. For example, coaches can call upon the self-control skills, such as "Keep Calm," when athletes have difficulty controlling their emotions during a game. Constructive criticism and team building are also important sportsmanship skills. After-school and summer programs also can provide both direct instruction and reinforcing practice activities in social and decision-making skills. Workshops have been developed to incorporate SDM/SPS as foundation skills for training of students involved in student government, peer leadership, peer mediation, and service learning.

How does SDM/SPS include parents and family members?

Parent and family involvement is a critical area for extending classroom-based instruction to the home and family. Two widely available paperback publications by Elias, Tobias, and Friedlander, *Emotionally Intelligent Parenting* (2000) and *Raising Emotionally Intelligent Teenagers* (2002), and a related Web site (www.eqparenting.com) have helped us to reach parents. The University of Medicine and Dentistry of New Jersey's Social Decision Making Program has developed the *Leader's Guide for Conducting Parent Meetings,* which provides a detailed plan to conduct a sequence of parent workshops on social decision making.

In addition, we have collaborated with district teams in the development of a wide variety of outreach activities and materials, based on the creative problem solving of educators and our staff. For example, a variety of local cable video programs have been produced as successful ways to reach many parents in a community. A parent survey to assess the best times for parents to tune in can help set a schedule in line with a variety of viewing times for busy parents. No baby-sitter or other logistical planning is needed for participation. Copies of the video are then distributed by the school for home viewing. In addition, we help districts adapt a brochure for parents describing the program, based on some standard prototypes we have designed in the past. Parents are also reached through materials incorporated into the curriculum that are designed to provide information that parents and guardians can post on their refrigerators for easy, regular viewing.

A wide variety of school-based events have also been effective in some communities, such as evening sessions including dinner and baby-sitters and bagel breakfasts in which parents are invited to join a morning class session where children help their teachers share what they are learning. Such events are designed and marketed in collaboration with our school colleagues, who are most knowledgeable regarding the local needs, access points, and obstacles in the community.

How does SDM/SPS encourage school-business partnerships?

Local businesses and corporations are very interested in working with schools to prepare students to enter the workforce. Recent studies have shown the importance of social and emotional competencies in the workplace. Learning these skills early in life has been shown to be beneficial in finding employment and in receiving promotions throughout a whole career. Local businesses have supported meetings at which students have displayed work done as part of the SDM/SPS curriculum, provided mentors for projects, visited classrooms, and provided resources in support of various projects and activities.

How does SDM/SPS address the effects of mass media?

SDM/SPS addresses the media in constructive ways. Students are taught critical viewing skills and to recognize situations in which they are being persuaded to buy a particular product or to agree with a certain point of view. In the Grade 5 materials, specific emphasis is placed on teaching students to recognize how advertisements play on their emotions and vulnerabilities. Mass media are also useful tools in teaching social and emotional learning. Various movies, television shows, and videos can present real-life and hypothetical situations that can be used to teach problem-solving and decision-making skills. Part of the SDM/SPS pedagogy is the TVDRP technique, a combination of television (or other audiovisual or digital media), discussion (that will facilitate thoughtful decision making), and guided rehearsal and practice (or other forms of experiential activity).

How does SDM/SPS link with academic achievement?

SDM/SPS and academics have strong empirical and conceptual links. Research studies carried out over the past three decades are summarized in Appendix A.

SUMMARY

SDM/SPS can help schools meet their mandates and perceived needs in a broad variety of areas. The skills it establishes are an essential part of developing a safe, caring school. The program helps educators build learning communities with character and lay a foundation for students' social-emotional development and for prevention of violence and substance abuse.

Sample Letter to Parents and Guardians to Introduce SDM/SPS

Dear Parents or Guardians:

I would like to take this opportunity to introduce you to a program that we are initiating in our school. The program is called Social Decision Making/Social Problem Solving (SDM/SPS). It teaches children valuable skills in the areas of self-control, problem solving, decision making, and getting along with others. We will be doing SDM/SPS lessons once a week, usually every _____ at
_____.

These skills require time and practice to develop. You will be receiving information and ideas for activities that will assist you in helping your child practice these skills. I would like to encourage you to reinforce these skills when your child is at home and during extracurricular activities. Your continued support and encouragement will enable your child to gain strength in this area and experience success now and in the future.

I am excited about implementing this program in our school. Please feel free to contact me or our building principal with any questions or ideas.

Sincerely,

_____   _____
(Teacher signature)   *(Date)*

RECOMMENDED TOPICS FOR GRADE 4

Rules and Tools

Emotional Regulation

Social Decision Making and Social Problem Solving

Supplemental

Topic

Grade 4 Worksheets

Topics 1–8

1 Introduction to Social Decision Making/Social Problem Solving (SDM/SPS) Lessons

OBJECTIVES
- To introduce and orient students to SDM/SPS lessons
- To establish ground rules for SDM/SPS meetings
- To introduce participation in a *Sharing Circle*
- To introduce and provide opportunities to practice Speaker Power and establish *Speaker Power* as shared language and a skill prompt
- To introduce and provide opportunities to practice Listening Position and establish *Listening Position* as shared language and a skill prompt
- To build a sense of group trust, belonging, and cohesiveness

MATERIALS
Chalkboard or easel pad

Speaker Power object

Poster board and markers

Whole-class display of the steps in Listening Position (Worksheet 4.1.1)

PREPARATION
The Sharing Circle will eventually be used as the vehicle for working through the problem-solving steps and class discussions of problem solving. Determine a location for the Sharing Circle and decide how to have students settle into it.

NOTE
After the group has compiled a list of rules, write or have students write them on a sheet of poster board and display them in the classroom. Change the poster as rules are refined and new rules added.

INSTRUCTIONAL ACTIVITIES

1. Introduce the lessons.

Begin by telling students that they will be having lessons that will help them learn skills for getting along with other people and making good decisions. Knowing how to make decisions that will help solve problems and getting along with other people are important in fourth grade and will also help them to be successful and healthy as they grow up.

Inform the students that these skills will help the class work together as a problem-solving team.

2. Assess the current skill level.

Ask if any children have had lessons like this before. Often, it is valuable to have children who have had SDM/SPS lessons in the past explain in their own way what they have learned. School conditions change from year to year, and this exercise provides an opportunity to assess prior knowledge and skills and to structure children's expectations toward what you actually plan to do this year. If you are working in a district with an established scope and sequence of skills for grade levels, it is a good idea to ask students to describe and demonstrate skills they already know to help gauge the need for review.

3. Establish rules and agreements.

Tell the class that to work as a problem-solving team, you will first have to establish some rules to be followed so the meetings will go well. Ask the children to volunteer some rules that would help make everyone feel good about being a member of the class team. Keep a list on the chalkboard or easel pad. Ask them to think about what would make them feel good about sharing their ideas and how they would like to be treated. Then ask them to list some things that would make them not feel good about being a part of this team.

Usually, most of the children's suggestions fall into general categories that overlap nicely with skills that will be covered during upcoming lessons and later given a label (or skill prompt). Therefore, when you're just getting started, team rules should be brief and positive, leaving room for more explicit phrasing to be added later.

Let the children know that as they learn about specific ideas that can help the team work well, the rules will be updated, but it is valuable to post some initial ideas. Here are some common rules to begin with:

- Listen to each other without interrupting.
- Respect each other in words and what we do.
- Remember that behavior outside the rules has consequences.

4. Introduce the Sharing Circle.

Explain that the first activity is called a *Sharing Circle.* To participate, everyone (children, teachers, visitors in the room) in turn will at least say their name and answer a Sharing Circle question.

5. Introduce Speaker Power.

Select an object (magic wand, stuffed animal, ball, ruler, pen . . .) that will be passed to the person speaking to designate a turn to talk. Say:

A Speaker Power object helps remind us to respect the person who is speaking, and the job of the other team members at that time is to listen carefully without interrupting.

Explain that everyone will have a chance to have Speaker Power—either by receiving the object as it gets passed around the group or by raising a hand to ask for it.

Remind students that, as the teacher, you always have a kind of invisible Speaker Power. You will ask for the object when it fits into the lesson to do so, but it's also your job to speak whenever you regard it as necessary.

6. Introduce Listening Position.

Explain that this lesson will also help the class explore what listening is and how to go about doing it better. To be a good listener it is necessary to pay attention. Establish the behavioral components of *Listening Position:*

1. Sit or stand straight.

2. Face the speaker or source of sound.

3. Look toward the speaker or source of sound.

7. Conduct a practice exercise using Speaker Power.

Begin by asking a simple and nonthreatening question that will allow everyone in the group to have a turn. Let students know that there are no right or wrong answers and they can share with the group anything that comes to mind, as long as it addresses the question. During the initial Sharing Circle, it is a good idea to set the tone for further circles. Tell children that they are not being asked to agree with everything that is being said; they can agree or disagree with someone's statement but still respect the person.

When first getting started, it can be helpful to go first and model what is expected. Students often enjoy learning things about their teachers, and this helps build an interest in what other people feel and think about a similar question.

Sample questions to ask:

- What happened to you lately that made you feel surprised?
- What is your favorite radio station?
- If you could live in a jungle for one day, what kind of animal would you want to be?

As time permits, ask the students two or three additional questions that will gradually reveal something new about them to their classmates. After each question, have four to six children answer, then move onto the next question. The following questions have been found to be quite useful for an initial group-building exercise:

- What is your favorite food? (Why?)
- What is your favorite time of day? (Why?)
- If you were going to be the star of a television show, what show would you pick? (Why?)
- If you could meet anyone you wanted to whom you have never actually met, who would you pick? (Why?)

8. Introduce a Reflective Summary.

As outlined in the Introduction, ask students to reflect on the question "What did you learn from today's lesson?" Reinforce key themes, then go over any follow-up work.

9. Follow up.

The following steps will help make sure that the students have a chance to continue working with the new concepts.

Assignment

Inform students that you will be using the cue words *Speaker Power, Listening Position,* and *Sharing Circle* during all subjects and at many times during the day.

Take-Home

Distribute a letter to parents or guardians like the one presented in the Introduction at this time (if it hasn't been sent earlier or distributed at Back to School Night) to introduce the Social Decision Making/Social Problem Solving skill-building lessons to the students' families.

Plans to Promote Transfer and Generalization of Skill

Plan ahead to provide opportunities for students to practice a Sharing Circle, Speaker Power, and Listening Position as part of an academic lesson or class discussion.

TIPS FOR TEACHERS

1. Class size and maturity are important factors in determining how the Sharing Circle will best operate. Here are some other Sharing Circle questions teachers have found useful in addition to or instead of those suggested earlier:

   - If you were the ruler of the world, what would you do?
   - Do you think boys or girls have it easier? Why?
   - What are you the most proud of having done? What would make you even more proud?
   - If you could be an adult for one week, what would you do during the week?
   - If you could have the ability to talk to one kind of animal, which would you choose and why? What would you talk about?
   - If you could take a friend home with you after school, what would you show off first?
   - If you had to pick a new name, what would you choose?

2. It is permissible to allow students to pass should they not wish to respond to a particular question. However, this option should be exercised sparingly.

3. Sharing Circle questions should allow for self-expression but not call for personal information considered confidential. Children may not be aware of these limits, so it is important for teachers to avoid questions that pull for such information and to politely interrupt, support, and redirect any responses that are inappropriate for a classroom skill-building lesson. For example, you can say:

   I can tell that you have strong feelings about this, and I want to hear about it. But it is better to talk about private things that happen at home privately, not in a large group. We can talk about this after we finish the lesson to respect the privacy of your family. Can you think of an example that happened to you at school or with your friends?

   Be sure to follow up and refer to another staff member if what students share is outside your area of professional training.

4. Research has found that it is most beneficial to use formal lessons to teach social and emotional skills in combination with ongoing opportunities to practice the skills throughout the day. Prompts

and cues (set phrases such as *Speaker Power*) serve as meaningful shared language that can be used to evoke the behavioral components of a skill taught in the lesson. How well students develop and internalize these skills will be directly related to the number of opportunities they have to practice.

5. Clear consequences should be established for disruption of the group by either aggressiveness or silliness. One strategy that has been successful for some students and groups is to first remind disruptive students about their agreement to keep the rules, such as respect each other and listen to each other, to prompt desired behavior. If this reminder does not work, try having such students sit out for a few minutes, letting them know that you will be checking back with them to ask if they are ready to come back and stick to the team agreements. This strategy is effective when the students enjoy the activities and don't want to be left out. As with any behavior management technique, it is important to find reinforcers and consequences that work for a particular child or group.

6. Integrate skills as you teach them into your existing behavior management system. Many teachers we have worked with report that it becomes natural and automatic to include skill prompts and practice of SDM/SPS skills within academic subject areas throughout the course of the day once students have mastered the basic skills. At initial stages of implementation, however, it is best to think ahead each week and include specific activities for skill practice within the lesson plans of all subject areas.

7. It is helpful to identify situations and subject content areas where the practice of SDM/SPS skills would fortify existing objectives. It is also useful to document these plans and monitor the opportunities students have to practice and generalize the skill they are learning to academic and real-life situations. This effort helps ensure that teaching practices remain faithful to the instructional design that led to research-validated outcomes. It also helps teachers—in their role as adult learners—to integrate new skills within the complex repertoire of teaching skills needed.

Listening Position

1. Sit or stand straight.

2. Face the speaker or source of sound.

3. Look toward the speaker or source of sound.

Worksheet 4.1.1

2   Respectful Listening

OBJECTIVES
- To deepen and further develop listening skills
- To introduce active listening and establish *Repectful Listening* as a skill prompt
- To provide an opportunity to practice paying attention

MATERIALS
Whole-class display of the steps in Respectful Listening (Worksheet 4.2.1)

INSTRUCTIONAL ACTIVITIES

1. Review the basic approach to SDM/SPS lessons.

Begin by eliciting from students ground rules and descriptions for Sharing Circle, Speaker Power, and Listening Position. Review all behavioral skill components.

2. Conduct a Sharing Circle.

Introduce the topic by saying:

Think of a person you respect. Before we share, let's talk about what the word respect *means. What do you think?*

Provide a summary from the dictionary if necessary. Then ask:

What do you think of someone who listens carefully and respectfully to you? What do they do to make you know they are listening?

Take time at intervals during Sharing Circle to ask students to show how well they were listening by sharing their recollection of what other students who spoke previously had to say. Reinforce good listening skills and Listening Position.

3. Introduce Respectful Listening.

Explain why it is important to be able to listen effectively:

The new kind of listening we'll be talking about today is a way to be sure you understand what you have listened to and to show people speaking to you that you respect them.

To be sure that you have paid attention and are right about what you heard, you can repeat what you think you heard. You might say, "I heard you say that . . . ," and say back to the other person what you heard them say. And then you ask them if you are right by saying something like "Did I understand you?"

Display the components of *Respectful Listening:*

1. Use Listening Position

2. Pay attention to what the other person is saying.

3. Repeat what the other person said.

4. Check to see if you are right.

4. Model the skill.

Ask for a student volunteer to role-play with you on the question "What is your favorite thing to do after school?" Place two chairs in the front of the room, facing each other, and remind your partner that both of you are going to use Listening Position and Respectful Listening. Then ask what your partner's favorite thing to do after school is. Ask a question for more detail if response is too brief. Say, "Thank you; let me see if I understand what you have been saying so far," if it runs on too long.

Repeat what the student said. Ask if you are right: "Is that your favorite thing?"

5. Conduct a practice activity.

Pair two students and ask them to practice what they have seen.

Tell them that they will need to decide who will listen and who will talk first. (Give them a minute to decide.) Then say:

I will be giving you a question or topic to talk about. If you're the person you decided would go first, you will talk about what I've suggested. If you're the listener, you will use Listening Position and Respectful Listening, and then repeat and check to see if you heard what your partner said. Then the two of you will switch, and the person who talked first will be the listener and the person who listened first will be the speaker.

Ask if there are any questions. Here are some useful practice topics:

- What movie would you recommend to a friend? What is good about it?

- Pick an animal that you think makes a good pet. Why do you think it makes a good pet?
- If you could eat the perfect meal, what foods would you have?

  Listeners, if your partner mentions foods that you do not recognize, you can ask for a description.

  Speakers, if your listener does not know about the food that you would like to have, describe one or two things and help your partner understand why you like that food instead of just listing a lot of things they have never eaten and know nothing about.
- If you could have the perfect playground, what would it look like? What would be there?

Stop after the first round and ask students what the exercise was like for them. Did the listener use Respectful Listening? Ask the speaker to tell the listener one thing the listener did that let them know that they were listening. Here are some questions:

- Listeners, did you check to see if you listened accurately? What happened? Did you get it right or did you forget something? What was difficult or easy about listening?
- Speakers, how did it feel when someone repeated what you said? How does it feel when you know someone is listening to you?

Repeat the activity with a new question, as time permits. Switch partners for the next topic or question if logistics, group management, and maturity allow.

6. Introduce a Reflective Summary.

As outlined in the Introduction, ask students to reflect on the question "What did you learn from today's lesson?" Reinforce key themes, then go over any follow-up work.

7. Follow up.

The following steps will help make sure that the students have a chance to continue working with the new concepts.

Assignment

Ask students if they can think of some times when it would be a good idea to check and be sure that they are accurately hearing what other people say. Generate a list of ideas, such as when someone is explaining something to do, when someone is telling you why they think doing something is a good or bad idea, and when listening to instructions or reminders about homework. Have students pick one of these ideas to try and write it on their homework list or in their assignment book. Let them know that they will have time to talk about how well they listened during the next lesson.

Plans to Promote Transfer and Generalization of Skill

Plan ahead to provide opportunities for students to practice Respectful Listening. For example, after morning announcements, ask students who had good Listening Position and can remember what was said. When someone speaks up accurately, praise that student for Respectful Listening.

TIPS FOR TEACHERS

1. Prompt for Listening Position and Respectful Listening throughout the school day. Prior to giving directions, encourage the class to use these skills to remember what they are to do, so they won't need to come to you to ask you to repeat directions.

2. Praise students for exercising good Listening Position and Respectful Listening throughout the school day.

Respectful Listening

1. Use Listening Position.

2. Pay attention to what the other person is saying.

3. Repeat what the other person said.

4. Check to see if you are right.

Worksheet 4.2.1

TOPIC

3 Strategies for Remembering

OBJECTIVES
- To review and practice good listening skills
- To help students discover various *Strategies for Remembering*
- To increase awareness of metacognitive strategies for remembering
- To practice using strategies for remembering

MATERIALS
Six to twelve common household or classroom items; a scarf or large sheet of paper to cover the items

Chalkboard or easel pad

Poster board and markers

NOTE
After the group has compiled a list of strategies, write or have students write their ideas on a sheet of poster board for display in the classroom. If students come up with other strategies, add them to the list.

INSTRUCTIONAL ACTIVITIES

1. Review Topic 2.

Go over Listening Position and Respectful Listening. Ask students to share their experiences with the listening technique they wrote down as the last lesson's homework.

2. Introduce the idea of remembering things on purpose.

Ask:

When is it important to remember things?

Ask for examples that relate to school and home. One important example is in the area of homework. Ask for all the different aspects of homework that need to be remembered. Examples include remembering to write the assignment in the assignment book; remembering to bring home all the necessary books, materials, and supplies; remembering how to do the assignment; remembering to put the completed assignment in the book bag; remembering to bring materials to school.

Elicit from students the consequences of not remembering things that they are told. Make the point that part of being a responsible person is to remember things.

3. Discuss strategies.

Have students describe any strategies that they already use to remember things.

4. Introduce the Memory Test activity.

Tell the students that they are going to play a game that will help them learn about remembering. Say that you have placed a number of items under a scarf or large sheet of paper, point out the surface where the objects are hidden, and explain that the object of the game is to be able to list as many of the objects as possible after a quick look. (Start off with five or six items, but don't tell students how many items to expect.)

Remove the cover. Have the students look at the items for about thirty seconds. Then cover the items and ask the students to write or draw all the items that they can remember. Give the class a few minutes, then have the students share their lists.

5. Conduct a Sharing Circle.

Ask the students to share the various means by which they remembered the items. Generate a list, noting common strategies and most effective strategies. (Some examples include counting the items; taking a mental picture of the items; saying the names of the items over and over; grouping the items by color, size, or use; or telling a story or making personal associations between the objects and things that are happening.)

After the list is compiled, ask students if they have heard a strategy that one of their classmates used to help them remember that they never thought of before. Explain that actively using a strategy for remembering improves the chances of remembering.

6. Repeat the Memory Test activity.

Tell the students that you will play the game again (using different objects).

Instruct the students to select a strategy to use to help them remember the objects—and to try a different strategy even if they used one that worked well the first time. Allow students to view the new set of items for thirty seconds and then quiz them on their recollections.

7. Have another Sharing Circle.

Ask about strategies used and how well the new strategies worked. Did students trying a strategy for the first time or using a different strategy remember more items this time?

8. Discuss uses of strategy.

Elicit examples from students of different situations in which they can use the Strategies for Remembering that they brainstormed during the lesson. For example, they can use the strategies when they need to memorize their spelling words or math facts, or to complete homework assignments.

9. Introduce a Reflective Summary.

As outlined in the Introduction, ask students to reflect on the question "What did you learn from today's lesson?" Reinforce key themes, then go over any follow-up work.

10. Follow up.

The following steps will help make sure that the students have a chance to continue working with the new concepts.

Assignment

Ask students to pick a time when they can use a strategy to help them remember and to write it down on their homework list. Tell them that at the start of the next meeting they will have a chance to share a time when they used a strategy to help them remember and tell their classmates how it worked.

Take-Home

Send home a copy of the Strategies for Remembering list the class worked out. Add these ideas:

Parents and guardians can help children improve their memory skills by giving them common household chores and discussing what Strategies for Remembering can help the child accomplish the task. For example, make a grocery list and have the child try to memorize some or all of the items on the list. Bring the list to the store and see how many items the child can remember. Another way to practice using remembering skills is doing a trip recall. After returning from a family trip or vacation, have the child write a story or draw pictures of the activities that you did. Have the child try to remember as many details as possible, such as the names of places or the events that happened in the order they occurred.

Plans to Promote Transfer and Generalization of Skill

Academic

Assign students or student groups the task of coming up with a strategy for remembering how to master challenging spelling words, math facts, or information for upcoming tests in any academic area. Also try asking students to come up with a strategy to help them remember what they need to do as homework.

Social Practice

As a group-building activity, especially at the beginning of the school year, play a name game to help students remember the names of their new classmates. For example, have the students sit in a Sharing Circle. Ask one student to start by saying her name. Then ask her to call on another student, who repeats her name, says his name, and calls on another student, who does the same thing. Continue until everyone is named by the last child called on. When the list gets to fifteen or more names, you can allow classmates to help each other out. If they have trouble, lead a discussion on possible strategies they can use to help them remember the names.

TIPS FOR TEACHERS

1. This lesson can be modified and repeated to promote remembering with varied stimuli (concrete objects, pictures, sounds and spoken words, and so on).

2. This activity is also about developing students' metacognitive skills; the students are beginning to think about how they learn and remember. As they become better aware of their own learning styles, they can be encouraged to employ a particular strategy for specific tasks.

TOPIC

4 Role-Playing

OBJECTIVES
- To explore techniques for role-playing
- To help students understand reasons and needs for role-playing
- To help students understand responsibilities of the audience

MATERIALS   None

PREPARATION   Before conducting the activities in this Topic, review the "Role-Playing, Rehearsal, and Practice" section in the Introduction for a full description of the four steps in role-playing. Prepare outlines for more complex role-plays for use in Step 6.

INSTRUCTIONAL ACTIVITIES

1. Review good listening and remembering skills.

Go around a Sharing Circle and discuss the memory strategies the students explored since the last lesson. Then point out that the skills just reviewed will be very important in today's lesson because today the topic will be role-playing. Brainstorm some ideas about what role-playing is and assess the students' existing level of experience with role-playing.

2. Introduce role-playing.

Explain that *role-playing* is acting out situations, something the class will do often in future meetings. Continue by saying that everyone has an important part in every role-play. The actors must use their following directions skills, and the audience members must use their listening skills. Stress that sometimes the role-plays may seem funny, but that there is a serious reason behind doing each role-play.

3. Begin with pantomimes.

Scenes without speaking parts are useful for easing students into role-playing. For each of the following situations, or similar ones that you may choose, whisper the role to a student. Have the student play the part while others try to guess what is being pantomimed.

- Shopping
- Driving a car
- Reading a book
- Waking up from a nap
- Brushing teeth
- Eating dinner

4. Describe the process of role-playing.

Explain to students that role-plays follow these four steps:

- *Prepare the script:* Choose a situation, identify characters, and select the students who will perform the role-play (the actors).
- *Run through the action:* Discuss the situation with the whole group (the audience), getting constructive suggestions for what the actors should say and do. Then have the actors discuss what they will say and do and rehearse, if time allows.
- *Action on the set:* The actors enact the situation, while the teacher serves as a director-coach, helping the actors as they need it.
- *Review the performance:* The audience shares its views of the thoughts, views, and actions expressed by the actors.

5. Conduct a practice exercise.

This example illustrates the main principles involved in role-playing. These principles can be emphasized to the students as well. Choose a situation such as one of these:

- You have a new student in your class, and you want to welcome the newcomer.
- You are having trouble doing a math problem, and you want to ask the teacher for help.
- You are a new student in the class, and you want to make friends.

Choose volunteers and brief the role-players on their parts. Have them plan what they will say and possibly let them rehearse by themselves. Remind them to have good eye contact with one another when talking.

Assign the rest of the class specific actors to watch and things to watch for—for example, how an actor looked around, felt, and so on. Remind the audience to use good listening skills.

Have the student-actors enact the situation. Provide coaching and assistance as needed.

Provide feedback to the actors. Ask the audience:

Did the actors have good eye contact?

Did they speak loudly and clearly?

Did they accomplish their task?

You can add other questions here if they seem appropriate to a given role-play.

6. Complete more complex situations.

Use general situations from the classroom (for example, a child never gets picked to play kick ball; a child always cuts in line; and the like). Follow the procedures from Step 5, role-playing practice.

7. Introduce a Reflective Summary.

As outlined in the Introduction, ask students to reflect on the question "What did you learn from today's lesson?" Reinforce key themes, then go over any follow-up work.

8. Follow up.

The following steps will help make sure that the students have a chance to continue working with the new concepts.

Assignment

Have the students write situations that can be role-played. Point out that they can create role-plays for both academic and social situations. Have them hand in their situations so you can use them during SDM/SPS activities or at other times during the school day, as needed.

Take-Home

Students can show their families how to role-play by acting out scenes from a movie, television show, or book. The families can then use role-playing to act out solutions to situations and problems that arise at home or during extracurricular activities.

Plans to Promote Transfer and Generalization of Skill

Academic

Role-playing can be very effective when it involves characters in books or stories being read in language arts. It can also be used in history lessons to reenact events or create different solutions or endings.

Social Practice

Have students role-play positive ways to solve playground problems or other interpersonal situations that arise in the classroom, in the lunchroom, or outside school.

TIPS FOR TEACHERS

1. For children to handle interpersonal situations successfully, they must be able to take the perspective of the other persons involved. Role-playing is useful for improving children's social awareness and for practicing how to cope with problems that arise. Because it is such a powerful tool, it is often useful to devote more than one full lesson to orienting the children to it. For the teacher, the initial lesson serves as a way of assessing how ready each child is for role-playing and what skills need to be developed slowly to enable a child to participate comfortably.

2. Role-playing also provides an opportunity for children to practice and receive feedback on many of the readiness skills. Further, many subsequent activities rely on the use of role-playing. The Introduction includes more information on the purposes of role-plays and techniques for conducting them.

3. Here are additional topics for pantomimes and role-plays:

   Pantomimes
   - Getting dressed
   - Taking a test
   - Talking on the phone
   - Participating in gym class

   Role-plays
   - You are at lunch, and someone accidentally trips you. You become upset. They apologize and try to help.
   - You are playing at lunchtime, and a group of kids you don't know ask you to play a game you don't know.
   - You are in the library and can't find a book you need.
   - You want to ask someone to play in school; you want to ask someone to play at your house.
   - You have lost your lunch money and need help.
   - You are lost and need directions.
   - Someone is having trouble with their spelling, and another student is trying to help.
   - You and a sibling don't get along well and now have to share a room. How can you work it out?
   - You want something for your birthday that your parents think is expensive and you don't need, and you try to convince them to buy it.

5 Be Your BEST

OBJECTIVES

- To help students learn to distinguish between passive, aggressive, and assertive styles of behavior and communication
- To teach students a strategy for effective communication
- To provide students with practice using assertive and confident behaviors as shown by their body posture, eye contact, words used, and tone of voice
- To practice BEST behaviors in role-plays of simple teammate interactions, such as greetings and saying good-bye

MATERIALS

Whole-class display of the steps in "Be Your BEST" (Worksheet 4.5.1) and the "Be Your BEST Grid" (Worksheet 4.5.2)

Copies of the "Be Your BEST Grid" for students to take home

PREPARATION

Before the lesson, establish a role-play situation and work it out with another adult—or with a student, if no other adult is available. Prepare the other person away from the class, to ensure that the class is unaware of how the role-play is going to look. One suggestion is to pretend that you are the main character and that you took some pictures with your cell phone or digital camera, including one of your friend sleeping. The other person in the role-play will pretend to be the person whose picture was taken and will become upset that you took the picture and that you plan to show it, along with the others, to friends. The focus of the role-plays will be on the main character; instruct the other person to respond in a normal and appropriate way.

Role-Play 1

For the first role-play, the main character will act *aggressively*. For example, when the person in the picture says not to show the picture to anyone, you (the main character) will react by standing up, getting into their face and space, glaring at them, and yelling at them, using words that are mean, nasty put-downs. (If you are role-playing with a student and not another adult, you would tone down this example.)

Role-Play 2

For the second role-play, repeat the first lines of the first one. This time, when the other person says that they do not want you to show the picture, you (the main character) will react *passively* by slumping your shoulders and hanging your head, looking down at the floor, mumbling, and whining your disagreement in a very quiet tone of voice, while you slowly leave the scene.

Role-Play 3

For the third role-play, when the other person says that they do not want to you to show the picture, you (the main character) will act *assertively* by sitting or standing up straight (depending on whether the other person is sitting or standing), maintaining direct eye contact, and using polite and appropriate language and an even tone of voice to try to explain that you thought it would be funny and didn't realize it would be embarrassing. End by apologizing and deleting the picture.

NOTE   A sample Be Your BEST Grid, including possible student responses, appears as Worksheet 4.5.3, at the end of this Topic. Your students' responses may be different.

INSTRUCTIONAL ACTIVITIES

1. Review good listening and remembering skills.

Go around a Sharing Circle and discuss the importance of listening carefully and remembering what people say. Stress that using Listening Position during this lesson will be very important.

2. Introduce the new topic: BEST.

Tell the students about the importance of communicating effectively and say that today's activity will involve viewing several role-plays and looking for the components of behavior that go by the acronym *BEST*.

Ask the students if they have ever heard of "Be Your BEST." With the help of the class, define the components of BEST:

    B stands for Body Posture.

    E stands for Eye Contact.

    S stands for Speech (Say something nice).

    T stands for Tone of Voice.

Elicit from the students a definition of each of these components. Tell them that when you ask them to "Be Your BEST" or "Use your BEST" skills, you are reminding them to think about BEST before they act.

3. Direct students' attention to the BEST Grid.

Introduce the terms *aggressive, assertive,* and *passive.* Tell the students that they will be watching three role-plays and that they will have to guess whether the main character is acting aggressively, assertively, or passively. The class can be split into four different groups so that each group can focus on a particular BEST component.

4. Demonstrate aggressive behavior.

Use the first of the role-plays you practiced for this Topic.

After the role-play, have the class guess how you were acting (aggressively). Refer students to the whole-class display of the BEST Grid, and elicit from them the behaviors that fit into each square under the heading "Aggressive." Explain to students that in the first role-play, you were respecting your rights and what you wanted, but you were not respecting the rights of the other person.

Before doing the next role-play, tell the students that they will be guessing whether the main character is being passive or assertive.

5. Demonstrate passive behavior.

The second role-play should be the passive situation.

After the second role-play, have the class guess how you were acting (passively). Again, elicit from the students the behaviors that fit into each square on the grid under "Passive." Explain to students that in the second role-play, you were respecting the rights of the other person and what they wanted, but you were not respecting your own rights.

6. Demonstrate assertive behavior.

The last role-play should be the assertive, or BEST, situation.

After the third role-play, elicit the behaviors that fit into each square under "Assertive." Explain to the students that in the third role-play, you were being respectful of your rights and of the rights of the other person. Further, explain to students that being assertive, being their BEST, is their best shot at being successful and that people are much more likely to respond in a positive manner when someone is being assertive rather than passive or aggressive.

7. Discuss the way people tend to respond when others are passive or aggressive.

Ask students for their opinions on this question. Some possible responses from the recipient of passive behavior include annoyance, pity, and guilt. Passive behavior may also bring out an aggressive response, including bullying. Aggressive behavior may bring out an aggressive response from its recipient—or a passive one if the recipient is afraid of the aggressor.

8. Conduct a practice activity.

Have students practice being assertive by doing some role-plays. Have students practice only the assertive behaviors, not the passive or aggressive behaviors.

End the lesson by having students brainstorm when they will try to use assertive behaviors, both in and out of school.

9. Introduce a Reflective Summary.

As outlined in the Introduction, ask students to reflect on the question "What did you learn from today's lesson?" Reinforce key themes, then go over any follow-up work.

10. Follow up.

The following steps will help make sure that the students have a chance to continue working with the new concepts.

Assignment

Since BEST is a difficult skill to learn and one that may not meet with much success in an aggressive surrounding, teachers should provide follow-up and discussion, especially as this relates to improving school climate.

Give students the assignment to try to use BEST during disagreements with their peers, both in school and during extracurricular and social situations. Have the students write a brief description of the situation, without using any names of those involved. Tell students that during the next lesson they will be sharing their experiences and how well their attempts worked or did not work.

At the next lesson, have students share their experiences, with the focus on the situations and not the names of the people involved. Have the students practice doing more role-plays using these situations and have a class discussion regarding how the students can be assertive and influence others to act assertively rather than acting passively or aggressively.

Take-Home

Send home a copy of the BEST Grid and these suggested activities.

BEST on Television

Have a discussion with your child regarding the assertive, aggressive, and passive behaviors seen in movies, videos, and television programs that you watch together. Also, discuss the impact of one character's assertive, aggressive, or passive behaviors on the other characters on the show.

Assert Your Beliefs

Help your child think of ways to take a stand instead of going along with the crowd because it is easier. Initially, have the child practice being assertive with seemingly small issues. This builds skills for the times when tougher issues arise.

Plans to Promote Transfer and Generalization of Skill

Language Arts

Have students find a character in a story who acted aggressively or passively and discuss the consequences of their behavior. Discuss how the story might have been different if the character had acted assertively. Have students write a different ending to the story, based upon the character's assertive behavior. Another option is to have the students create a role-play showing the character acting assertively rather than passively or aggressively. Have students change the story to reflect the impact that the assertive behavior would have on the action.

Social Practice

Assertive communication is a key component in preventing bullying. Discuss instances of bullying that occur in your school or in the neighborhoods of your students. Have the students discuss and practice using assertive communication to combat common bullying situations. One effective strategy that can be used with persistent teasing and bullying is illustrated by the following sequence of steps:

1. Ignore the bullying or teasing.

2. Say, "Please stop."

3. Say, "Please stop—you are bothering me."

4. Say, "If you don't stop, I am going to tell [the adult in charge]."

5. Go to the adult in charge. Use BEST as you describe what is happening and ask for help with the situation.

TIPS FOR TEACHERS

1. It should be noted that there are cultural and ethnic differences in what might be regarded as proper BEST behavior. For example, some children may be less likely to make eye contact with adult males, out of respect. These behaviors may be open to potential misinterpretation. Educators should keep in mind that behavior in the BEST areas strongly influences impressions in social interactions but that there are cultural differences in how and when certain of those behaviors should be displayed (Banks, 1991, 1992; Banks & McGee, 1989).

2. It has been helpful to state explicitly that everyone uses passive, aggressive, and assertive behaviors at times. We are not talking about different types of people here but about different styles of behavior.

3. When discussing bullying, talk about the role of the bystanders and how their passivity affects the situation. Have the children practice being assertive when they are bullied and when they see others being bullied. Use the following examples as needed.

BEST Bullying Role-Plays

- A group of girls in fourth grade are playing at recess, but they will not let Rosa play with them. Rosa walks away from the group and finds Alicia, and they begin playing together. Then the group walks over to Alicia and says to her, "Why do you want to play with Rosa? Don't you know that nobody likes her?"

- Alex is a boy in the fourth grade. Alex likes to read and do puzzles in his free time. Several of the boys in Alex's class tease him and make fun of him because he does poorly at sports. When the teams are picked in gym, he is always picked last. The boys call him a loser and tell him that they don't want him on their team.

- Veronica is a new girl in the fourth-grade class. She moved from a town in Canada. She is nice, but she speaks with an accent and uses words and phrases that the other kids in the class don't understand. A group of girls laugh and make fun of her by imitating her, and now they won't let her sit at the fourth-grade girls' lunch table.

- Bobby is a fourth grader and has difficulty learning math. He needs to go to the resource room teacher every day during math class. Several of the boys in his class call him "stupid" or "idiot." Every morning, they take the special math book that he uses and toss it to each other on the playground before school while they tease him about not knowing the answers to simple math problems.

- Jason is in the fourth grade, and he has become very sad and angry since his parents' divorce. Charlie is a boy in Jason's class. Lately, Jason has been picking on Charlie by pushing and tripping him in the hall and then yelling at Charlie for getting in his way and for being clumsy.

Advanced Conversation Topics Using Respectful Listening

- Talk about ways that you can help a friend.
- Talk about how you can include a new child in your games at recess.
- Talk about how you can help a child who is being picked on.
- Talk about what you can do when another child picks on you.
- Talk about what makes a good friend.

Be Your BEST

B — Body Posture

E — Eye Contact

S — Speech (Say something nice.)

T — Tone of Voice

From *Social Decision Making/Social Problem Solving: A Curriculum for Academic, Social, and Emotional Learning (Grades 4–5).*
Copyright © 2005 by Maurice J. Elias and Linda Bruene Butler. Research Press (800-519-2707; www.researchpress.com)

	AGGRESSIVE	ASSERTIVE (BEST)	PASSIVE
Body Posture			
Eye Contact			
Speech			
Tone of Voice			

	AGGRESSIVE	**ASSERTIVE (BEST)**	**PASSIVE**
Body Posture	Fists clenched "In your face" Tense Too close Grab, hit, slam Pound, push	Listening Position Relaxed Standing tall Straight	Slumping shoulders Shuffling feet Head down
Eye Contact	Glaring Staring	Direct Good eye contact	Looking down Looking away No eye contact
Speech	Insults Put-downs Bossy, bad words Mean words	Clear Nice words Polite	Unclear Muttering Mumbling
Tone of Voice	Yelling Screaming	Mostly calm Medium	Soft Low Whiny

6 BEST Applied: Good Teammate Behaviors

OBJECTIVES

- To identify characteristics of a good teammate *(Good Teammate Behaviors)*
- To identify undesirable characteristics of a teammate *(Not-Good Teammate Behaviors)*
- To identify and practice BEST skills in communicating with teammates
- To promote tolerance, acceptance, and empathy for teammates

MATERIALS

Chalkboard or easel pad

Copies of "What Makes a Good Teammate?" (Worksheet 4.6.1; *optional)*

NOTE

In the SDM/SPS curriculum for Grades 2–3, this concept is taught as Good Friendship Behaviors and Not-Good Friendship Behaviors. The idea in using *teammate* instead of *friend* for this level is that friendship is personal, whereas anyone can be a good teammate to anyone else.

INSTRUCTIONAL ACTIVITIES

1. Review BEST.

Discuss the components on the BEST Grid—Body Posture, Eye Contact, Speech, and Tone of Voice—and remind the class that these four categories add up to styles of behavior that can help or hurt people. Point out that the goal of today's activity is to examine and describe what people do (their behavior)—and not to use any names.

2. Introduce the idea of Good Teammate Behavior.

Ask students to think about what makes people good teammates. List their ideas on the chalkboard or easel pad. Help the children define their terms. Students often start with vague words such as *nice* and *good*. Ask them what a nice or good person *does*. What are some ways that teammates show that they care about each other? Be sure the list includes *give help, give praise, listen when you are talking,* and so on.

3. Introduce the idea of Not-Good Teammate Behavior.

Now ask students to consider behaviors that we do not like in a teammate. What are unfriendly or nonsporting behaviors? Have the children generate a list of behaviors and characteristics they do not like. Discuss some ways teammates show that they do not care about each other by their behavior.

4. Talk about the difference behavior makes.

Focus discussion on how teammates communicate with one another. Compare and contrast how teammates communicate and the way people who are not teammates communicate (or fail to communicate).

5. Conduct a practice activity.

Divide the class into pairs. Have each pair develop a role-play scenario of a situation taking place in the school cafeteria or on the athletic field. Have students first role-play an example of unfriendly behavior. Then have students role-play friendly behavior. Allow students opportunities to practice applying the skills of BEST in role-plays.

With the entire class, ask the partners how they felt when doing the unfriendly role-play. See if you can bring out any sense of discomfort or tension. Contrast this with their feelings associated with the friendly role-play.

6. Introduce a Reflective Summary.

As outlined in the Introduction, ask students to reflect on the question "What did you learn from today's lesson?" Reinforce key themes, then go over any follow-up work.

7. Follow up.

The following steps will help make sure that the students have a chance to continue working with the new concepts.

Assignment

Have students keep a journal about friendly and unfriendly communication they give or receive for a one-week period.

Plans to Promote Transfer and Generalization of Skill

1. Have students monitor effective communications with teammates. They can watch for BEST communications in the classroom, schoolyard, and so on, and then list them on index cards or in a

computer file. Set up a box or e-mail location for student submissions and review contents in the Sharing Circle format.

2. Give each student a copy of What Makes a Good Teammate? (Worksheet 4.6.1) and have students complete it before the next meeting. Discuss their responses at the meeting.

TIPS FOR TEACHERS

This lesson helps students strengthen classroom relations. When conflicts arise between students subsequent to this lesson, it is helpful to have the parties each consider their own behavior in the context of teammate behaviors, as defined during this Topic. Such an exercise in self-rating is beneficial in the development of social interaction skills and fosters accountability.

Student _____ Date _____

Things I like about my teammates

1. _____

2. _____

3. _____

4. _____

5. _____

6. _____

7. _____

8. _____

9. _____

7 BEST Applied: Giving and Receiving Praise

OBJECTIVES
- To define the words *praise* and *compliment*
- To develop skills for giving and receiving praise, using BEST
- To teach children to look for positive qualities in their peers and themselves
- To promote acceptance of classmates

MATERIALS
Whole-class display of the steps in "Giving Praise" (Worksheet 4.7.1)

Copies of "I'm a Star!" (Worksheet 4.7.2)

INSTRUCTIONAL ACTIVITIES

1. Review the past lesson in a Sharing Circle.

Ask:

What did we do in our last session? What teammate behaviors did you observe during the week? When did you observe them?

Prompt for specific examples of BEST skills in communicating with teammates. Students may wish to read their examples or develop role-plays for them.

2. Introduce the skill of Giving and Receiving Praise.

Ask students to define the terms *praise* and *compliment.* Have students offer examples of compliments.

3. Discuss how praise works and why it is important.

Ask students to remember a time when they praised or complimented someone else. Have students share what they said and how they said it.

Ask:

Why is it important to give praise?

Some examples:

- If you thank people when they do something for you, they are more likely to do it again.
- If you compliment someone, that person is more likely to compliment you at another time.
- We all like to get compliments.
- If you thank and compliment people, they will enjoy being around you.

Encourage students to remember and share compliments they have received and to describe how receiving the compliments made them feel. Ask students how they responded after receiving the compliment—what they said or did.

4. Present and model the behavioral components of Giving Praise.

Direct students' attention to the whole-class display of the steps in the skill:

1. Look for something you like about the other person.

2. Be honest. Don't try to praise someone for something that is not true.

3. Be simple. Say clearly what you like.

Ask students to name some things you could say that you like about a person. (Their responses should include appearance, behavior, and accomplishments.) Also point out that it is important to choose the right time and place to give your praise. Ask why this is important. (Students' responses should include the idea that if you don't choose a good time and place, the situation may embarrass you or the other person.) Finally, stress the importance of using BEST to deliver the praise.

5. Model and discuss giving effective compliments and praise.

Use the following examples:

- You have a friend you like to listen to music with. How could you praise your friend? You could say, "I like listening to music with you. It's fun."
- You like someone's new outfit. What could you say? You could say, "That's a nice-looking shirt" or "You look good in that shirt."

6. Model and discuss receiving compliments and praise in ways that encourage the giver.

Use the following example:

Your teacher says, "Your handwriting on that paper is very neat. Good work." You should use BEST: Look at the teacher, smile, and say, "Thank you."

Ask students to share some good ways to receive praise. Then ask:

Why is it important to receive praise in a friendly and appreciative way?

Some examples:

- To encourage (not discourage) people to continue to praise you.
- To show that you appreciate praise.
- To show your respect for the other person's opinion.
- To help you feel good about yourself.

7. Conduct the "I'm a Star!" activity.

Distribute copies of the worksheet, and have the students write their own names in the middle of their stars. Collect the stars and put them in a pile or a small bin. Have each student pick a star (not their own). On one point of the star, have students write a compliment about the student whose star they have picked. Remind students that it is OK to say what they see if they cannot think of a specific compliment. Collect and redistribute stars until every student gets back a star with five compliments (adapt the procedure as necessary). Have students read and share their feelings about receiving and giving compliments.

8. Introduce a Reflective Summary.

As outlined in the Introduction, ask students to reflect on the question "What did you learn from today's lesson?" Reinforce key themes, then go over any follow-up work.

9. Follow up.

The following steps will help make sure that the students have a chance to continue working with the new concepts.

Assignment

Have students keep track of the types of compliments they give and receive during the week. Ask students how they felt when giving and receiving praise.

Take-Home

Have students write or speak compliments to individuals in their lives outside of school. Practice the BEST approach with parents, siblings, coaches, caregivers, and others.

Plans to Promote Transfer and Generalization of Skill

Language Arts

Have students keep a journal of compliments they have given or received.

Social Studies

Students can watch the news or a talk show. Have students makes notes on the ways in which newsmakers, politicians, and celebrities give and receive praise. Do these individuals demonstrate BEST skills?

TIPS FOR TEACHERS

1. Students are typically highly motivated to receive compliments. The compliment collection activity can be used to reinforce and practice SDM/SPS skills when you have a short block of free time between more formal SDM/SPS meetings.

2. A compliments collection (picking one student to whom each person in the class gives a compliment in a Sharing Circle format while the teacher records what everyone says) can be used in conjunction with Student of the Week activities, to honor a student's birthday, or as part of a good-bye send-off when a student, teacher, or teacher's helper is leaving the school. It is important to be aware that some children may actually find it difficult to receive compliments and reject them because of the threat they pose to a negative self-image.

Giving Praise

1. Look for something you like about the other person.

2. Be honest. Don't try to praise someone for something that is not true.

3. Be simple. Say clearly what you like.

Worksheet 4.7.1

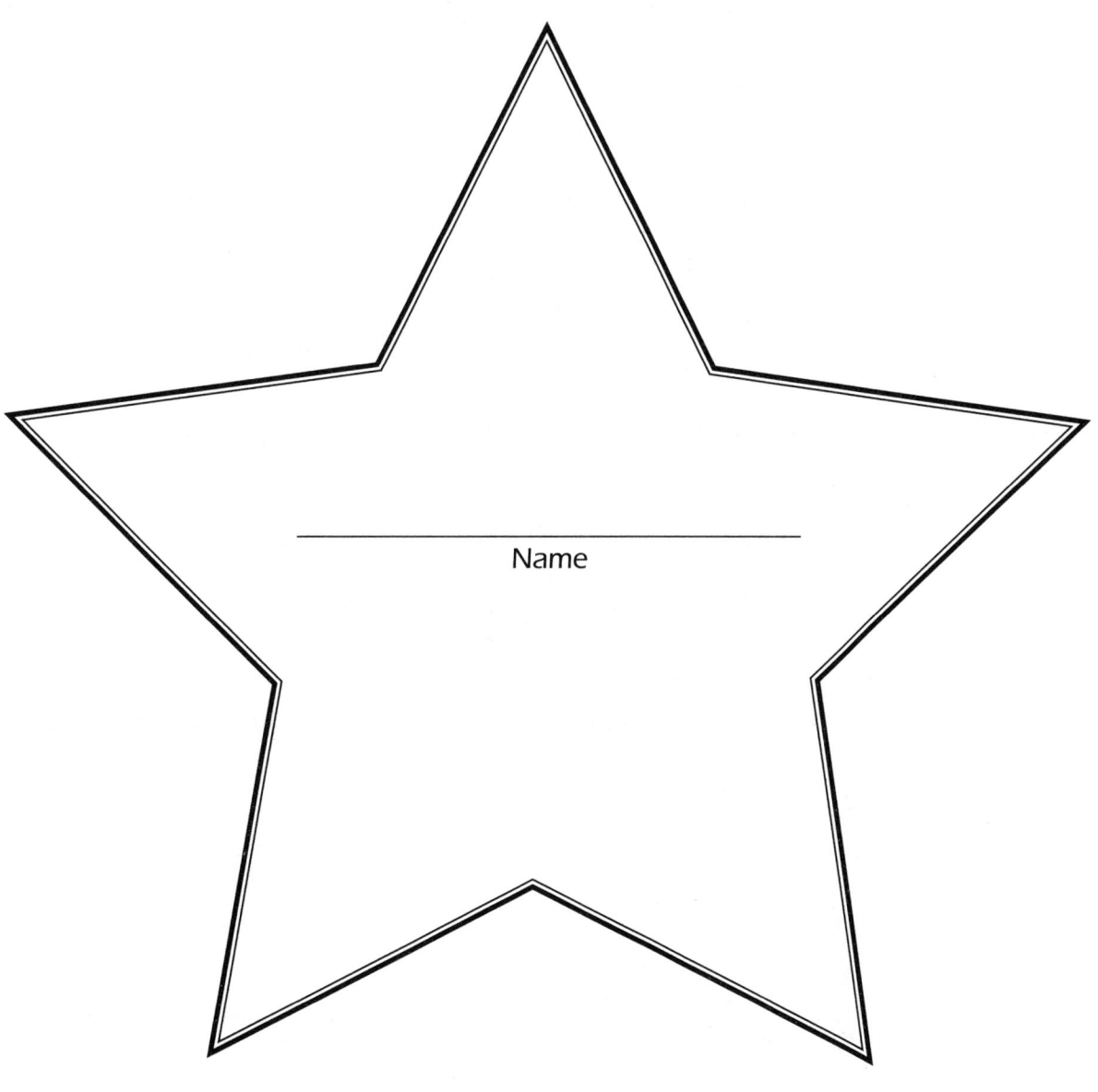

_____

Name

8 Packing Your SDM/SPS Toolbox

OBJECTIVES
- To provide students with an opportunity to review the social decision making and social problem solving skills they have learned to date

- To make a "toolbox" to house SDM/SPS skills—now called *tools*

- To provide teachers and students with an opportunity to assess skill gains

MATERIALS
Whole-class display of "Tools for the SDM/SPS Toolbox (Topics 1–7)" (Worksheet 4.8.1)

Copies of "Checking Your SDM/SPS Tools (Topics 1–7)" (Worksheet 4.8.2)

Shoe boxes or large envelopes, crayons or markers, drawing paper, scissors (or index cards and markers)

NOTE
You can perform the activity described here with a figurative or literal "toolbox." Some classes manage well by simply *thinking* of the concepts as tools. In this case, you may distribute index cards and have each student write down the skill names, one per card. Students then keep these decks of cards handy. Other classes do better with *concrete symbols.* The "Instructional Activities" section describes the process for having students develop and illustrate actual skill symbols. They then keep these tools in the SDM/SPS Toolboxes they create.

INSTRUCTIONAL ACTIVITIES

1. In a Sharing Circle, review the assignment from the last topic.

Ask students to report on their experiences giving or receiving praise.

2. Review the SDM/SPS skills to this point.

Refer students to the Checking Your SDM/SPS Tools worksheet and ask:

Think of a time when you used a skill you learned and it helped you. What was it?

What is your favorite skill?

The skills and concepts learned thus far, and the Topics in which they were introduced, are as follows:

- Sharing Circle; Speaker Power; Listening Position (Topic 1)
- Respectful Listening (Topic 2)
- Strategies for Remembering (Topic 3)
- Role-Playing (Topic 4)
- Be Your BEST (Topic 5)
- Good Teammate Behaviors (Topic 6)
- Giving and Receiving Praise (Topic 7)

3. Introduce the idea that the skills are mental tools.

Say:

I would like you to imagine that our class is a construction team that has been hired to build a house. Before heading out to the job site, let's pretend that we are organizing our toolbox.

The conversation could go like this:

Teacher: If we needed to put two pieces of wood together, which tool or tools would we use?

Student: Hammer and nails.

Teacher: Great. What if we needed to cut a few inches from the bottom of a door?

Student: Saw. (Or "plane.")

Teacher: Super. And what if we were going to put a lock into a door?

Student: Drill, screws, and a screwdriver.

Teacher: Excellent!

Reinforce students for knowing what tool to use in each of the situations when it was needed. Explain that social and emotional situations follow the same pattern: You need to consider the situation and then determine which tool to use.

Inform students that for today's activity, they are going to create their own SDM/SPS Toolbox, which they will keep in or on their desks for future use.

4. Have students create their tools and toolboxes.

Distribute the art supplies and instruct students to create their symbols. Students may work individually or in teams to design and color the tools. (If a computer or clip art are available, students could use them to express their ideas.) Each student should decorate an envelope or shoe box to hold the tools.

5. Conduct a practice activity.

After the toolboxes (or decks) are complete, explain that you are going to give the students a chance to see if they are as good at choosing the right social decision making tool as they are at choosing what tools they need to build a house. Let them know that you will be reading descriptions of something that might happen to them, and they should hold up the tool they would use in that situation.

What tool would you use if . . .

The principal is standing in front of the school in the auditorium, waiting to start a show. (Listening Position and Respectful Listening)

The fire alarm goes off. (Respectful Listening and Remembering)

You notice that a student who is new to our school is alone on the playground, looking a little shy. (BEST, Good Teammate Behaviors)

A teacher tells you that you have been very helpful in class. (Receiving Praise)

Ask the class to describe how they would put these tools to work. Reinforce the idea that sometimes you can use more than one skill.

6. Evaluate progress.

Distribute the "Checking Your Social Decision Making Tools (Topics 1–7)" self-report worksheet and let students know that you are interested in hearing from them about what tools they are using and what tools they have a difficult time remembering to use. Let students know that you are going to be asking them to show you which tools they could use when situations come up throughout the week.

7. Introduce a Reflective Summary.

As outlined in the Introduction, ask students to reflect on the question "What did you learn from today's lesson?" Reinforce key themes, then go over any follow-up work.

8. Follow up.

The following steps will help make sure that the students have a chance to continue working with the new concepts.

Assignment

Whenever you introduce a new classroom activity, have students identify which SDM/SPS tools they will use to cope with it. Do the same before other transitions within the school day.

Take-Home

Encourage students to take their toolboxes (or tool cards) home for a weekend to use in situations that arise in their homes. Discuss their use at the beginning of the next meeting.

Plans to Promote Transfer and Generalization of Skill

1. Before activities that involve group work, movement to a new area, or attending an event, ask students to think about their toolbox and which tools they will use.

2. Some students benefit from a visual reminder of a skill they are having trouble remembering to use. If you notice someone forgetting a tool, have them put the tool symbol or prompt on their desk where they can see it.

3. Scan ahead for situations characters face in language arts, social studies, health lessons, or movies or videos when the use of social decision making skills would be beneficial. Students can be asked to do as follows:

   - Think ahead about what tools a character might want to take out of their toolbox before heading into a situation.
   - Think about what social decision making tools a fictional character could have used and what would happen as a result of using or not using the tools.

TIPS FOR TEACHERS

1. Provide students with visual reminders of skill application by posting tool symbols in various areas of the classroom where skills would apply and by posting symbols to correspond with periods of the daily schedule.

2. Encourage students to refer to their SDM/SPS toolbox when conflicts arise within the classroom. Prompt for use of specific skills when appropriate.

Tools for the SDM/SPS Toolbox (Topics 1–7)

1. Sharing Circle

2. Speaker Power

3. Listening Position

4. Respectful Listening

5. Strategies for Remembering

6. Role-Playing

7. Be Your BEST

8. Good Teammate Behaviors

9. Giving and Receiving Praise

Student _____ **Date** _____

So far, you have practiced many skills to help you get along with other people and learn to make good decisions. Use this worksheet to check your progress in learning these new skills. Circle how well you think you can use the tool listed, then fill in the blanks.

1. **Participating in a Sharing Circle**   OK   Good   Great

   One Sharing Circle question I liked was _____.

2. **Listening Position**   OK   Good   Great

   This tool helps us by _____.

3. **Respectful Listening**   OK   Good   Great

   A time when it was important for me to listen was _____.

4. **Strategies for Remembering**   OK   Good   Great

   A strategy I use to remember is _____.

5. **Role-Playing**   OK   Good   Great

   A role-play I learned from was _____.

6. **Be Your BEST**   OK   Good   Great

   BEST stands for:

   B _____

   E _____

   S _____

   T _____

7. **Good Teammate Behaviors**   OK   Good   Great

   I use these two: _____

   _____

8. **Giving and Receiving Praise**   OK   Good   Great

   Someone praised me for _____,

   and it made me feel _____.

EMOTIONAL REGULATION

Topics 9–13

9

Trigger Situations and Feelings Fingerprints

OBJECTIVES

- To help students become aware that some situations elicit or trigger strong emotions *(Trigger Situations)*
- To increase awareness of the unique way strong feelings manifest themselves in the body *(Feelings Fingerprints)*
- To teach students about fight-or-flight reactions and how strong feelings impair the ability to think clearly
- To introduce the importance of taking responsibility for using Feelings Fingerprints as warnings to calm down before trying to think and act

MATERIALS   Chalkboard or easel pad

INSTRUCTIONAL ACTIVITIES

1. Begin with a Sharing Circle.

Ask for examples of how social decision making tools came in handy during the preceding week.

2. Introduce the idea of Trigger Situations.

Ask:

How many of you have ever heard chalk squeak on a chalkboard? How do you feel when you hear it?

Take a few minutes discussing this and share how you feel. Tell the students that all people find that some situations they're in lead them to feel upset. These are called *Trigger Situations.* When someone runs into a Trigger Situation, they experience physical reactions such as a faster heartbeat or sweaty palms and feelings such as fear or anger.

Ask students to identify their own personal triggers. Provide examples to get things started—perhaps something like giving a speech, getting into an argument, and so on—and brainstorm a variety of common Trigger Situations with the group. List these on the chalk-board or easel pad.

3. Introduce the idea of Feelings Fingerprints.

Ask students if any of them know what a *Feelings Fingerprint* is. If so, use their explanations to make the following points:

- Our bodies send us signals when we are very stressed or upset.
- The name for this signal is *Feelings Fingerprint.*
- Everybody has Feelings Fingerprints.

Tell students:

> *It is important to know what your own Trigger Situations are so that you can try to think about ways to handle situations before they happen.*

> *The next step is also very important. You need to know your own Feelings Fingerprints.*

Explain that everyone has their own special way that feelings show up. Anyone who is faced with a strong feeling, or Trigger Situation, will experience physical reactions, but each person might experience a different physical reaction in response to that strong emotion.

4. Discuss Feelings Fingerprints as physical signs of stress.

With the class, brainstorm Feelings Fingerprints, or physical signs of stress. Start out with some of your own Feelings Fingerprints, then have the students each share what they experience when faced with Trigger Situations. The list may include headache, increased heart rate, stomachache, clenched teeth, sweaty palms, tense shoulders, rapid breathing, shaky knees, and so on.

Mention people with different occupations and ask why, when, and where they might experience Feelings Fingerprints. The list may include athletes, musicians, police officers, firefighters, librarians, cashiers, and others (choose occupations your students have the back-ground to appreciate).

> *Do any of you watch sports?*

Give an example of athletes' getting nervous before a competition:

> *Athletes feel many different Feelings Fingerprints, or physical signs of stress. For example, they get butterflies in their stom-achs, their hands get sweaty, or their shoulders tense up. Just as athletes have a lot of pressure on them to perform, you can also be under a lot of stress. The ability to recognize Feelings Fingerprints is an important first step in learning to stay calm*

and to think clearly in stressful Trigger Situations that can lead to trouble.

5. Point out that acting under stress is often useless.

Explain that sometimes people jump ahead to try to solve a problem before they are ready or able to do so. If this happens, nothing gets accomplished because they are too upset and out of control to think about what they might be able to do.

Have students generate examples of situations where they have felt nervous, restless and unable to concentrate, or about to lose their temper.

You may suggest that students close their eyes and try to remember that situation. Ask them to try to visualize the experience and feel how their bodies felt at the time.

Ask:

> *Are there any ways you can think of to get self-control when you run into a problem?*

Give the class a few minutes to come up with suggestions.

6. Introduce the idea of "fight or flight."

Explain that human bodies are equipped to respond to upsetting situations with a "fight or flight" response: What happens in a Trigger Situation is that the body makes a chemical called adrenaline, which causes various physical reactions and provides a lot of energy. When people have strong feelings, it is a lot easier for them to get angry (fight) or run away (flight) than to think because adrenaline also makes it hard to use the thinking part of the brain.

Then say:

> *It is important to be aware of your triggers and how they affect your body. Try to notice where you feel the stress. This sign of stress, or Feelings Fingerprint, is the clue that the fight-or-flight response may happen. By being aware of your triggers and Feelings Fingerprints, you can learn to calm yourself down to regain control and have access to your thinking skills.*

7. Introduce a Reflective Summary.

As outlined in the Introduction, ask students to reflect on the question "What did you learn from today's lesson?" Reinforce key themes, then go over any follow-up work.

8. Follow up.

The following steps will help make sure that the students have a chance to continue working with the new concepts.

Assignment

Have students record Trigger Situations and the corresponding Feelings Fingerprints in journal format. Keep their ideas on hand for future practice.

Present students with potential Trigger Situations by staging role-plays, acting out a situation yourself, or showing a video or pictures and then having students add examples of their own to those presented. The following situations may be used:

- It is your turn to read aloud.
- The big math test is this morning.
- You are late for your friend's birthday party.

Take-Home

Encourage students to begin to notice other people's Trigger Situations and Feelings Fingerprints when they see them on television, at the mall, on the bus, at school, and so on. Students should record their observations in a journal without naming specific people.

Plans to Promote Transfer and Generalization of Skill

Social Studies

Have students identify current events from newspapers and magazines, broadcast media, or Internet sources in which individuals encountered Trigger Situations. Instruct students to identify the Trigger Situation and the resultant actions.

TIPS FOR TEACHERS

Modeling and calling the students' attention to your own Trigger Situations and physiological responses to stress is an effective teaching tool at this point. Likewise, calling attention to the triggers and Feelings Fingerprints of characters in literature and the media is another means of developing children's awareness of these situations.

10   Keep Calm

OBJECTIVES
- To point out problematic situations where students can use self-control to calm down before reacting
- To teach students to regulate their emotions and maintain control in problematic situations
- To practice the *Keep Calm* exercise

MATERIALS

Whole-class display of the steps in Keep Calm (Worksheet 4.10.1)

Copies of the "Keep Calm Reminder Cards" (Worksheet 4.10.2) *(optional)*

INSTRUCTIONAL ACTIVITIES

1. Review Topic 9.

Go over the vocabulary from the last lesson, with a focus on Trigger Situations and Feelings Fingerprints. Encourage students to share their observations and experiences.

2. Conduct a Sharing Circle.

Ask students to share a time when they find it helpful to calm themselves down.

Make the point that it is possible to handle almost every type of problem or difficulty better if you are able to stay calm. Say something along these lines:

> *To help us learn to be better at keeping calm, we are also going to learn a specific four-step strategy called* Keep Calm. *This strategy can help you think through a problem before you try to do something about it.*

3. Introduce the Keep Calm exercise.

Say:

> *The key to keeping calm is to slow down your breathing. Athletes, performers, and people in the martial arts have used*

methods of controlling their breathing to achieve a high level of concentration and calmness that can help them perform their best.

Provide examples of sports figures or fictional characters your students will relate to, then continue:

Learning to regulate the way that you breathe increases your ability to think clearly and to do things with more skill and control.

Ask if anyone has ever heard of Keep Calm. If so, have them help you explain the four steps in using this skill:

1. Tell yourself to STOP.

2. Tell yourself to KEEP CALM.

3. Slow down your breathing with two long, deep breaths.

4. Praise yourself for a job well done.

4. Demonstrate the steps to the class.

Direct students' attention to the whole-class display of the skill steps.

Follow this procedure: Present a situation in which you could be irritated or nervous. Describe the situation, then model the following:

First, I would tell myself to STOP.

Then I would tell myself to Keep Calm.

Then I would take two long, deep breaths. First, I would let out all the air in my lungs through my mouth. Then I would take a slow and smooth breath of air in through my nose to the count of five. I would hold that breath for the count of two and then slowly let the air out through my mouth to the count of five, while I say to myself (inside my head), "Keep Calm." I would do the breathing again.

Then I would say to myself, "Good job." Using self-control can be hard work, and you need to praise yourself.

Demonstrate the procedure, counting with your fingers to five while taking a breath in, and to two while holding your breath, and again to five while breathing out. Bring your hands down to your sides while you are releasing the breath through your mouth—indicating that you are saying, "Keep Calm." Smile after completing the breathing to indicate you are telling yourself you've done a good job.

5. Conduct a practice exercise.

Have the class practice Keep Calm in the same way.

Look for students who are doing the procedure correctly. Be specific in praising—you can say things like "Nice, smooth breathing." If children need correction, describe what to do in positive terms. For example, say, "Slow down your breathing" rather than "Don't go so fast."

6. Discuss use of the exercise.

Have the class generate situations when Keep Calm may come in handy. Most situations fall into three main categories:

- When you are nervous. (Examples include things like being about to take a test, going up to bat, or giving a speech or other type of performance.)
- When you really need to concentrate. (Examples include things like working on a test, getting back in the mood to work after recess, or feeling distracted by noise in the room.)
- When you are angry or frustrated and about to lose your cool. (Examples include things like beginning to yell during an argument.)

7. Conduct additional practice.

Present students with situations to role-play, either acting out a situation yourself or showing a video or pictures and then having students add examples of their own to those presented. Have students practice using Keep Calm to help them in these situations:

- Feeling fidgety and talking in class
- Feeling nervous about a test or a report
- Being lost in a shopping center
- Going to a new school
- Competing in a sports event

8. Introduce a Reflective Summary.

As outlined in the Introduction, ask students to reflect on the question "What did you learn from today's lesson?" Reinforce key themes, then go over any follow-up work.

9. Follow up.

The following steps will help make sure that the students have a chance to continue working with the new concepts.

Assignment

Encourage students to find a time when they can use Keep Calm and try it. Let them know that you will expect an example of how they used Keep Calm at the next lesson.

Take-Home

If you wish, send Keep Calm cards home with students. Parents and guardians can find many situations in which the skills will be useful.

Plans to Promote Transfer and Generalization of Skill

Social Studies and Current Events

Instruct students to seek examples of people taking deep breaths before performing certain tasks. Encourage students to observe athletes, politicians, surgeons, or others in real life or on TV. Have students keep track of observations of deep breathing used for calming.

Language Arts

Instruct students to identify points in stories during which a character could use Keep Calm. Have students predict what might have happened if the character had used Keep Calm and how that might differ from what did occur in the story.

Art Project

Have students submit posters illustrating the steps of Keep Calm.

TIPS FOR TEACHERS

1. Some children may need a real-life example of what it's like to be nervous or antsy or to lose their temper. This can be illustrated in several ways. Use a mirror to show differences in physical appearances before and after using Keep Calm. Jogging in place to increase breathing can be used to show the contrast before and after Keep Calm.

2. During problem situations that come up during the week, encourage children to use the Keep Calm technique before discussing the situation with their teacher or classmates. If you wish, you may distribute Keep Calm Reminder Cards (Worksheet 4.10.2).

3. It may be a good idea to remind children about Keep Calm before potentially stressful situations, such as joining a new class or attending special classes like art, music, and physical education. The technique is especially useful for students with special education needs who are joining a regular classroom.

4. Some students will learn to use their Feelings Fingerprints as a sign to use Keep Calm. Others will be prompted by Trigger Situations or other sets of cues. Regardless, the skill will be learned to the extent that children are prompted and reminded to use it in salient everyday situations, such as when moving from class to class, before a test, before an important meeting, or when they are upset at home.

5. Here are some sample prompts to use when a child is upset or is beginning to lose control:

   - Use your Keep Calm steps.
   - Stop and think about what's happening.
   - Let's Keep Calm and get focused.
   - Let's take a look at what's going on. Tell me what you see. (Or "what you saw, what happened, how you are feeling.")
   - Take a deep breath and Keep Calm—then we can talk about it.

6. Testimonials about the use of Keep Calm (or times when Keep Calm could have been used) are highly valuable for students to share. These should be solicited regularly to promote future use of self-control. Students should be helped to use Keep Calm to prepare themselves for actual or possible Trigger Situations.

Keep Calm

1. Tell yourself to STOP.

2. Tell yourself to KEEP CALM.

3. Slow down your breathing with two long, deep breaths.

4. Praise yourself for a job well done.

From *Social Decision Making/Social Problem Solving: A Curriculum for Academic, Social, and Emotional Learning (Grades 4–5)*.
Copyright © 2005 by Maurice J. Elias and Linda Bruene Butler. Research Press (800-519-2707; www.researchpress.com)

Worksheet 4.10.1

From *Social Decision Making/Social Problem Solving: A Curriculum for Academic, Social, and Emotional Learning (Grades 4–5).* Copyright © 2005 by Maurice J. Elias and Linda Bruene Butler. Research Press (800-519-2707; www.researchpress.com)

KEEP CALM

1. **Tell yourself to STOP.**

2. **Tell yourself to KEEP CALM.**

3. **Slow down your breathing with two long, deep breaths.**

4. **Praise yourself for a job well done.**

KEEP CALM

1. **Tell yourself to STOP.**

2. **Tell yourself to KEEP CALM.**

3. **Slow down your breathing with two long, deep breaths.**

4. **Praise yourself for a job well done.**

KEEP CALM

1. **Tell yourself to STOP.**

2. **Tell yourself to KEEP CALM.**

3. **Slow down your breathing with two long, deep breaths.**

4. **Praise yourself for a job well done.**

KEEP CALM

1. **Tell yourself to STOP.**

2. **Tell yourself to KEEP CALM.**

3. **Slow down your breathing with two long, deep breaths.**

4. **Praise yourself for a job well done.**

Keep Calm Reminder Cards

11 Practice Keep Calm and Be Your BEST

OBJECTIVES
- To practice combining Keep Calm with Be Your BEST to respond to Trigger Situations
- To provide students with practice in dealing with conflicts and criticism through the use of specific exercises taught in the program

MATERIALS
Whole-class display of the Be Your BEST Grid (Worksheet 4.5.2); copies of the grid for students to take home

Whole-class display of the steps in "Keep Calm" (Worksheet 4.10.1)

INSTRUCTIONAL ACTIVITIES

1. Review BEST.

Go over the components of BEST (Body Posture, Eye Contact, Speech, and Tone of Voice) and discuss the passive, aggressive, and assertive behavior associated with each component.

2. Establish the importance of the lesson.

Obtain students' interest by saying that today they are going to practice using Keep Calm and Be Your BEST so the techniques will be easy in situations where it is very important to use these skills.

Say:

> One of the most important times to use these skills is when someone makes you angry. (An example of this could be when someone takes something of yours or is disrespectful to you.) If you let yourself get upset, it makes it harder to get what you want—get your stuff back or make the other person treat you with respect.

3. Demonstrate how the exercises work in practice.

Read the following scenario and role-play as follows:

- You are waiting for your turn on the computer, and you are next in line. Pat gets on in front of you. You are not sure what to do next. Ask:

How would you feel if this happened to you? Using what we learned, what would be the first thing to do? (Keep Calm.) What would you do next? (Use Be Your BEST.)

Choose two students to role-play this situation, demonstrating Keep Calm and Be Your BEST. Give them time to practice. While they are practicing, divide the audience into four groups. Assign each a different task: One group is to concentrate on the tone of voice, one on body posture, one on eye contact, and one on speech.

After the chosen pair present their role-play, review it by discussing each component of BEST. Here are some discussion questions to use:

- Were the actors calm?
- Did they have an even tone of voice?
- Did they look at each other or away?
- Did they say appropriate things?
- Did they stand tall? Or were they slumped over or hunched?

Complete a whole-class version of the Be Your BEST Grid with the class to illustrate the example.

4. Conduct a practice activity.

Continue role-playing, selecting different pairs of students as time allows. Discuss the results and chart them on another Be Your BEST Grid, as in Step 3. Here are some useful scenarios:

- You are on the playground and two children start making fun of the way you kicked the ball during the kick ball game. How would you feel if this happened to you?
- You show a friend a new shirt you bought. You are very proud of it. Your friend looks at it and says, "That's ugly." How would you feel?

Reinforce the concept by saying:

In these situations, having a calm voice, good eye contact, nice speech, and tall posture could help you and whoever you're talking to be comfortable.

5. Review the need for calming exercises.

Ask:

How can you tell when you are upset and may lose control?
How can you remind yourself to use Keep Calm and Be Your
BEST?

6. Introduce a Reflective Summary.

As outlined in the Introduction, ask students to reflect on the question "What did you learn from today's lesson?" Reinforce key themes, then go over any follow-up work.

7. Follow up.

The following steps will help make sure that the students have a chance to continue working with the new concepts.

Assignment

Tell the class to pay attention over the next week and think about a time when they used or could have used Keep Calm and Be Your BEST. They should come to the next lesson prepared to describe what happened and how it turned out.

Take-Home

Have students bring home a copy of the Be Your BEST Grid to explain to their parents or guardians and siblings. Suggest that students keep a journal of times they try to use Be Your BEST skills at home.

Plans to Promote Transfer and Generalization of Skill

Language Arts

During any story you are reading, focus on what leads up to the conflict. Ask students to determine if characters involved in the conflict used Keep Calm or tried Be Your BEST.

Social Application

Remind students frequently to do the following: Use Be Your BEST when giving a report in front of the class, talking to the principal or a teacher, or trying to join a group of unfamiliar children in an activity.

TIPS FOR TEACHERS

1. Continue to use Keep Calm and Be Your BEST as prompts to encourage students to move smoothly between school activities and to help children who appear to have strong feelings that they would like to get under control.

2. It's almost impossible for the class to get too much practice with Keep Calm and Be Your BEST. Add one or more lessons on this topic to give the students a chance to demonstrate using Keep Calm and Be Your BEST in the scenarios that follow. You can also intersperse such practice opportunities when five to ten minutes are available at any point during the school day. Supplement this list with hypothetical versions of common situations that are triggers for your students:

   - You are working on a math problem, and nothing you try checks out. Time is running out, and you feel yourself getting angrier and angrier. You think you might lose control.

   - You spent a lot of time working on a math paper. Instead of subtracting, you added all the problems. The teacher tells you to do it over again. You are very frustrated.

   - Two kids want you to take something out of someone's desk. You know it is wrong and say no. They make fun of you for being a chicken. You are very upset.

   - Today you need to take a note signed by your parent or guardian to school so you can go ice skating with your class. You love to go ice skating. You remember to check for the note five minutes before the morning school bus will arrive. You know that someone signed the note, but now you can't find it. If you don't have the note, you cannot go skating. The bus will be here in four minutes now! Your parent or guardian is in the kitchen, very busy caring for your baby brother.

   - You are riding your bike with your friends. You slip on a wet spot in the road, and your front wheel runs into another bike, causing one of your friends to fall and get hurt. Your other friends think you caused the crash on purpose and are angry at you.

   - Your class has to stay inside during lunch hour because it's raining, and several classmates start to play a game together. You ask to join them, but they say you can't because they have enough people to play already.

12 Be Your BEST and Trigger Journal

OBJECTIVE ▪ To continue to practice monitoring triggers and dealing with conflicts and criticism through the use of Keep Calm and Be Your BEST

MATERIALS Copies of the "Trigger Journal" (Worksheet 4.12.1)

INSTRUCTIONAL ACTIVITIES

1. Review skills.

Go over good listening skills and remind students of the importance of using Listening Position during this lesson. Then review the Keep Calm and Be Your BEST skills by asking students to remember the four steps of Keep Calm and the components of Be Your BEST.

2. Conduct a Sharing Circle.

Ask the students to share a recent Trigger Situation that ended in a way they didn't like.

3. Introduce the Trigger Journal.

Tell the students that keeping a journal will help them deal with difficult Trigger Situations, especially ones that occur frequently.

Distribute the "Trigger Journal" worksheets and have the students take turns reading the questions aloud. Talk about the kinds of things each question calls for to ensure that everyone is clear on how the worksheet should be completed.

4. Have the students complete the Trigger Journal.

Ask students to use a Trigger Situation from a time when they were younger. Tell the students that they will be reading their Trigger Journals to the class, so they should use a situation that they are comfortable sharing now. Have students pay special attention to whether or not they remembered to use Keep Calm and Be Your BEST skills. Also have them pay attention to the last question, which requires them to create a positive alternative solution that they could try if a similar situation arises.

When the students have completed their Trigger Journals, have them take turns reading in front of the class or from their desks. Remind students to use Keep Calm if they become nervous and to use their Be Your BEST skills as they are reading aloud.

5. Role-play some of the situations.

After all the students have had a turn to read, choose some situations that seem particularly relevant to your class to use for role-playing. Discuss a situation with the class, emphasizing Question 9, "What is something else you could have done to handle the situation?" Have the students role-play the situation as it happened, then have them role-play using the positive alternative.

Divide the class and have each group watch for a specific BEST component in the role-play. Have the class analyze the second role-play and talk about whether the alternative might have come out better than what was done originally. Have students create additional solutions that might work and practice these as role-plays.

6. Conclude the lesson by discussing your expectations for the Trigger Journals.

The "Follow up" and "Tips for Teachers" sections discuss several options that you can use alone or in combination. Select the ones you plan to use and describe them here.

7. Introduce a Reflective Summary.

As outlined in the Introduction, ask students to reflect on the question "What did you learn from today's lesson?" Reinforce key themes, then go over any follow-up work.

8. Follow up.

The following steps will help make sure that the students have a chance to continue working with the new concepts.

Assignment

Distribute copies of the Trigger Journal and have students complete them for homework using a situation that arises during the upcoming week. Have the students bring them to the next Sharing Circle and repeat Step 5 of this lesson by having the students share their completed Trigger Journals. Again, role-play the situations that you feel are most relevant to your students. Emphasize that there is always more than one way to handle a difficult situation. (This activity is getting the students ready for more advanced problem solving and decision making.)

Take-Home

The Trigger Journal is a tool that can be used by teachers and other school staff when working with parents and guardians on difficult Trigger Situations. Reviewing Trigger Journals with parents provides good examples of situations students face in school and can be used during conferences or disciplinary meetings, allowing for joint planning to approach these issues in the future. Consequently, parents and guardians can use this tool to help their children deal with Trigger Situations at home.

Plans to Promote Transfer and Generalization of Skill

Academic

Have the students pretend that they are a character in a story and complete a Trigger Journal from the character's point of view. Have the students share their completed journals during a language arts lesson.

Social Practice

The Trigger Journal has many creative uses. Often, teachers have a stack of blank forms available. When students have a problem or encounter a Trigger Situation, they can complete the worksheet. Students can keep the completed worksheets to themselves, even stapling several together to form a diary, or take them home to share with their families. Some teachers leave a box for completed Trigger Journals to be turned in and used as future situations for role-plays and discussion. Often teachers have students complete a Trigger Journal to help the students solve their problems or prevent future difficulties. Trigger Journals are also useful tools for guidance counselors, child study team members, and principals and vice principals who need to help students who are dealing with difficult situations.

TIPS FOR TEACHERS

1. This Topic gives children an opportunity to practice using Keep Calm and Be Your BEST and also to show that they can recognize

when these skills are not being used correctly. The Trigger Journal encourages students to use these skills outside the formal lesson context. Teachers can then use Trigger Journals in an ongoing manner as a way to help students think through problem situations that occur during the week and also to recall the situations for discussion during SDM/SPS lessons.

2. Some children have difficulty with writing, and provisions can be made for them to talk to an aide, teacher, counselor, or peer who can help them complete the worksheet.

3. There is much benefit to reviewing the use of the Trigger Journals several times throughout the week. Have students complete Trigger Journals regularly at times when you feel that it is important for them to self-monitor.

4. Sometimes it is difficult for students to share actual Trigger Situations with the group because the class lacks the cohesion and trust to support the activity, or some or all of the students are not sufficiently mature to handle it. If you have such a group, you can collect the completed Trigger Journals in advance and create anonymous, hypothetical Trigger Journals based on the real-life situations presented by students. It can be beneficial to actually complete a Trigger Journal and display it in a whole-class format so the entire class can see it and work on it together.

Student _____ **Date** _____

1. Briefly describe a difficult Trigger Situation that you were involved in.

   What happened? _____

   _____

   _____

   Who with? _____ Peer/Adult
                                                        (Circle one.)

   When/where? _____

2. How did you feel?

3. What did you say and do?

4. What happened in the end?

5. How calm and under control were you before you said or did something? *(Circle one number.)*

1	2	3	4	5
Under control	Mostly calm	So-so	Tense and upset	Out of control

6. How satisfied were you with what you did? *(Circle one number.)*

1	2	3	4	5
Not at all	Only a little	So-so	Pretty satisfied	Very satisfied

7. What did you like about what you did?

8. What didn't you like about what you did?

9. What is something else you could have done to handle the situation?

13   More Tools for the Toolbox

OBJECTIVES
- To provide students with an opportunity to review the social decision making and social problem solving skills they have learned to date
- To update the SDM/SPS Toolbox with new SDM/SPS tools
- To provide teachers and students with an opportunity to assess skill gains

MATERIALS

Whole-class display of "Tools for the SDM/SPS Toolbox (Topics 9–12)" (Worksheet 4.13.1)

Copies of "Checking Your SDM/SPS Tools (Topics 9–12)" (Worksheet 4.13.2)

Crayons or markers, drawing paper, scissors (or index cards and markers)

NOTE

Display the whole-class version of "Tools for the SDM/SPS Toolbox" (Topics 1–7; Worksheet 4.8.1) along with the display of skills and concepts covered in Topics 9–12. As discussed in Topic 8, you may have students depict the tools or write the tool names on index cards.

INSTRUCTIONAL ACTIVITIES

1. Review skills learned and practiced so far.

Read from the list of skill prompts and list skills on the worksheet. Inform students that today they are going to update their SDM/SPS toolboxes and review all of the skills that they have learned so far.

The skills and concepts taught in Topics 9–13, and the Topics in which they were introduced, are as follows:

- Trigger Situations; Feelings Fingerprints (Topic 9)
- Keep Calm (Topic 10)
- Trigger Journal (Topic 12)

2. Conduct a Sharing Circle.

Here are some suggested Sharing Circle questions:

- Of all the SDM/SPS skills we have learned and practiced so far, what is your favorite skill?
- Can you think of a time when you used a skill that you learned during our SDM/SPS lessons, and it helped you?
- What is one thing that you like about our problem-solving team?
- Share times that you have tried to use the SDM/SPS skills outside the classroom. Were you successful? What could you try to make things work better next time?

3. Expand the toolboxes.

Have students get into groups with their toolboxes or card decks and add Trigger Situations, Feelings Fingerprints, Keep Calm, and Trigger Journals. Then have one person in the group hold up a tool picture or flashcard—for example, Keep Calm. The other members of the group must demonstrate the skill by listing the steps or showing the procedure and giving an example of a good time to use this skill. Have students repeat for all the tools in their toolboxes as time allows.

4. Evaluate progress.

Have students complete and hand in the "Checking Your SDM/SPS Tools (Topics 9–12)" (Worksheet 4.13.2).

5. Introduce a Reflective Summary.

As outlined in the Introduction, ask students to reflect on the question "What did you learn from today's lesson?" Reinforce key themes, then go over any follow-up work.

6. Follow up.

The following steps will help make sure that the students have a chance to continue working with the new concepts.

Assignment

Have students choose a skill that they think requires more practice. Have them think of ways that they will practice it, reminding them that they will share what they did at the next meeting.

Plans to Promote Transfer and Generalization of Skill

Language Arts and Social Studies

Remind students to use the tools in their toolboxes before cooperative learning activities.

Social Applications

Remind students to use their toolboxes at lunch, recess, on the playground, and in the hallway.

TIPS FOR TEACHERS

1. These skills need to be learned and relearned until they become automatic; this "overlearning" is very important; indeed, it is key to the success of the program. Continue to prompt and encourage students to use their tools in all aspects of their academic and social activities.

2. After you review "Checking Your SDM/SPS Tools (Topics 9–12)" (Worksheet 4.13.2), give the students feedback. Feedback may include any or all of these components:

   - Returning the sheets, praising honest and accurate self-appraisal of areas of strength

   - Meeting with individual students to make a plan to improve areas that need improvement

   - Working with students whose appraisals are unrealistic to improve their self-monitoring (especially, but not only, if they are too lenient in their self-appraisal)

   - Continuing to have students complete worksheets; collect the worksheets and give feedback as needed

Tools for the SDM/SPS Toolbox (Topics 9–12)

1. Trigger Situations

2. Feelings Fingerprints

3. Keep Calm

4. Trigger Journal

From *Social Decision Making/Social Problem Solving: A Curriculum for Academic, Social, and Emotional Learning (Grades 4–5)*.
Copyright © 2005 by Maurice J. Elias and Linda Bruene Butler. Research Press (800-519-2707; www.researchpress.com)

Worksheet 4.13.1

Student _____ **Date** _____

Now you have practiced even more skills to help you get along with other people and make better decisions. Use this worksheet to check your progress in learning these new skills. Circle how well you think you can use the tool listed, then fill in the blanks.

1. Trigger Situations   OK   Good   Great

   A trigger for me is _____

   _____.

2. Feelings Fingerprints   OK   Good   Great

   My body reacts to a Trigger Situation by _____

   _____.

3. Using Keep Calm   OK   Good   Great

   A time I should have used Keep Calm was _____

   _____.

4. Using a Trigger Journal   OK   Good   Great

   Filling out a Trigger Journal helps me to _____

   _____.

SOCIAL DECISION MAKING AND SOCIAL PROBLEM SOLVING

Topics 14–26

14 Introducing FIG TESPN

OBJECTIVES
- To help students recognize the cognitive process underlying problem solving
- To help students discover the links between emotions and problem solving

MATERIALS

Chart paper, markers, tape

Whole-class display of the "FIG TESPN Ladder" (Worksheet 4.14.1); copies of the ladder for students to take home

NOTE

Keep the "FIG TESPN Ladder" and any other student-made FIG TESPN posters mounted where students can readily see them.

INSTRUCTIONAL ACTIVITIES

1. Conduct a Sharing Circle.

Briefly review the lessons to date, then ask the students to share the results of their skill practice from the preceding session.

2. Introduce the idea of using a strategy for decision making.

Explain to students that up to now, the class has worked on skills to help them become a cooperative problem-solving team and deal with strong feelings and Trigger Situations. Now it is time to develop a set of skills for problem solving and decision making. Say something along these lines:

We take many steps in the course of solving a problem. By using a consistent strategy that everyone can learn and practice together, over time, we can get so good at it that we can even use it during times of stress or crisis. This strategy is called FIG TESPN.

3. Conduct a practice activity.

Tape two pieces of chart paper to the wall. On the first, write the heading "Problems and Decisions I Faced in K–3." On the second, write "Future Problems and Decisions." Have students divide into two groups and assign each group to begin at one of the two posters. Have students brainstorm a list for their heading. After a few minutes, have each group switch to the other poster. Have each group read the list and have them brainstorm more ideas to add to the list. After the brainstorming, ask students about their feelings associated with the problems and decisions that they listed.

(Some teachers call this activity "The Carousel" because of the way the students move around the room.)

4. Introduce *skill* components of FIG TESPN.

Ask students what skills they have learned that seem likely to help them tackle these problems. Introduce the FIG TESPN steps by saying:

We know how emotional decisions and problems can be. Today, we are going to learn how to use FIG TESPN to guide us in thinking through problems and decisions.

Present and review FIG TESPN, using the whole-class display.

Illustrate a simple problem, such as deciding which jacket or shoes to wear to school on a day that it might rain hard. Run through the FIG TESPN steps, getting student input as time allows.

F —Find the Feelings
I —Identify the Problem
G —Guide Yourself with a Goal
T —Think of Many Possible Solutions
E —Envision Consequences
S —Select the Best Solution
P —Plan and Be Prepared for Pitfalls
N —Notice What Happened (Now What?)

Conclude by saying:

In the next few weeks, we will be discovering and practicing each of these steps to help us become better problem solvers.

5. Introduce a Reflective Summary.

As outlined in the Introduction, ask students to reflect on the question "What did you learn from today's lesson?" Reinforce key themes, then go over any follow-up work.

6. Follow up.

The following steps will help make sure that the students have a chance to continue working with the new concepts.

Assignment

Tell the students to think about a time when they had trouble solving a problem or making a decision. They should be prepared to share their situations at the next class meeting.

Take-Home

Have the students inform their parents or guardians that their class will be working on problem solving. Distribute copies of Worksheet 4.14.1 for students to take home.

TIPS FOR TEACHERS

1. Each of the eight FIG TESPN steps taught in this curriculum is a complex skill that must be addressed individually to be fully understood and used in the decision-making process.

2. It is most effective to teach the FIG TESPN model through the use of facilitative questioning—that is, through turning each of the eight steps into questions designed to guide students through the FIG TESPN process. This approach will allow you to move from being the solver of your students' problems to becoming the facilitator of your students' own thinking and decision-making skills—and that is the heart of a teacher's mission. You can find guidelines and examples for building students' problem-solving skills in the Introduction, especially in the section titled "The Facilitative Approach of Open-Ended Questioning."

3. An important aspect of these lessons is the consecutive building of one step upon another. It doesn't matter how familiar the students are with the names of the steps (the list may have been posted in the classroom before the introduction of this set of lessons, and many students may have memorized the steps in Grade 3), the material should still be presented as follows:

   - One step at a time
   - Consecutively, in the order given in this volume
   - With the preceding skills reviewed cumulatively as each new step is presented

4. To ensure transfer and generalization of these skills, which is the point of teaching them, they must be *overtaught*, using repetition and as much practice of each skill as possible. Teachers must look

for opportunities within content areas and the life of the school to generate social problem solving and social decision making practice, enlarging upon the curriculum as individual classes and circumstances allow. These lessons should be considered the jumping-off point for a creative process of program planning to find numerous, regular, and visible opportunities for students to use their problem-solving and decision-making skills (that is, FIG TESPN, supported by all of the skills previously learned for team building and emotional regulation) throughout the school day. This approach will work best when coordinated with other teachers in your grade, as well as with all school support staff and administration.

5. Students need visual reminders of FIG TESPN. Many teachers find it useful to have the class create their own FIG TESPN posters. These posters should be posted in the classroom (as well as in other places in school, such as the gym, lunchroom, hallways, guidance office, and main office). You can point to a poster as a prompt whenever you want students to use FIG TESPN or rethink one or more steps.

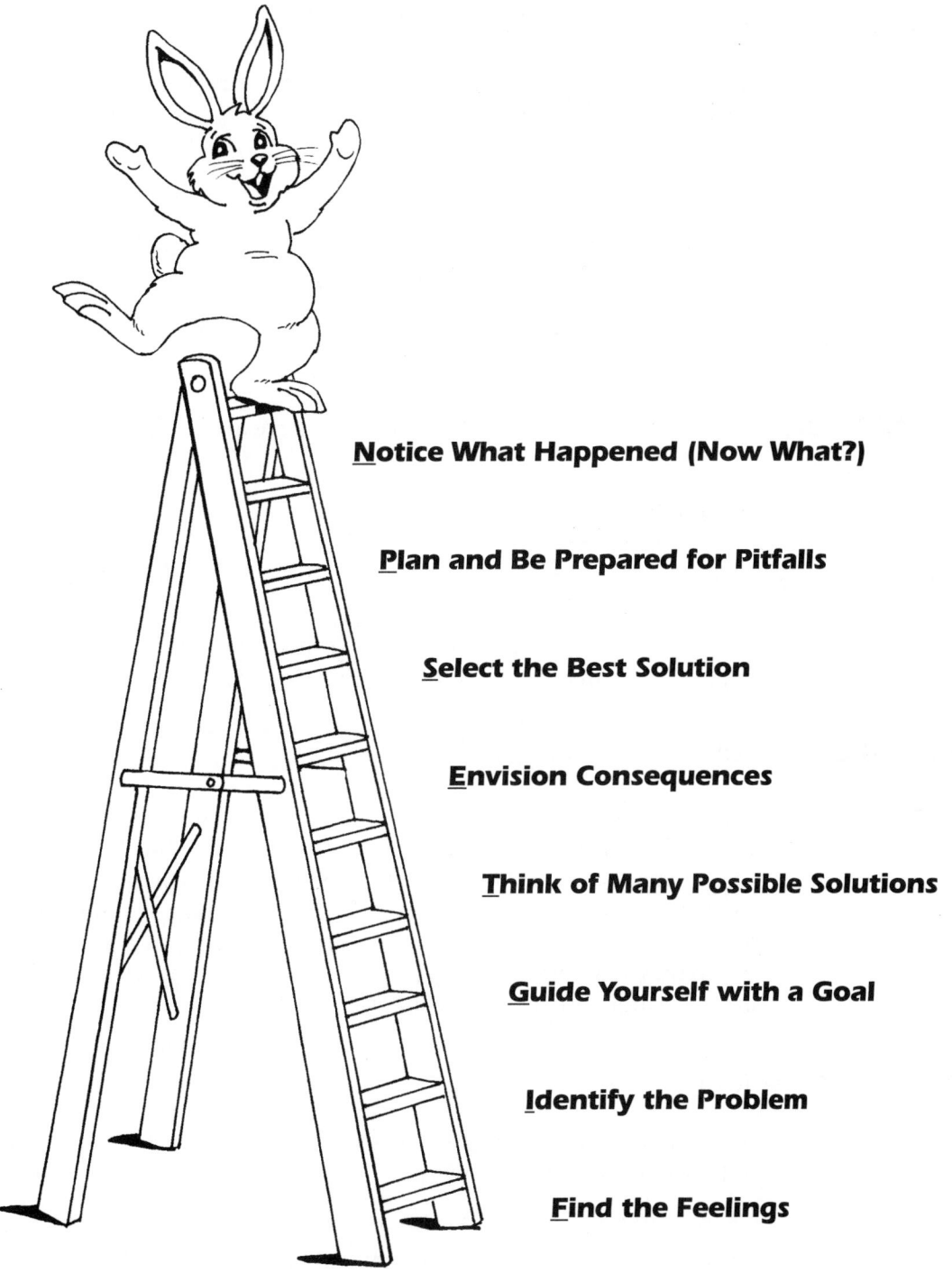

Notice What Happened (Now What?)

Plan and Be Prepared for Pitfalls

Select the Best Solution

Envision Consequences

Think of Many Possible Solutions

Guide Yourself with a Goal

Identify the Problem

Find the Feelings

15

FIG TESPN: Step 1.
F = Find the Feelings

OBJECTIVE
- To sensitize students to personal feelings and the feelings of others to teach students to recognize and verbalize those feelings

MATERIALS
"Feelings Flashcards" (Worksheet 4.15.1)

PREPARATION
Photocopy and cut apart the Feelings Flashcards.

INSTRUCTIONAL ACTIVITIES

1. Conduct a Sharing Circle.

Briefly review the concept of FIG TESPN, then ask the students to share the results of their skill practice from the preceding session.

2. Discuss the importance of feelings.

Introduce and explain the skill—that good problem solvers learn to pay attention to the messages that other people send through their facial expressions (an uplifted eyebrow to show surprise or doubt, for example) and their posture (slouching or slumping over the desk as a sign of being tired or bored). Good problem solvers also recognize when they have strong feelings themselves, and they learn to tell others accurately what those feelings are.

3. Introduce skill components.

Ask students how they will be able to tell what others are feeling. Elicit at least the following answers:

- By looking at people's facial expressions and how they act
- By listening to what people say and how they say it (tone of voice, volume, speed, expression, and so on)
- By asking, "How are you feeling?"

4. Discuss the way feelings affect behavior.

Ask students to think of a time when they may have been in a bad mood (overtired, cranky, irritated, or angry) and someone approached them to ask a favor (for example, "Can I use your bike?" or "Can I borrow some money?") Ask what happened. Have the class discuss how mood affects responses in a situation like that.

Two important points can be made:

- The irritated person should recognize being in this mood and be able to express it—for example, "Look, I'm sort of angry right now. Maybe we could talk about this later." Things will be much less irritating down the line if the person responds like this rather than with an angry outburst such as "No way! I'll never lend you anything."
- The person doing the asking should be able to read signs of the other person's feelings, which would be a clue to wait until another time to ask.

5. Conduct a basic practice activity.

Use the following situations and ask several different students how they would feel if these situations happened to them. (Or insert hypothetical names and ask how they think that person would feel.)

Sample situations:

- Someone took your iPod without asking your permission.
- You've just been chosen for an important part in the school play.
- Your best friend just told you about plans to move far away.
- Someone just cheated in a game you were playing.

Encourage clarification by asking why the students might feel that way. It can also be useful to ask how the other person in each scenario might be feeling.

6. Additional practice: Feelings Charades.

Divide the class into two teams. Give one student a flashcard with a feelings word on it. The student must act it out nonverbally while teammates try to guess what it is. Then the other team gets a turn. The goal is to see which team can recognize their actor's words most quickly.

If you prefer, you can add your own feelings words to the list and choose those appropriate for your students.

7. Additional practice: Mirroring.

In this exercise, students demonstrate what feelings look like. Choose two students: one as the Communicator and the other as the Mirror. Explain that as you read the following scenarios, the Communicator will make a facial expression that reflects each feelings word. The Mirror's job is to copy exactly what the Communicator does.

Sample scenarios:

- Jacquetta is *excited* about a gift she has just received and *curious* about what it could be. She becomes *frustrated* when she can't untie the ribbon, but finally opens it and is *surprised* to find it empty!

- José is *worried* about his dog, Spike, who has stayed out overnight. He hears a scratching sound at the door and is *suspicious* about what it could be. When he opens the door and sees Spike, he is *joyful*. But then he remembers how upset he was and becomes *angry*. But not for long!

- Angela is *disappointed* when a class trip is canceled but is *happy* when her dad suggests a movie that evening.

- A student is *contentedly* working on a math assignment when he encounters difficulty and becomes *frustrated*. After trying several solutions, he solves the problem and feels *proud* and *satisfied*.

8. Introduce a Reflective Summary.

As outlined in the Introduction, ask students to reflect on the question "What did you learn from today's lesson?" Reinforce key themes, then go over any follow-up work.

9. Follow up.

The following steps will help make sure that the students have a chance to continue working with the new concepts.

Assignments

1. Make up a daily schedule sheet for your class that shows all the periods of the day for a full week but has blank spaces so students can write some things. Ask them to look for signs of different feelings in themselves and, for the entire week, to write down the feelings they noticed in themselves after each period. This "Feelings Log" can be collected and discussed.

2. Ask the class to think of one other student (don't tell who!) and to pay particular attention to the signs of different feelings that this person shows. This assignment can be kept informal or written up as an anonymous report.

Take-Home

Send home a note asking parents to reinforce feelings skills with the following activity:

Have your child identify the feelings of characters using a video or DVD of a favorite television show or movie. Stop the action at key points and ask your child how a character was feeling and what the character did to show how they were feeling. Go back and freeze the frames to get a more detailed look at facial expressions and gestures.

Plans to Promote Transfer and Generalization of Skill

Language Arts

When reading stories or books, have the class notice different writers' techniques for portraying characters' feelings. You may have students keep a list of feelings words or phrases used by writers. When students are writing, encourage them to use more and new feelings words, perhaps by assigning them. (For example, you might say, "In this assignment, you must use eight feelings words from this list before you use *happy, sad,* or *mad.*")

Art

Have students express certain feelings using colors, shapes, textures, and other abstract means; no words or specific objects or figures are allowed. Share, discuss, and display.

Social Applications

Ask students to watch two of their favorite TV shows in a different way this week. Their job is to pick two or three main characters and to list ways the characters showed different feelings. Ask them to see if a character has a favorite facial expression or body posture for showing one or more feelings.

TIPS FOR TEACHERS

1. Students have been exposed to looking for signs of different feelings in themselves during the lessons in Topics 9 and 10, for Feelings Fingerprints and the Keep Calm exercise. You can refer to those lessons if students find the activities in this topic difficult.

2. Students who are less verbal or have communication difficulties can use flashcards during the practice activities, or they can draw pictures of people exhibiting the feelings being discussed.

3. Feelings Find: An excellent in-class or homework assignment involves having students look through magazines or newspapers to find people who are exhibiting a feeling. You can use these pictures in many ways:

- Have the students share their pictures with the group.
- Group like feelings together on a large sheet of paper with the feeling written on the top.
- Compile the pictures into a feelings notebook.
- Post the pictures on a feelings bulletin board.
- Use your own creative idea!

4. Students enjoy these activities and benefit greatly from the practice, so consider spending more than one session on this topic or working in practice opportunities when brief periods of time arise during a school day.

angry	proud	excited
surprised	annoyed	embarrassed
frustrated	joyful	curious
happy	sad	worried
disappointed	suspicious	confident

16 FIG TESPN: Step 2. *I* = Identify the Problem

OBJECTIVE
- To help students recognize and identify a problem and make a clear problem statement

MATERIALS
Chalkboard or easel pad

Copies of "Feelings, Problems, and Goals" (Worksheet 4.16.1)

INSTRUCTIONAL ACTIVITIES

1. Conduct a brief review.

Ask students for feedback on their identification of feelings since the last lesson. Have students read all the FIG TESPN steps aloud with you, then reread Step 1 (Find the Feelings) and Step 2 (Identify the Problem).

2. Define the term "problem."

Say:

After we have looked for signs of different feelings in ourselves and in others, we need to describe the problem in a specific way. We need to create a clear, concise problem statement. In this way, "I feel silly" becomes "I feel silly because I did my math homework but forgot to bring it in."

Ask students what the word *problem* means. Be sure their ideas include a problem as something that happens to someone or between two people that makes one or both of them unhappy.

Ask students why it is sometimes difficult to put problems into words. (Look for at least the following: Emotion gets in the way, the first or obvious problem is sometimes not the real problem, sometimes there are many problems, or the problem is very complex.) Allow students to share examples (real or hypothetical) of these difficulties.

3. Work on putting problems into words.

Have students brainstorm things that might help them make a problem statement. Examples:

- Look at feelings first, yours and others'—they often point to a problem.
- Look at the facts—what is happening is often the problem.
- Consider other points of view—this helps clarify a problem.

Tell the students that one strategy is to say, "I feel [feelings word], because [describe what happened]" or "I feel [feelings word], when you [describe what the person does that bothers you]."

4. Conduct a basic practice activity.

Ask students to identify possible problems for the following feelings:

- I feel confused because . . .
- I feel annoyed because . . .
- I feel nervous when . . .
- I feel embarrassed when . . .

5. Additional practice: "Billy Reads Out Loud."

Let students know that they will hear about a boy named Billy, and while they listen they should be thinking how the people in the story might feel and noticing different problems that people in the story have. They should be prepared to describe these problems.

Billy Reads Out Loud

It was Tuesday afternoon in Mrs. Hartwick's class. The children had just returned from recess and were in a playful mood as they got their reading books out. Billy knew that Mrs. Hartwick would call on him to read out loud. He was very nervous because, although he could read well silently and understand what he read, he would often make mistakes when he read to the class. He began to shift around in his seat and bounce his leg up and down, and he even began to perspire a bit.

Sure enough, Mrs. Hartwick soon called out, "Billy, would you start us off by reading the story out loud?" Some of the children who sat near Billy laughed as he began to read. Billy made many mistakes, and more of his classmates began to laugh. One boy whispered to him, "Boy, Billy, are you dumb!"

Ask:

How was Billy feeling before he started to read?

Have several of the children role-play a person being nervous or embarrassed.

Ask:

> *How was Billy feeling after he read?*

Have several students demonstrate expressions that show different feelings Billy might have had.

Ask the class to describe Billy's problem, then ask them to describe Mrs. Hartwick's problem. List answers on the chalkboard or easel pad. Warn the students to be careful not to confuse the problem with the goal or a possible solution. If they veer toward solutions, advise them that the problem can often be a simple statement of what happened. If necessary, guide them to say things like "Billy makes mistakes when he reads aloud" or "The other kids are rude to Billy" instead of things like "Billy needs to practice reading aloud so he gets better at it" or "Mrs. Hardwick needs to make the other kids be polite to Billy."

6. Introduce a Reflective Summary.

As outlined in the Introduction, ask students to reflect on the question "What did you learn from today's lesson?" Reinforce key themes, then go over any follow-up work.

7. Follow up.

The following steps will help make sure that the students have a chance to continue working with the new concepts.

Assignment

Give students a copy of the "Feelings, Problems, and Goals" worksheet. Ask students, individually or in small groups, to watch for and record problem situations they observe. The situations may be on television, in literature, or in real life. Students should identify the feeling the person in the situation is having and make a clear statement of the problem. Students will record goal statements at the next meeting (Topic 17).

Take-Home

Send a note home to parents suggesting that they try this activity.

Problems in the News

The news is filled with problems. Read a story with your child from a newspaper or magazine. Discuss the problems related in the article. Ask your child to create a clear problem statement for each of the problems discussed in the article. You may want to discuss how these problems affect the different people involved in the news item. *Note:* Television or radio news items are often not as useful for this activity because these stories are so brief that they usually define the problem for viewers and listeners.

Plans to Promote Transfer and Generalization of Skill

Language Arts

To reinforce this lesson, ask students what a character's feelings and problem are as stories are read, videos watched, history lessons presented, school-based situations encountered, and so on.

Social Applications

Have students describe some common classroom, hallway, cafeteria, and playground problems by creating clear problem statements that can be used in later meetings. Have students decide if several problem statements may arise from a single situation or incident.

TIPS FOR TEACHERS

1. The use of the concept of "a problem" has special value. First, it encourages children to describe social matters with the same familiar language that they use in math or science. Second, placing a social difficulty into a problem context suggests, optimistically, that it may be solvable.

2. Another important aspect of this skill is that if students can put what is bothering them into words, a seemingly overwhelming situation becomes manageable. "I feel sad" becomes "I feel sad because I forgot to feed the dog."

3. For extra skill-building practice, here is a game students can play in a small-group format.

Problem Finding

Problem Finding is a skill-building game. First, you need a list of problem situations like the following. You can use a written list or index cards:

- Someone took Connor's new skateboard for a ride without asking his permission.
- Someone drew on Isabella's new blouse on purpose.
- Alex and Terry just cheated in a game you were playing.
- The teacher just yelled at Leslie for not paying attention.
- Rico is thinking about having someone do his homework for him.

You can add other problems to the list. Have students form groups and have one of them pick a card or a number. Then have someone read the following items (which can also be put on index cards):

- How do you think _____ would be feeling if that happened?
- What are some *signs* that would tell us how _____ is feeling?
- If you were _____, you would have a problem. Put the problem into words, then tell us your problem statement.

After the person has a turn, ask if anyone would say something different about this problem.

Student(s) _____ Date _____

Situation 1

Feelings _____

Problem _____

Goal _____

Situation 2

Feelings _____

Problem _____

Goal _____

Situation 3

Feelings _____

Problem _____

Goal _____

FIG TESPN: Step 3. *G* = Guide Yourself with a Goal

OBJECTIVE
- To show students how to decide what they or another person would like to have happen

MATERIALS
Students' "Feelings, Problems, and Goals" worksheets (4.16.1), assigned at the last meeting

INSTRUCTIONAL ACTIVITIES

1. Conduct a brief review.

Review FIG TESPN by having students stand and read all the steps while balancing on one foot. Then, have students repeat Steps 1 and 2 while seated. When discussing Step 3, always begin by addressing the feelings and problem identification steps. You may state what these steps mean or ask students to discuss the meanings.

2. Ask students to define "goal."

The answers should include how you would like things to end up or what you would like to see happen. Ask what other words or ideas are similar to *goal*. (The students should understand and recognize *target, bull's-eye, purpose,* and *finish line* as similar to *goal*.)

3. Introduce skill components.

Explain to students that the goal is often the opposite of the problem. For example, if the problem is "David is teasing me," the goal might be "I want the teasing to stop" or "I want to stay calm and cheerful even if people tease me." Students should begin a goal statement with "One goal is that . . . "

It is important that students understand that a given situation can pose several problems and that different people can have different goals. They also need to be able to tell the difference between goals and solutions, which are easily confused.

For example, suppose the statement is "I am upset (feeling) because Ken took my place in line (problem)." A good goal statement would be "One goal is that I get my place in line." Students who confuse goals with solutions are apt to say things like "One goal is that the teacher should send Ken to the principal's office" or " . . . should tell Ken's family."

Model your own goal setting by saying things like "My goal is to see us finish this work early so we can play a game" or "I'd like to see everyone sitting quietly—that's my goal."

Ask students which example is most likely to guide them in the best direction, and why.

4. Conduct a practice activity.

Have students share what their goals are in the following actions:

- Doing homework
- Doing a favor for a family member
- Studying for a test
- Saving money

Discuss realistic and unrealistic goal setting:

- Joe wants to be a millionaire by the time he is twenty-one. Is that a realistic goal? Why or why not?
- Tanya wants to buy her cousin a new house for Christmas.
- Bill wants to get an *A* in math.
- Magda wants to be a doctor someday.

Students may add circumstances to these scenarios to support their claim of realistic or unrealistic. This "what if" thinking is OK and adds to the discussion. It also helps students sort out their own goals.

5. Introduce a Reflective Summary.

As outlined in the Introduction, ask students to reflect on the question "What did you learn from today's lesson?" Reinforce key themes, then go over any follow-up work.

6. Follow up.

The following steps will help make sure that the students have a chance to continue working with the new concepts.

Assignment

Ask students to use their "Feelings, Problems, and Goals" worksheets to list goal statements that correspond to the feelings and problems they identified. Students will need these worksheets again in Topic 19.

Plans to Promote Transfer and Generalization of Skill

Language Arts

When reading a story or book, have students discuss the author's goal in writing the story. What did the writer want to have happen? As opportunities arise, ask students what a character's problem and goal are.

Social Application

Within the context of setting goals, discuss the idea of New Year's resolutions.

TIPS FOR TEACHERS

1. Problems and goals are often confused. Remember that the goal is the reverse of the problem. This will help students clarify the difference. It is also important for students to realize that a given situation can pose several problems and that different people have different goals.

2. Goals and solutions are also commonly confused. Goals are end states; solutions are actions. Have students practice deciding if a goal they suggest is how they want things to end up or what they'll do to get there.

18

Giving Constructive Criticism: Find the Feelings, Identify the Problem, and Guide Yourself with a Goal (FIG)

OBJECTIVES
- To identify the difference between constructive (that is, positive) and negative criticism
- To link constructive criticism with the first three steps of problem solving and with "I-messages"
- To practice giving criticism in a constructive manner (FIG)

MATERIALS
Whole-class display of steps in "Giving Constructive Criticism" (Worksheet 4.18.1)

Copies of "I-Messages" (Worksheet 4.18.2; *optional*)

INSTRUCTIONAL ACTIVITIES

1. Conduct a brief review.

Go over FIG TESPN by having students read the steps while balanced on one foot, with one eye covered. Have them repeat Step 1 (feelings), Step 2 (problem), and Step 3 (goal) once seated.

2. Introduce the idea of constructive criticism.

Obtain students' interest by presenting these contrasting stories.

Story 1

Students from a class are getting together after school to work on a project. Peter is in charge of bringing the arts and crafts materials, but he was not paying attention when the teacher gave a list of what was needed. Now he has only some of the items. Yolanda, the group leader, yells at Peter, "What's wrong with you? You never listen! I don't want you in my group anymore!"

Story 2

Students from a class are getting together after school to work on a project. Peter is in charge of bringing the arts and crafts materials, but he was not paying attention when the teacher gave a list of what was needed. Now he has only some of the items. Yolanda, the group leader, says to Peter, "I am angry at you because you weren't paying attention when the teacher read the list of what we needed, and now we can't finish the project today. If we are going to be able to finish the project, you have to listen carefully and pay attention."

Ask the students:

What was Yolanda doing to Peter in these stories? (She was criticizing him.)

Ask the students:

What is criticism? (It's telling someone when you disagree with what they are doing or asking someone to change or stop the behavior you do not like or think is wrong.)

To get the class thinking about the difference the kind of criticism makes, ask:

How did Peter feel in the first story when Yolanda criticized him? How do you think he reacted?

How did Peter feel in the second story when he was criticized? How do you think he reacted this time?

3. Emphasize the importance of constructive criticism.

Point out:

Sometimes it is important to ask someone to change what they are doing. Letting someone know that you have a problem with their behavior and asking them to change or stop is called criticism. It is important to criticize in the correct way so that the person will listen to what you have to say. In which story was it easier for Peter to listen to the criticism? Why?

Explain that to criticize in a positive manner, students can use the first three steps of FIG TESPN.

F: Say what you see and feel.

I: Give a reason why you do not like it (identify the problem).

G: Tell what you want instead (your goal).

4. Conduct a practice activity.

Read Story 2 again and review the steps from the FIG chart. Ask:

What words did Yolanda use to say what she saw? (You were not paying attention when the teacher read the list.)

What words did Yolanda use to show why she did not like Peter's behavior? (We can't finish the project today.)

What words did Yolanda use to show what she wanted instead? (Peter must listen carefully and pay attention.)

Give the students an opportunity to practice using FIG to criticize in constructive, positive terms. The display of steps in giving constructive criticism will provide a framework for deciding what to say.

5. Discuss ways to express criticism.

Explain and model that sometimes you may not like something about a person.

Suppose someone comes in with a haircut, and it does not look very nice; what could you do?

You could say nothing about it and talk about something else—or you could say, "Boy, your hair looks funny" or "Hey, I see you got a haircut." Which would be the better thing to say? Why?

In this case, it is better to say what you see rather than to say how you feel. Why do you think it might be better to say what you see rather than what you feel?

Help the students recognize that insults may hurt the other person's feelings and provoke them to ignore anything the speaker has to say. Ask for examples of ways to describe a haircut without being critical. If needed, follow up with examples relating to clothes.

6. Introduce a Reflective Summary.

As outlined in the Introduction, ask students to reflect on the question "What did you learn from today's lesson?" Reinforce key themes, then go over any follow-up work.

7. Follow up.

The following steps will help make sure that the students have a chance to continue working with the new concepts.

Assignment

Have students practice giving constructive criticism by asking them to use the first three steps of FIG TESPN when they need to give feedback to others. Have them look for positive criticism given by others and be prepared to share this at another time.

Plans to Promote Transfer and Generalization of Skill

Social Application

Have students use FIG when they encounter problems or are giving feedback during cooperative learning activities, physical education, and recess.

TIPS FOR TEACHERS

1. Giving constructive criticism is similar to giving "I-messages," a technique described in a wide variety of cooperative learning and conflict resolution programs. If you wish, you can copy the two "I-Messages" patterns given in Worksheet 4.18.2, use them for practice, or make them available to students for times they need to give constructive criticism.

2. Especially as students are learning to give constructive criticism, they may be more "critical" than "constructive." Sometimes it is a good idea to use a Sharing Circle or naturally occurring opportunity to talk about receiving criticism. Role-play practice can take place during academic feedback activities.

3. With special needs students, it is best to monitor criticism given by students continually and consistently.

4. Be aware of insults given by students. Have them rephrase their insults as constructive criticism. For example, when students put each other down, say to each of them, "It's important for you to say things to each other in a careful, constructive way. How can you use FIG (refer to the whole-class display of the steps in giving constructive criticism) to say what you said in a constructive way?"

5. You may find it useful to keep a record of the number of insults before and after lessons and compare this to the amount of constructive criticism given by students.

6. Discuss with the class how teasing and put-downs are insulting. Discuss what teasing is. How does it hurt the person who is being teased? What are some reasons a person teases?

Giving Constructive Criticism

F —Say what you think and feel.

I —Give a reason why you don't like it (identify the problem).

G—Tell what you want instead (your goal).

Worksheet 4.18.1

I-Message 1

Student _____ **Date** _____

Problem situation _____

I feel _____

_____

when you _____

_____

because _____

_____,

and I want _____.

I-Message 2

Student _____ **Date** _____

Problem situation _____

I feel _____

_____

when you _____

_____,

and I want you to _____.

19

FIG TESPN: Step 4. *T* = Think of Many Possible Solutions

OBJECTIVE
- To help students think flexibly and creatively and consider a variety of alternative responses to a given situation

MATERIALS
Students' "Feelings, Problems, and Goals" worksheets (4.16.1), continued from Topic 17

Paper and pencils

Miscellaneous objects (ruler, shoe box, string, marker, paper clip, or the like)

Chalkboard or easel pad

Whole-class display and copies of "FIG TESPN: Eight Steps for Social Decision Making and Social Problem Solving" (Worksheet 4.19.1)

NOTE
After this Topic, Worksheet 4.19.1 is referred to as the "FIG TESPN steps worksheet." Keep the whole-class version of the worksheet posted for future reference.

INSTRUCTIONAL ACTIVITIES

1. Conduct a brief review.

Refresh the students' memory of FIG TESPN by having them say all of the steps in a quiet whisper. Then repeat the FIG steps—feelings, problem, and goal.

2. Introduce skill components.

Define *alternative solutions* as all the ways that a problem could be solved. Talk about *brainstorming*—a process already familiar to the students from many earlier topics, although they may not necessarily have heard the word—as being a way of coming up with alternative solutions by listing as many as possible.

3. Conduct a practice activity for brainstorming.

Present an object (ruler, shoe box, string, marker, paper clip) and have students take thirty seconds individually to list as many uses for that object as they can on a piece of paper.

Have everyone share their lists; make a master list on the chalkboard or easel pad.

Repeat the activity as a large group, using a different object and posting the master list as students call out possible uses. Then ask:

Who had more ideas—the whole group or any one person?

What are the benefits of brainstorming in a group?

4. Enlarge the practice activity.

Divide the class into "thinking teams" of three or four students. Tell them you are going to ask them a question, and each team should write down as many answers as possible. (One student on each team should be a designated recorder.) Set a time limit of three minutes.

After the activity, regroup and compare and contrast solutions generated by various groups. Emphasize alternative solutions to the same problems and questions, making sure that the students realize there is usually more than one good way to solve a problem. Repeat as time allows.

Sample questions:

- How many games can you create with a ball, tape, and a ten-foot rope?
- How many things can you think of that go up (down, backward, in a circle, noisily, slowly, underwater, and so on)?
- How many things can shock you? (*Shock* may be defined as an emotion or an electrical charge—but let students discover that!)
- If you were lost in the woods in February in Alaska, what could you do?

You can ask other questions, of course—just choose something your class will find interesting and relevant to their lives.

5. Introduce a Reflective Summary.

As outlined in the Introduction, ask students to reflect on the question "What did you learn from today's lesson?" Reinforce key themes, then go over any follow-up work.

6. Follow up.

The following steps will help make sure that the students have a chance to continue working with the new concepts.

Assignment

Give students (either individuals or small groups) a copy of the FIG TESPN steps worksheet. Have them choose one situation from their "Feelings, Problems, and Goals" worksheet, and instruct them to copy the feelings, problem statements, and goals from that situation where indicated on the FIG TESPN steps worksheet. Students should then brainstorm as many solutions as they can to the problem they selected. Students will need this sheet in Topic 20.

Plans to Promote Transfer and Generalization of Skill

History and Language Arts

As opportunities arise in stories, films, and content areas, stop when a problem is presented and encourage students to brainstorm ideas. For example, suppose you are showing the film or reading the book *Johnny Tremain*. The colonists are outraged over taxes imposed by the king, especially the new one on tea. Stop the story at an appropriate place. Ask students what feelings the colonists are expressing. What is the problem and the colonists' goal? Now have students brainstorm solutions. What could the colonists do to reach their goal? Resume the story to see what idea the colonists chose.

Language Arts and Vocabulary

For each of the words listed in this section, ask students to look up the definition and write as many synonyms as they can. Then have them write a story using all the words. Students may share their stories. To emphasize the idea of alternatives, you can have students write another story using the same words.

idea	*criticize*
solution	*success*
alternative	*answer*
brainstorm	*act*
think	*impulsive*

Social Application

Have students write, in a journal format, instances at school during the week in which they got upset or irritated. They should write next to each situation at least three ways they could have handled it.

TIPS FOR TEACHERS

1. It is important that students be encouraged to respond with as many ideas as possible when they brainstorm for this Topic. Adhere to the basic principles of brainstorming:

   - Defer judgment (verbal or nonverbal).
   - Allow original, offbeat responses.
   - Go for quantity—the more ideas the better.
   - Build on ideas—the wildest suggestion can spark something useful.

2. Here are some words and phrases that will stimulate students' thinking and promote expansion of ideas:

   - Who or what else instead? Other material? Other process? Other ingredients? Other power? Other place? Other approach?
   - How about a blend, assortment, ensemble? Combine purposes, ideas?
   - What else is like this? What other idea does this suggest? What could I copy? Who could I emulate?
   - New twist? Change meaning, color, motion, sound, order, form, shape?
   - What to add? More time? Stronger? Higher? Longer? Thicker? Duplicate? Multiply? Exaggerate?
   - New ways to use it as is? Other uses if modified?
   - Smaller? Lower? Shorter? Lighter? Split up? Understate?
   - Omit? What to subtract?
   - How about opposites? Other pattern? Other layout? Other sequence? Transpose cause and effect? Change pace? Change schedule?

   Never underestimate the power of substituting, combining, adapting, modifying, putting to other uses, eliminating, reversing, or rearranging!

FIG TESPN: Eight Steps for Social Decision Making and Social Problem Solving

Student _____ Date _____

1. Feelings _____

2. Problem _____

3. Goal _____

4. **Think of many solutions.**   5. **Envision consequences.**

A. _____ ————————————— (+)

                                  ————————————— (−)

B. _____ ————————————— (+)

                                  ————————————— (−)

C. _____ ————————————— (+)

                                  ————————————— (−)

D. _____ ————————————— (+)

                                  ————————————— (−)

6. **Select the best solution:** _____

7. **Plan and be prepared for pitfalls.**

   In your plan, consider who, what, when, where, and how.

   _____

8. **Notice what happened. (Now what?)**

20 FIG TESPN: Step 5. *E* = Envision Consequences

OBJECTIVES
- To help students learn to think ahead to two or three consequences that might follow each alternative
- To practice applying the first five FIG TESPN steps and deciding on a solution based on the information presented

MATERIALS

Whole-class display of the FIG TESPN steps worksheet

Students' FIG TESPN steps worksheets, continued from Topic 19

INSTRUCTIONAL ACTIVITIES

1. Conduct a brief review.

Go over the FIG T steps. Have students repeat them.

2. Discuss the idea of consequences.

Ask students what the word *consequence* means. Take at least four or five answers. Then define the word as follows:

A consequence *is a feeling or action that follows or happens after something else.*

Then ask students what they think the word *envision* means. Take another four or five answers. Then define the word as follows:

To envision *something is to make a mental picture of what you can't see. Sometimes the subject is just out of sight, and sometimes it hasn't happened or been built yet.*

Then say:

When we brainstorm many solutions to a problem, we sometimes get excited and rush ahead, acting on a solution without thinking it through. What can happen when we do this?

Draw from your own experience and offer an example of how "envisioning the consequences" was very helpful for you (buying a used or new car, picking books or materials to use with your class, selecting the means of transportation to take a trip). Be sure to emphasize how you would try to picture the possibilities and explain to students that this is what it means to envision the consequences of a decision.

3. Introduce skill components.

Explain that this step encourages students to forecast, or predict, what is going to occur by picturing what might happen.

Discuss the way students envision the consequences of their actions. What factors influence what they think might happen?

- Past experience
- Knowledge of persons involved
- Rules, regulations, or laws
- Other

Ask which kinds of consequences most influence their choice of a solution.

Have students discuss the difference between short-term and long-term consequences. Include discussion of consequences for themselves and for others.

4. Conduct a practice activity.

Ask students to close their eyes and picture the back of the room or a part of the room behind them. (Don't let them turn around to look at the back.) After a few seconds, ask students to call out what they envision. Confirm what is accurate, ask for details, give hints. Help students get a good picture of the back of the room, then have them open their eyes and turn around and take a look.

Explain that *envisioning* also means picturing what might happen if you do something. Ask students to envision coming home without their keys and finding that no one is home. Have them picture themselves realizing that they don't have their keys. Ask them to share how they are feeling. Then have them envision what would happen next. Ask them to share with the group exactly what they would do.

Have students use the same type of procedure to envision possible consequences of these actions:

What might happen if . . .

- You do not do your homework for a week.
- You clean your room without being asked.
- You borrow your friend's bike, and it gets stolen.
- You go up one grade level in every subject.

5. Refer students to the whole-class display of the FIG TESPN steps worksheet.

Present the following situation for use with the FIG TESPN steps worksheet:

The other kids give you a hard time when you play kick ball.

Briefly review some feelings and possible goals. Select a goal and have the class generate alternative solutions.

Use the worksheet to illustrate how students can diagram two solutions and two consequences for each solution.

Have the students do the same thing with other pairs of solutions from the list of possibilities generated for the kick ball problem.

Discuss the types of consequences mentioned (long-term and short-term; positive and negative).

Here is an example of how to diagram solutions and consequences:

Problem: The other kids give you a hard time when you play kick ball.

Solution 1: Talk to the kids about how you feel.

Consequence 1: They might tease you.

Consequence 2: They might let you play.

Solution 2: Go tell your teacher.

Consequence 1: Your teacher might tell you to handle it yourself, using your problem-solving steps.

Consequence 2: The other children might get angry.

For this exercise, you can use situations relevant to your class and phrase them hypothetically if necessary. Situations involving peer pressure, breaking rules or laws, and getting along with others provide an endless supply of problem-solving opportunities. Some examples:

- You see a friend cheating on a test.
- You are falsely accused of spilling paint all over the floor.
- Your best friend is hanging out with a new student and has no time for you.

6. Introduce a Reflective Summary.

As outlined in the Introduction, ask students to reflect on the question "What did you learn from today's lesson?" Reinforce key themes, then go over any follow-up work.

7. Follow up.

The following steps will help make sure that the students have a chance to continue working with the new concepts.

Assignment

Refer to the assignment in Topic 19. Have students think of the positive and negative consequences for the solutions that they brainstormed, using the FIG TESPN steps worksheet.

Take-Home

Send home a note to parents and guardians with this suggestion:

Television and movie plots provide practice opportunities for anticipating consequences. At various points in a show, ask your child, "What do you think will happen next?" Videos and DVDs work well for this activity because they can be paused for a brief discussion. Television shows also work well because commercial breaks often occur at key moments in the plot for decision making and problem solving. A commercial break is a good time for a brief discussion regarding possible solutions and consequences.

Plans to Promote Transfer and Generalization of Skill

Language Arts

As you assign various stories and plays to read, encourage students to think about "what-ifs"—things like what if certain characters acted differently or what if stories were set in a different time, place, or culture.

Social Application

For added practice, have students write the consequences that might occur if any of these conditions were true:

- You could accurately predict the future.
- School met all year long.
- Everybody had the same amount of money.
- You no longer watched television.
- Everyone in school got into a fight whenever they had a disagreement.

For additional real-world practice, whenever a class problem comes up, have students focus on the long-term and short-term consequences of a course of action and the effect these consequences might have on the students and others.

TIPS FOR TEACHERS

1. The following questions help elicit consequences:
   - What might happen if you try _____?
   - What do you think might happen?
   - Anyone else have some ideas?
   - How would you feel if _____ were tried?
   - If you try _____, what else might happen?
   - Is that what you want to happen?
   - What else could you try?

   Encourage a balance, where appropriate, of positive and negative consequences.

2. When a student gives an unrealistic or inappropriate consequence, try to encourage more appropriate thinking. Here are several possibilities:
   - Asking what the *most likely* consequence would be.
   - Asking, "How would you react or feel if [the proposed solution] were tried on you?"
   - Bringing other children into the discussion by saying, "OK, let's hear what some other people think. Are there things that are more likely to happen?"

3. Help students practice envisioning in literature, social studies, and current events lessons.

21 FIG TESPN: Step 6. *S* = Select the Best Solution

OBJECTIVES
- To show students how to consider different solutions and consequences and decide which solution is best for them in their situation
- To help students begin to assume responsibility for thinking through and trying to solve their problems

MATERIALS
Whole-class display of the FIG TESPN steps worksheet

Chalkboard or easel pad

Drawing paper, crayons or markers

Students' FIG TESPN steps worksheets, continued from Topic 20

INSTRUCTIONAL ACTIVITIES

1. Conduct a brief review.

Go over the FIG TE steps in an interesting manner. For example, have students say each step in alternating high (alto) or low (bass) tones of voice or while standing on one foot but switching off to the other after each step.

2. Introduce skill components.

Have students discuss the idea of "selecting your best solution." Be sure they know what the word *select* means. Ask if they recognize that different people make different decisions based on different knowledge and perspectives—that making a good decision is a special, personal act. Discuss "making up your own mind."

When selecting their best solution, students must be sure that the solution leads to their goal. It is important to remind students to consider the link between goal and solution throughout this lesson. Students should also consider these questions:

- Will the solution harm anyone?
- What will it mean now, and how will I feel about it later?
- How will this choice affect others?

Offer an example or two from your own experience of how you arrived at a "best solution" or "best decision" for you or a member of your family (for example, where to go on vacation, how to deal with a difficult friend or relative, how to select activities for the class to do).

3. Conduct a practice activity.

Present the following scenario:

Marsha wants to join a club of girls at school. The leader, Anne, tells Marsha that she must steal a bracelet from the mall in order to join the club. Marsha is lonely and would like very much to be a member of the group.

Lead a discussion using these or similar questions:

- How do you think Marsha was feeling?
- What do you think Marsha's problem is?
- What could Marsha's goal be in this situation?
- What are some possible solutions for Marsha's problem?

Encourage the class to generate at least four to six possible solutions. Say:

If we choose the first solution, what might happen?

Consider consequences for each solution, writing them on the chalkboard or easel pad for ready reference.

On the basis of all the thinking we have done, which solution is the best one for Marsha?

Be sure to have students explain why they chose a solution as the best one. Have the class vote to select the two best solutions, and then have students role-play each one. This will allow them to see that there may be more than one workable solution and that it is OK to disagree with classmates about which one is best.

4. Illustrate the concepts.

Have students work in groups of four to make cartoon strips showing themselves in one or more of the following situations:

- Being offered drugs or alcohol
- Being asked to smoke
- Being asked to cheat on a test
- Being asked to take something that doesn't belong to them

Be sure that the cartoon strips show the first five FIG TESPN steps in action and that the last cartoon block clearly shows the decision made.

5. Introduce a Reflective Summary.

As outlined in the Introduction, ask students to reflect on the question "What did you learn from today's lesson?" Reinforce key themes, then go over any follow-up work.

6. Follow up.

The following steps will help make sure that the students have a chance to continue working with the new concepts.

Assignment

Refer to the assignment from Topic 20. Have students choose the best solution for the problem that they were working on.

Plans to Promote Transfer and Generalization of Skill

Social Applications

1. Journaling is useful for lessons on decision making. Encourage your students to keep a running list of all the large and small decisions that they make over one or two full days. Have them list decisions chronologically throughout the day, starting with waking in the morning and including breakfast time, school time, afternoon, dinnertime and evening—whether to lie in bed a few extra minutes, what to wear, what to eat for breakfast, and so on.

2. When a class problem comes up, have students decide what their best solution to the problem would be. Have students focus on the effect their decision might have on themselves and others. Encourage use of the FIG TESPN steps worksheet to help structure their thinking process.

TIPS FOR TEACHERS

1. When having the class choose a solution, you may sometimes call for a vote. It can be helpful to review the consequences to help students clarify which solution is associated with positive or negative consequences.

2. You may sometimes want to have students individually choose a solution in order to practice independent thinking.

3. Ask students to share what they do to give themselves the confidence it takes to choose a best solution, even if it means going against the crowd. Encourage them to choose their best solutions and not be followers.

22 FIG TESPN: Step 7. *P* = Plan and Be Prepared for Pitfalls

OBJECTIVES
- To help students learn to plan the time, place, and circumstances of executing a chosen solution
- To help students learn to anticipate obstacles to the implementation of their plan

MATERIALS
Students' FIG TESPN worksheets, continued from Topic 21

Whole-class displays of the FIG TESPN worksheet and "Plan and Be Prepared for Pitfalls" (Worksheet 4.22.1)

INSTRUCTIONAL ACTIVITIES

1. Conduct a brief review.

Have students review the FIG TESPN steps while they stand on one leg, switching legs after saying each step. Tell them that today's focus will be on Step 7, "Plan and Prepare for Pitfalls."

2. Discuss the concepts.

Ask students to define the word *plan*. Be sure that they include the following in the definition: the detailed steps necessary to carry out a solution and the how, when, where, with whom, and to whom of putting an idea into action.

Instruct students to consider the following elements when planning:

- Timing
- Tone of voice
- The right people to ask for help
- The past experience that would be useful in this case

Ask students to describe and help define the words *pitfall* and *obstacle* as well. Define "plan and prepare for pitfalls" as thinking of possible obstacles to carrying out the plan and planning for those possibilities.

Explain that sometimes even good solutions won't work. Ask these questions:

How do you feel when you stop and think of a good solution, try it, and things still don't get better—the problem is still there?

How can you be ready, just in case your first solution doesn't work?

Warn the students that they need to think about obstacles ahead of time and plan to have another solution ready.

3. Talk through a scenario.

Have students discuss plans for the following decision:

You have decided to invite your friend for a sleepover. What do you need to think about to make it work? What is the first thing you should do? Next? Then what?

Then extend the discussion to cover some contingencies:

What would you do if you are asked to baby-sit for your little cousin that night?

What would you do if your friend isn't feeling good?

What would you do if your brother asks to have a friend sleep over on the same night?

Refer students to the "Plan and Be Prepared for Pitfalls" worksheet. Ask students to comment on any other aspects of the plan for the situation.

4. Conduct a practice activity.

Have students problem solve, using the FIG TESP steps. Use the FIG TESPN steps worksheet, especially for students working in small groups. Help students generate realistic obstacles and plan around them. Either use one of the following sample situations or have the students generate their own hypothetical but realistic examples of trying to get into a group, coping with rejection, or coping with the desire to get even with others.

- You have been invited to Jamie's party, and the only person you know there is Jamie. She's very busy talking to other people. You are standing alone not talking to anyone.

- You have just started at a new school. You have different class periods; you're not sure where your classes are. When you stop someone in the hall to ask for help, he says, "Tough luck, punk. You're on your own."

- You get a disappointing grade on a math test. You decide to study more, but you don't feel that you're learning the material.

5. Introduce a Reflective Summary.

As outlined in the Introduction, ask students to reflect on the question "What did you learn from today's lesson?" Reinforce key themes, then go over any follow-up work.

6. Follow up.

The following steps will help make sure that the students have a chance to continue working with the new concepts.

Assignment

Refer to the assignments in preceding FIG TESPN lessons. Have students use the best solutions they have generated to formulate a plan and then create role-plays that they can improve with feedback from their classmates. Have students brainstorm obstacles and generate additional plans, again using role-playing to practice and improve their ideas.

Take-Home

Send a note home to parents and guardians with the following information:

Board games and table games are very valuable tools to help teach planning and dealing with obstacles. For example, checkers, chess, and tic-tac-toe teach children to plan their moves and look out for obstacles. Various board games require strategy, planning, and rethinking at the roll of the dice.

Plans to Promote Transfer and Generalization of Skill

Academic and Social Applications

Use situations and content areas that are complex enough to demand problem solving, extensive and ongoing planning, and some degree of persistent rethinking. Examples:

Publishing a classroom newsletter

Fund-raising for a class trip

Social Studies

Have students research famous persons and write a description of any obstacles they had to overcome to fulfill their missions.

TIPS FOR TEACHERS

1. Research shows that students' ability to handle obstacles and plan effectively for pitfalls are among the most important predictors of future adjustment for coping with stressful situations. Practice in this area, including the introduction of hypothetical obstacles for students (in groups, pairs, or individually) to think through at various times during the school day, is one of the best ways to promote transfer and generalization of skills.

2. Everyone has their own perspective on the time and energy they will expend to reach a certain goal. It is important to know when to walk away from a problem. However, it is also important to develop persistence so that valued goals are reached despite obstacles.

3. The use of hypothetical situations is helpful until the students become familiar with the framework and are comfortable using it. Role-playing provides an important link in the transfer and generalization of the skills from the hypothetical to real life.

Plan and Be Prepared for Pitfalls

Who: Who will be involved?

What: What will you do?

When: When will you carry out the plan?

Where: Where will you do this?

How: How will you carry out the plan?

Worksheet 4.22.1

23

FIG TESPN: Step 8. *N* = Notice What Happened (Now What?)

OBJECTIVES
- To help students learn to enact a plan
- To help students learn to evaluate a plan's success and, using the problem-solving process, decide what to do next time
- To help students learn to solve problems by using the full FIG TESPN process

MATERIALS
Chalkboard or easel pad

Whole-class display of the FIG TESPN steps worksheet; copies of the worksheet for students to take home

Students' FIG TESPN worksheets, continued from Topic 22

INSTRUCTIONAL ACTIVITIES

1. Conduct a brief review.

Have students read the FIG TESPN steps, alternating between a loud voice and the quietest possible voice.

Point out that getting things done, enjoying life, and accomplishing goals involve the eighth step—trying out plans and then rethinking the action to learn from the situation. Discuss with students whether they think trying out a plan is risky. Why or why not? *(It might not work, people might laugh, you might not get what you want, and so on.)*

2. Present the main decision-making story.

Prepare the students for the story by saying:

One of the most uncomfortable feelings that we can have is feeling bad when we are not invited to a party or other kind of gathering that we would like to attend. It happens to almost everyone at some time or another, and when it happens to you, you can think of it as a problem to be solved.

3. Read the story.

Pamela's Party Problem

Pamela was one of the friendliest children in Mrs. Brown's class. She always seemed to be involved with her classmates in recess games and special projects, and she was one of the most helpful students. She was a person you could always count on to share her things. Pamela was also a happy girl who enjoyed school and did well in class.

One Monday afternoon, Pamela overheard two of her classmates, Cathy and Justine, discussing Cathy's birthday party, which was coming quite soon. Pamela was busy at the moment finishing her spelling work, so she didn't join in the conversation. However, she did hope to herself that she would be asked to come.

On Thursday afternoon, Pamela saw Justine and a number of the other girls happily opening up the invitations they had received to Cathy's party. At that moment, Pamela knew that she probably was not invited.

4. Conduct a practice activity.

Practice the first seven problem-solving steps as they relate to Pamela's story. Students may use the FIG TESPN steps worksheet. Add to the situation by telling students the result of their planning—what happened (hypothetically) when they tried their plan. Have them rethink the situation and decide what to do.

- Ask the students to name at least three different feelings that Pamela might be experiencing.
- Ask someone to state Pamela's problem in words, and then request that another child write the problem on the chalkboard.
- Have the class suggest at least two possible goals, and then select one of them.

  Ask:

  What are some of the things that Pamela could do to solve her problem?

  What are some of the possible consequences that she should be thinking about?

  If you were Pamela, which solution would you choose?

  Use FIG TESPN Step 7—"Plan and Prepare for Pitfalls"—to develop role-plays setting up the situation and the solution.

5. Introduce the new step: "Notice What Happened (Now What?)"

Before the children do their role-play, explain that you are emphasizing the rethinking process. Let them know that you would like to have them do the role-play, and then rethink it by looking at consequences. Invite the class to offer constructive new ways of planning and trying out the solution (or even deciding on a different solution). After the class responds, ask the same actors to role-play it again.

After each role-play, compliment both the actors and the children who offer constructive alternatives.

6. Repeat the exercise.

Role-play other practice situations as time allows and students' skills warrant. Here is another sample story.

James's Story

James was bringing his book home to study for tomorrow's test. Caleb said he lost his book and asked James if he could borrow James's book for the afternoon and bring it to his house at dinnertime. James didn't know Caleb well, but he said it was OK. Dinnertime came and went, and it was 7:30 and James still did not have his book. He also realized that he didn't know Caleb's last name.

7. Introduce a Reflective Summary.

As outlined in the Introduction, ask students to reflect on the question "What did you learn from today's lesson?" Reinforce key themes, then go over any follow-up work.

8. Follow up.

The following steps will help make sure that the students have a chance to continue working with the new concepts.

Assignment

In a Sharing Circle, have students talk about things they have learned from problems that they could not solve, despite trying. What did they learn for next time? (You can also have them first write personal or fictional stories about this and then use the circle format to share them.)

Take-Home

Share the following exercise with parents and guardians at an appropriate time. Provide a handout of the FIG TESPN steps worksheet (Worksheet 4.19.1).

Family Problem Solving

Problems and decisions are an everyday occurrence in all households. Family members can share their problems and decisions and use each other as sources of support and ideas. "Family Problem Solving" is a way to bring this kind of activity into your home. Pick a time during the week and designate it Family Problem-Solving Time. Each week, designate a different person to share a problem that they are having or one that they would like to consider. (Some families like to write problems on index cards and shuffle the cards and pick a different problem each week.) One suggestion is to start with an easy problem and work into more difficult and personal problems as your family becomes more comfortable with the framework. Using the eight-step FIG TESPN process, work through each step in order. When family members differ on aspects such as the best solution, take a vote or have the designated person decide. This activity fosters good problem solving and decision making and also keeps the channels of communication open between children and adults.

Plans to Promote Transfer and Generalization of Skill

Language Arts or Social Studies

Have students find characters in a story or real-life people in history or in current events who used problem-solving and decision-making skills. Have students write and discuss what these people did in the "Notice what happened (Now what?)" phase of their problem solving and decision making. What lessons could they have learned from what happened? Use the question "What did you learn about that for the next time?" as a prompt. Help students rethink problem-solving strategies that worked and did not work, so they can learn from both kinds of results—and learn to persist.

TIPS FOR TEACHERS

1. An important aspect of the final step of the decision-making and problem-solving framework is the review process. Constructively reviewing decisions and actions can be difficult for some people, but it is an essential aspect of the strategy.

2. Persistence is the major theme of the final step in the framework. Students need to see decision making and problem solving as a process that they can continually cycle through until they are able to reach their goal. By continually practicing the process in academic and social situations, students will gain the confidence they need to persist in their problem-solving and decision-making activities throughout their lives.

24
FIG TESPN: Putting It All Together—Teacher-Led Problem-Solving Practice

OBJECTIVES
- To allow students to demonstrate understanding of the eight-step FIG TESPN framework
- To systematically apply FIG TESPN to a variety of situations

MATERIALS
Chalkboard or easel pad

Whole-class display and copies of the FIG TESPN steps worksheet (Worksheet 4.19.1)

PREPARATION
If you want the students to start the lesson with hypothetical situations in mind for use in Step 4, assign the project of developing stories a few days before you take up this Topic.

INSTRUCTIONAL ACTIVITIES

1. Conduct a brief review.

Go over all eight FIG TESPN steps, using whatever memory game appeals most to the class.

2. Emphasize the importance of FIG TESPN.

Explain that being a good problem solver and decision maker is a habit and that practice helps people develop their habits. Tell the students that today they will use all eight steps to practice solving some challenging problems.

3. Conduct a practice activity.

Talk to the class about how even the best of friends can have problems with each other. When problems do come up, carefully planning solutions to problems is very important.

Read the main decision-making story.

A Friend Tells a Friend About a Friend

Terry and Erin met for the first time when school began this year. They quickly became best friends. They were in Ms. Mosley's class together; they would play with each other after school, and in school they would try to sit next to each other at special events.

Maureen was also in Ms. Mosley's class, and she had been Terry's friend for many years. One morning, before school opened, Maureen turned to Terry and said, "Terry, did you know that Erin was making fun of your new hairstyle yesterday?"

Use the following prompts to help the class practice the first seven FIG TESPN steps:

F: *If you were Terry, how would you be feeling? Show me how you would look.*

I: *Put the problem into words.*

G: *Tell us what your goal is.*

T: *See if you can think of several solutions.*

E: *Now, envision what would happen next after each solution.*

S: *Which one will you choose?*

P: *Now, let's plan how, when, where, and with whom you will try out your best solutions.*

Have one person (with the class's help) generate ideas about the best way to try out the solution, or divide the class into small groups to generate lists of ideas. In either case, write the ideas on the chalkboard or easel pad.

Role-play the solution. Ask the following question to turn the class's attention to the need to review and rethink what happened:

N: *Is that what you really wanted? What would happen next, and is there any way to make it better?*

Give the class time to discuss this, then have the actors from the first role-play try it again.

Repeat the activity with other students from other characters' perspectives.

4. Provide additional practice opportunities.

Have the students generate hypothetical stories (which can be based on real situations) either on the spot or as an assignment you gave earlier in the week. Have students use their worksheets in groups to apply FIG TESPN. Be sure that either all groups are working on the same problems or that at least two groups are working on the same problem so there can be an opportunity to share ideas, role-play different possibilities, think about obstacles, and rethink and replan their ideas.

5. Introduce a Reflective Summary.

As outlined in the Introduction, ask students to reflect on the question "What did you learn from today's lesson?" Reinforce key themes, then go over any follow-up work.

6. Follow up.

The following steps will help make sure that the students have a chance to continue working with the new concepts.

Assignment

Provide students with another copy of the FIG TESPN steps worksheet and tell them to use it during the week with an academic or personal problem or decision. Have students share their worksheets during the next SDM/SPS meeting.

Plans to Promote Transfer and Generalization of Skill

Language Arts or Reading

Have the students select three different characters from stories that they have read this year. Ask them to evaluate each character's problem-solving skills and suggest how the character might improve.

Health

Have the students use one of the problem-solving steps as a basis for discussing or writing about how to persuade another student not to smoke or use drugs or alcohol.

Social Application

As class, grade-level, or schoolwide situations arise, create hypothetical scenarios and have subgroups of students use worksheets to practice problem solving and comparing ideas, as suggested in Step 4 of the "Instructional Activities" section.

TIPS FOR TEACHERS

Establish a Problem-Solving Corner in a separate area of the room. Have copies of the FIG TESPN steps worksheet (Worksheet 4.19.1) available for student use.

25 FIG TESPN: Practicing Problem Solving—Find Your Strengths

OBJECTIVES
- To make the FIG TESPN steps personally significant for students
- To have each student identify a problem-solving strength

MATERIALS
Whole-class display of the FIG TESPN steps worksheet (Worksheet 4.19.1)

Copies of the "Personal Problem-Solving Planner" (Worksheet 4.25.1)

INSTRUCTIONAL ACTIVITIES

1. Conduct a brief review.

Go over all eight FIG TESPN steps, using whatever memory game appeals most to the class. Emphasize the point of Topic 24: Being a good problem solver and decision maker is a habit, and practice helps people develop good habits. Tell the students that today they'll have another chance to use all eight steps to practice solving some challenging problems.

2. Introduce the day's activity.

Ask the students to consider all of the eight problem-solving steps that they have learned and to choose one particular step that helps them out the most when they are in a difficult situation. Some students may feel that setting a goal is most helpful because it keeps them on track. For others, thinking about the consequences of their ideas may be the most helpful.

Go around and have each child share one main strength. Keep track of answers and have students form eight groups (which can vary in size, down to just one student), corresponding to the FIG TESPN steps. If nobody chooses one of the steps, ask for a volunteer to represent a group for that particular step.

3. Read the story.

Before you begin, tell the students that today's story is about an adult—a substitute teacher—with a tough problem and very uncomfortable feelings.

Mrs. Price's Problem

Mrs. Mason taught the fifth graders at Soundview Street School. She liked the children in her class, and the children felt the same way about her. They were working hard this year and were having fun learning at the same time.

One Monday, as had been planned, Mrs. Mason was not able to come in to school because she had to go to the hospital for an operation. The principal assigned a substitute teacher, Mrs. Price, to teach the class.

From the beginning of the day onward, the children just did not cooperate with Mrs. Price. They would talk out of turn or otherwise disrupt the class. In fact, some of the students, including Todd, even made faces at her when they thought that she was not looking.

It was about 1:30 P.M., and while Mrs. Price wrote some math problems on the board, she saw out of the corner of her eye Todd and some of the others making faces at her, and she also heard other signs that the children were not cooperating. Mrs. Price felt several different feelings all at once.

4. Lead a discussion of the story.

For each point, have the appropriate FIG TESPN group reply. Ask for additional comments from the next group in the sequence. Use this procedure throughout the lesson. At the end, have the "N" group comment on the whole process, suggesting anything that would help Mrs. Price the next time.

F: What are some of the feelings that Mrs. Price may be experiencing?

I: She may be experiencing several problems at once. Could someone select one of her problems and put it into words?

G: Name a goal that she should try to aim for.

T: Now, what are all the things that Mrs. Price could do to reach her goal?

E: What might happen next if Mrs. Price were to try these solutions out?

S: *OK, let's choose what looks like it could be the best solution for Mrs. Price.*

P: *Let's talk about when, where, and how Mrs. Price could
do this so that it will work out the best.*

5. Role-play the solution.

Have students in the "P" group provide the actors (helped by "N" or
"S" groups, as needed).

Cast the role-play in a way that reflects students' preferred problem-
solving steps.

After the role-play, reflect on how well it went, whether the students
would do the same thing in the same way next time, and how they
would rethink it. Encourage them to share what step would have been
the most helpful to them if they were Mrs. Price.

Repeat the activity with another of Mrs. Price's problems as the
focus.

6. Introduce a Reflective Summary.

As outlined in the Introduction, ask students to reflect on the question "What did you learn from today's lesson?" Reinforce key themes,
then go over any follow-up work.

7. Follow up.

The following steps will help make sure that the students have a
chance to continue working with the new concepts.

Assignment

Distribute the "Personal Problem-Solving Planner" and ask the students to think of a problem that they are experiencing or are concerned
about now. Have them complete the worksheet for the next meeting.

Plans to Promote Transfer and Generalization of Skill

Language Arts

Encourage the students to each keep a Personal Problem-Solving
Journal in which they can record problems that they are experiencing and decisions they are making. In the future, when faced with a
similar problem, students can review their journal entries to help them
think through the current problem. In addition, a journal will allow
for review of skill improvement. Students can use the "Personal
Problem-Solving Planner" worksheet for this purpose.

TIPS FOR TEACHERS

1. Learning students' problem-solving strengths helps pave the way for you to prompt children's use of FIG TESPN outside the formal lesson. For example, you may have only a few minutes to help a student (or a group) resolve a recess-time problem. In that case, it might be helpful for you to call attention to one or two steps that are each child's strengths as well as to any that you feel would be particularly relevant. (For example, if you were talking to an impulsive child, you may want to request a list of solutions and consequences. With an overly intellectual child, you may want to emphasize recognition of feelings as an important, motivating first step.)

2. Talk to the class about the fact that the problem-solving lessons help bring them all together. Tell them that one of your favorite steps is the one about deciding on your goal. One of your goals this year is for them to feel that they can use their classmates as a problem-solving team. When a situation comes up that they feel is a problem, or if they get stuck on something, they can ask someone for advice (perhaps someone who prefers a particular step) or suggest that the matter be discussed at a class meeting.

3. Add the Personal Problem-Solving Planner to the Problem-Solving Corner, if you created one after Topic 24.

Student _____ **Date** _____

1. I am feeling _____

   _____ .

2. My problem is _____

   _____ .

3. My goal is _____

   _____ .

4. I am going to stop and think of as many solutions as I can and think about their consequences.

   Solutions I might try: If I try this, these consequences
                                              might happen:

   _____   _____

   _____   _____

   _____   _____

   _____   _____

   _____   _____

5. My plan for solving my problem is _____

   _____ .

6. *(Wait awhile and recheck your plan.)* Here is how I think it will work:

   a. Very well   b. OK   c. Not so well   d. Terribly

7. What I think I'll change is _____

   _____ .

8. What actually happens when you try your plan? _____

   _____ .

26 Review SDM/SPS Tools and Celebrate Success

OBJECTIVES
- To provide students with an opportunity to review their social decision making and social problem solving skills
- To provide teachers and students with an opportunity to assess skill gains
- To anticipate and plan ways to use social decision making and social problem solving skills in the next grade

MATERIALS

Whole-class displays of the previous lists of SDM/SPS Tools (Worksheets 4.8.1 and 4.13.1) and the list for this Topic (Worksheet 4.26.1: "SDM/SPS Tools (Topics 14–25)"

Copies of the following worksheets:

"SDM/SPS Certificate of Achievement" (4.26.2)

"Student Progress Report" (4.26.3)

"SDM/SPS Summary and Recommendations" (4.26.4)

Students' SDM/SPS Toolboxes (from Topic 13)

Crayons or markers, drawing paper, scissors *(optional)*

INSTRUCTIONAL ACTIVITIES

1. Introduce the lesson.

Direct students' attention to the whole-class displays of SDM/SPS tools. Explain that this lesson will give students a chance to think about all of the skills and concepts they have learned so far as a part of social decision making and social problem solving.

The skills and concepts taught in Topics 14–25, and the Topics in which they were introduced, are as follows:

- FIG TESPN (Topic 14)
- Feelings Log (Topic 15)
- Giving Constructive Criticism (Topic 18)
- Plan and Be Prepared for Pitfalls (Topic 22)
- Personal Problem-Solving Planner (Topic 25)

If you taught "I-Messages" (Worksheet 4.18.2), you can add that tool to the list.

2. Have a Sharing Circle.

Have students get into a Sharing Circle and have them go around and say which skill or concept they found to be most helpful. If you wish, you can ask them to name two or three skills or concepts they found helpful.

3. Conduct a practice activity.

Give students drawing paper and crayons or markers, and have them illustrate the tools presented in Topics 14–25. Instruct them to put these new tools in their SDM/SPS Toolboxes.

4. Review progress and look ahead.

Let the students know that you are interested in hearing what tools they are using and what tools they have a difficult time remembering to use. Ask students how they feel about going into the fifth grade. Then brainstorm some possible problems they might have.

5. Wrap up and celebrate the unit.

Praise students for their accomplishments. Ask students if they have any praise for the accomplishments of the team.

Conduct a final Sharing Circle, asking everyone to praise the person to the left about some way that person was a good teammate. Be sure that all students are able to give and receive a compliment.

End with a ceremony in which every member of the team is presented with a Certificate of Achievement. Wrap up with a round of applause for the great teamwork they have shown all year.

6. Introduce a Reflective Summary.

As outlined in the Introduction, ask students to reflect on the question "What did you learn from today's lesson?" Reinforce key themes, then go over any follow-up work.

7. Follow up.

The following steps will help make sure that the students have a chance to continue working with the new concepts.

Assignment

Have students take their toolboxes with them as a reminder to use their skills during the summer and in the next grade. Remind students to help one another use and practice their skills.

Take-Home

1. Send the Student Progress Report home to give parents and guardians a summary of student skill gains and recommendations for helping their children celebrate their achievements and continue building skills.

2. Student portfolios or notebooks can be sent home as a reminder of skills and a record of all that was learned and achieved throughout the year.

Plans to Promote Transfer and Generalization of Skill

Students should practice using their skills in various academic and social settings for the remainder of the school year. It is recommended that teachers continue to adapt lessons accordingly.

TIPS FOR TEACHERS

1. Students can continue practicing their FIG TESPN steps, using problems regarding the transition to a new grade for the remainder of the school year.

2. Teachers may also want to spend more time on transition problem solving if students will be moving to another school in the district—for example, from an elementary to a middle school setting.

3. Complete and distribute the "SDM/SPS Summary and Recommendations." This form is designed for you, as the sending teacher, to let receiving teachers know what their students have covered, and provides recommendations for maintaining and building on skill levels attained, as shown in an end-of-year assessment.

SDM/SPS Tools (Topics 14–25)

1. FIG TESPN

2. Feelings Log

3. Giving Constructive Criticism

4. Plan and Be Prepared for Pitfalls

5. Personal Problem-Solving Planner

Worksheet 4.26.1

SDM/SPS
Certificate of Achievement

_____

(Student)

Has successfully developed many Social Decision Making and Social Problem Solving skills

Sincerely,

_____   _____

(Teacher)   (Date)

Student Progress Report

I appreciate your support and partnership as we have worked this year to help your child develop social decision making and social problem solving abilities. As the school year comes to a close, I would like to share my assessment of your child's progress and make some recommendations to you about ways that you can help to continue the development of these skills through the summer months.

Skill improvement

_____

_____

_____

Suggestions to help you reinforce and continue skill development

_____

_____

_____

Additional comments

_____

_____

_____

_____

Thank you!

_____
(Teacher signature)

(Please sign and return this bottom section.)

Student _____ **Date** _____

We received the report.   ❑ Yes ❑ No

Comments:

_____
(Signature of parent or guardian)

Teacher _____ **Date** _____

Students in my class worked on a Social Decision Making and Social Problem Solving (SDM/SPS) team this past year to develop a variety of skills. I have attached a copy of all of last year's SDM/SPS Topics we covered. The numbers of those we covered fully are checked; an *X* appears beside Topics we touched upon but that might need some review. In addition, I have noted below accomplishments and areas of focus for particular students:

1. **Students with general strengths in SDM/SPS:**

   _____   _____

   _____   _____

   _____   _____

2. **Students needing overall growth in SDM/SPS:**

   _____   _____

   _____   _____

   _____   _____

3. **Students with strengths in particular SDM/SPS areas:**

   Student   *Area*

   _____   _____

   _____   _____

   _____   _____

   _____   _____

4. **Students needing skill development in particular SDM/SPS areas:**

   Student   *Area*

   _____   _____

   _____   _____

   _____   _____

   _____   _____

SDM/SPS Topics Covered

Rules and Tools (Topics 1–8)

☐ 1. Introduction to Social Decision Making/Social Problem Solving (SDM/SPS) Lessons
☐ 2. Respectful Listening
☐ 3. Strategies for Remembering
☐ 4. Role-Playing
☐ 5. Be Your BEST
☐ 6. BEST Applied: Good Teammate Behaviors
☐ 7. BEST Applied: Giving and Receiving Praise
☐ 8. Packing Your SDM/SPS Toolbox

Emotional Regulation (Topics 9–13)

☐ 9. Trigger Situations and Feelings Fingerprints
☐ 10. Keep Calm
☐ 11. Practice Keep Calm and Be Your BEST
☐ 12. Be Your BEST and Trigger Journal
☐ 13. More Tools for the Toolbox

Social Decision Making and Social Problem Solving (Topics 14–26)

☐ 14. Introducing FIG TESPN
☐ 15. FIG TESPN: Step 1. F = Find the Feelings
☐ 16. FIG TESPN: Step 2. I = Identify the Problem
☐ 17. FIG TESPN: Step 3. G = Guide Yourself with a Goal
☐ 18. Giving Constructive Criticism: Find the Feelings, Identify the Problem, and Guide Yourself with a Goal (FIG)
☐ 19. FIG TESPN: Step 4. T = Think of Many Possible Solutions
☐ 20. FIG TESPN: Step 5. E = Envision Consequences
☐ 21. FIG TESPN: Step 6. S = Select the Best Solution
☐ 22. FIG TESPN: Step 7. P = Plan and Be Prepared for Pitfalls
☐ 23. FIG TESPN: Step 8. N = Notice What Happened (Now What?)
☐ 24. FIG TESPN: Putting It All Together—Teacher-Led Problem-Solving Practice
☐ 25. FIG TESPN: Practicing Problem Solving—Find Your Strengths
☐ 26. Review SDM/SPS Tools and Celebrate Success

Supplemental (Topics 27–30)

☐ 27. Solving the Problem of Moving to a New Grade or School
☐ 28. Using FIG TESPN to Tame Tough Topics
☐ 29. Using FIG TESPN to Plan Community Service Activities
☐ 30. Using FIG TESPN as a Book Report Guide

Topics 27–30

27 Solving the Problem of Moving to a New Grade or School

OBJECTIVES
- To help students realize that change can be considered a problem that can be solved
- To show students how to apply their problem-solving knowledge to develop strategies to cope with upcoming change
- To emphasize the importance of friendship in coping with change

MATERIALS
Copies of "Here Today, There Tomorrow" (Worksheet 4.27.1) and "Action Plan" (Worksheet 4.27.2; *optional*)

Chalkboard or easel pad

Paper and pencils

A folder for each student

INSTRUCTIONAL ACTIVITIES

1. Discuss transitions.

Elicit feelings about school transitions, such as moving to another grade or school. Tell the class:

We have learned many skills that will help us make the move to a new grade or a new school. Think about all of the different problem-solving and decision-making skills that we have learned that are in your personal toolbox. Which skills do you think you will need to use as you fit into your new place? Why?

2. Conduct a practice activity.

Group 1

Divide the students into groups. Have the students use the "Here Today, There Tomorrow" worksheet to describe the Feelings Fingerprints they have when thinking about the transition. Have them meet in groups, compare feelings, and then report to the whole class a summary of their group's feelings.

Have groups link supports, good things, and problems they anticipate to the feelings they identify. List some of the responses on the chalkboard or easel pad and discuss the goals each suggests.

3. Make an action plan.

Group 2

For each goal stated in the discussion of the worksheet, have a different subgroup of the class work together to brainstorm as many ways as they can to reach the goal. Have them compile a list of their ideas.

Have each subgroup envision the consequences for each of their solutions. Give them a fixed time for discussion, and have each subgroup give you their two best solutions. Put these on the chalkboard under the goals.

Group 3

Assign a subgroup other than the one suggesting a particular solution to plan the steps to make the solution work. When and where can it be done? Who should be involved? How should it be done?

Ask each subgroup to role-play its plan, and have the other students provide feedback as a final check. Then, under each solution, write the plan that the class (and you) feel will help make a solution work best.

4. Have students make transition folders.

Have the students copy these problem-goal-solution-plan sequences in some form that they are likely to keep, such as the "Action Plan" worksheet. Ask the students to make transition folders (or something similar) in which they can put the various suggestions.

5. Introduce a Reflective Summary.

As outlined in the Introduction, ask students to reflect on the question "What did you learn from today's lesson?" Reinforce key themes, then go over any follow-up work.

6. Follow up.

The following steps will help make sure that the students have a chance to continue working with the new concepts.

Assignment

Encourage students to review and use their toolbox skills in the future as they move on to the next school year.

Take-Home

> Folders can be sent home with a brief cover note asking the parents or guardians to save them and to review the options with the students before they begin their new classes.

Plans to Promote Transfer and Generalization of Skill

Social Application

Encourage students to use their toolboxes when faced with change, problems, and decisions.

TIPS FOR TEACHERS

1. This Topic is particularly relevant toward the end of the school year as students begin to look ahead to their next grade level. The activities are also useful when one or more new students enter a class after the middle of the school year to help sensitize students to the difficulties involved in such changes.

2. One valuable variation can involve asking the students to brainstorm about ways in which to make their present situation better. If the Topic is continued over more than one meeting, be sure to keep a record of the problem and goal sections for use next time.

3. An additional activity might be to ask the students what the class can do, as a group, to make a transition easier. Some ideas that might result include planning trips to the new setting, getting to know new teachers or older students (perhaps via interviews), and learning new rules in advance. School-related transitions are stressful for many children, and some research suggests that how they master the stress sets the tone for subsequent academic and interpersonal progress. This issue may thus require several meetings or follow-up activities.

4. When you send transition folders home to parents, it is useful to ask parents to acknowledge that they have received the materials, to tell you when they reviewed the contents with their child, and to share briefly with you their child's reaction. A form can be provided so that parents can do this easily.

Student _____ Date _____

Put a check mark in the box that best shows how you feel about the words in each pair (Sad-Happy and so on).

Your Old Class or School

	Very	Sort of	Just a little	In the middle	Just a little	Sort of	Very	
Sad	☐	☐	☐	☐	☐	☐	☐	Happy
Calm	☐	☐	☐	☐	☐	☐	☐	Worried
Unsure	☐	☐	☐	☐	☐	☐	☐	Sure
Lazy	☐	☐	☐	☐	☐	☐	☐	Persistent
Unfriendly	☐	☐	☐	☐	☐	☐	☐	Friendly
Safe	☐	☐	☐	☐	☐	☐	☐	In danger

Your New Class or School

	Very	Sort of	Just a little	In the middle	Just a little	Sort of	Very	
Sad	☐	☐	☐	☐	☐	☐	☐	Happy
Calm	☐	☐	☐	☐	☐	☐	☐	Worried
Unsure	☐	☐	☐	☐	☐	☐	☐	Sure
Lazy	☐	☐	☐	☐	☐	☐	☐	Persistent
Unfriendly	☐	☐	☐	☐	☐	☐	☐	Friendly
Safe	☐	☐	☐	☐	☐	☐	☐	In danger

Student(s) _____ Date _____

1. What is the problem?

2. What is the goal?

3. What is my best solution?

4. What plan will I use to solve the problem?

28 Using FIG TESPN to Tame Tough Topics

OBJECTIVE
- To use FIG TESPN as a strategy for starting and completing projects

MATERIALS
Chalkboard or easel pad

Copies of "Taming Tough Topics" (Worksheet 4.28.1)

INSTRUCTIONAL ACTIVITIES

1. Begin with a subject-matter assignment that will be a stretch for the students.

Choose one or two areas of study to assign to the class. Possible topics include dinosaurs, space travel, conservation, inventors, explorers, women in history, and religions.

2. Distribute the "Taming Tough Topics" worksheet.

Ask the students to write down the topic. Then ask the class to generate a list of more detailed questions that they might want to consider within the larger topic. Have someone keep a list on the chalkboard or easel pad as ideas are mentioned.

3. Apply FIG TESPN.

Ask the students to consider as many ways as they can think of to gather information about their topics. Have them share their ideas, and again record them on the board. Suggestions such as going to the media center or library should be broken down into specifics, such as Internet search, films, magazines, card catalog, and so on.

Have the class generate a list of ways in which to present the information. It often helps to ask the students to remember interesting reports that they have read or seen. These include a written report, oral report, demonstration, exhibit, PowerPoint presentation, comic strip, video, news broadcast, brief skit or play, mural, overhead projection, game, and the like. For the most frequently used method, the report, help the class think of formats other than a listing of facts. Some examples are illustrative anecdotes, different viewpoints on the same topic, how the topic affects life today, what the people (or animals) involved would think about or do if they were living today, and how ideas have changed over time and with circumstances.

Ask each student to complete an individual worksheet as the plan for doing the assignment. If feasible, collect the worksheets and give the students final feedback before they begin.

4. Introduce a Reflective Summary.

As outlined in the Introduction, ask students to reflect on the question "What did you learn from today's lesson?" Reinforce key themes, then go over any follow-up work.

5. Follow up.

The following steps will help make sure that the students have a chance to continue working with the new concepts.

Assignment

After students have successfully completed the worksheet and received your feedback, have them complete their project. Say that they will have a chance to talk about how the planning worked, and whether they can see ways to plan more effectively another time.

Take-Home

If the project will require help at home, students should be told to share their completed worksheet with their parent or guardian. It's also a good idea to send home any other materials or supplies that might be required to complete the project, rather than assume that all students will have the essentials available around the house.

Plans to Promote Transfer and Generalization of Skill

These activities are designed to fit into language arts activities and involve skills necessary for academic learning, such as library research and preparing and making a written report or other form of presentation.

TIPS FOR TEACHERS

1. In encouraging students to think about ways in which to gather information, do not be limited by feasibility. Ideas such as an interview of an important figure or someone who is dead may seem

impossible, but they can be turned into activities such as writing letters or searching for records of historical correspondence.

2. The step of generating a list of ways in which to present information can sometimes await the completion of some or most of the information gathering.

3. At the end of the project, complete and file a feedback survey to assess this topic and refine your approach for use with future classes.

Student _____ **Date** _____

First: Define your problem and goal.

1. What is the topic?

2. What are some questions you would like to answer or learn about the topic?

Second: List alternative places to look for information.

1. Write at least five possible places where you can look for information.

   a. _____

   b. _____

   c. _____

   d. _____

   e. _____

2. Which ones will you try first?

3. Who else can you ask for ideas if these do not work?

Third: List alternative ways to present the topic.

1. Write at least three ways in which to present the topic.

   a. _____

   b. _____

   c. _____

2. Envision the consequences for each way, select your best solution, and plan how you will do it.

Fourth: Prepare for pitfalls and fix what needs fixing.

1. Does your presentation answer the topic and the questions that you asked? Is it clear and neat? Is the spelling correct? Will others enjoy it?

29 Using FIG TESPN to Plan Community Service Activities

OBJECTIVE
- To use FIG TESPN to plan and carry out community service activities and projects

MATERIALS
Chalkboard or easel pad

Copies of the FIG TESPN steps worksheet (Worksheet 4.19.1)

INSTRUCTIONAL ACTIVITIES

1. Introduce the idea of community service.

Ask the students what problems they see in and around the school and in the surrounding community.

Tell students that all communities have problems and often the adults in the community are doing many things to improve conditions there. Tell students that they, too, can participate in improving life in their community by doing community service projects.

2. Develop a list of possible projects.

Using the chalkboard or easel pad, brainstorm a list of all the problems that they would like to address in their community.

Have students prioritize the list. Ask them to come up with examples of ways in which they can help in their community.

3. Form groups to address the problems.

Distribute the FIG TESPN steps worksheet and divide the class into groups based on the number of prioritized problems that you would like to address.

Have each group choose a different problem that they would like to work through (or assign a different problem for them to work through) using their FIG TESPN steps worksheet. For example, if littering is a concern, students might consider forming a club that can pick up trash at local parks and playgrounds, create an anti-littering campaign, and help collect items to be recycled.

When the groups are finished, have each group share their work with the class. Discuss any pitfalls and rework the necessary details. Finalize plans for each group to participate in a community service activity.

4. Introduce a Reflective Summary.

As outlined in the Introduction, ask students to reflect on the question "What did you learn from today's lesson?" Reinforce key themes, then go over any follow-up work.

5. Follow up.

The following steps will help make sure that the students have a chance to continue working with the new concepts.

Assignment

Encourage all the students to participate and carry out the plan that their group creates. Provide opportunities for students to tell the class about their projects and how their efforts are making a difference in the community.

Take-Home

Doing projects in the community often requires the cooperation of parents and guardians for transportation and supervision, so this is a wonderful opportunity to involve the whole family in community service. Families can be encouraged to participate together, and adults can serve as positive role models. Parents and guardians should also be encouraged to discuss their involvement in community activities with their child and possibly with the entire class to show students that this should be an ongoing part of their life and not just an isolated project.

Plans to Promote Transfer and Generalization of Skill

Language Arts

Students can write about their community service activities in their journals or in a longer report. They can also write letters to politicians and newspaper editors, as well as create other documents to support or publicize their community service work.

Social Studies and Science

Students can look for articles in their local newspapers on problems and issues facing their community. They can also find articles on how people are trying to solve these issues and problems.

Art

Students can create posters and other artwork to encourage others in their school to serve their community and to take more responsibility.

TIPS FOR TEACHERS

Instead of having several different groups within the class working on different projects, you could also have the class choose one project to focus on as a whole class. Another idea is to have each grade level in the school choose a project to do together.

30

Using FIG TESPN as a Book Report Guide

OBJECTIVES
- To help students demonstrate understanding of FIG TESPN
- To help students apply FIG TESPN systematically, using materials from literature
- To help students apply critical thinking in the writing of a book report

MATERIALS

Literature materials

Copies of the "Book Report Guide" (Worksheet 4.30.1)

INSTRUCTIONAL ACTIVITIES

1. Introduce the topic.

Distribute the "Book Report Guide" worksheet and introduce it as a guide that will help students write their next book report.

Read the worksheet with the class and discuss any questions that students may have.

2. Conduct a practice activity.

To make sure that all students understand how to complete the Book Report Guide, have students complete the worksheet using a book that has recently been read in class.

Review the completed Book Report Guides and have several students read theirs aloud. Discuss how students could use these guides to write a full book report.

3. Introduce a Reflective Summary.

As outlined in the Introduction, ask students to reflect on the question "What did you learn from today's lesson?" Reinforce key themes, then go over any follow-up work.

4. Follow up.

The following steps will help make sure that the students have a chance to continue working with the new concepts.

Assignment

Give students additional copies of the Book Report Guide. Assign a book report to be completed by using the Book Report Guide. Students should answer the questions on the sheet after they have read their books. The answers can then be rewritten as a running narrative and combined to produce the book report.

Take-Home

An explanation of the Book Report Guide can be sent home so that parents and guardians can help their child complete this long-term assignment. Parents and guardians should be encouraged to work with their child to create a time line for completion of the assignment. They can also help their child review the book using the Book Report Guide.

Plans to Promote Transfer and Generalization of Skill

Language Arts and Social Studies

The Book Report Guide can be used with books assigned not only in language arts but also in social studies—for example, by using biographies. The Book Report Guide can also be modified so that it can be used with nonfiction books in other academic areas.

TIPS FOR TEACHERS

1. The Book Report Guide can be modified to include additional questions or changed to provide a better fit with curriculum materials and required reading.

2. Even if the entire class is reading the same book, guides can be completed individually, in dyads, or in small groups. Class time can also be used, especially in the latter two situations, to keep students on track, to allow teachers to check on the process and supervise the teamwork, and to help provide group meeting time.

3. Long-term assignments may be difficult for some students with special needs. Additional steps may be necessary to break the assignment into manageable increments for these students.

Student _____ **Date** _____

Use these questions to help you write your book report.

1. How did you feel about what you read?

2. In a paragraph or two, tell what the story is about. Be sure to write the main idea of the book in one clear sentence and <u>underline</u> it.

3. Why do you think the author wrote this? What was the goal?

4. What clues in the story helped you to discover the author's goal?

5. What else could be added to the book to help you understand the story better? Think about the characters and the time and place of the story.

6. If you could write a book that could come before or after this book, what would it be about? Write a paragraph or two to describe your prequel or sequel.

RECOMMENDED TOPICS FOR GRADE 5

Social Decision Making and Social Problem Solving

Topic

Putting It All Together

Topic

Supplemental

Grade 5 Worksheets

SOCIAL DECISION MAKING AND SOCIAL PROBLEM SOLVING

Topics 1–15

1 Introduction to Social Decision Making/Social Problem Solving (SDM/SPS) Lessons

OBJECTIVES

- To introduce and orient students to SDM/SPS lessons
- To establish ground rules for SDM/SPS meetings
- To introduce participation in a *Sharing Circle*
- To introduce and provide opportunities to practice Speaker Power, and establish *Speaker Power* as shared language and a skill prompt
- To introduce and provide opportunities to practice *Listening Position* and *Respectful Listening* and to establish these terms as shared language and skill prompts
- To build a sense of group trust, belonging, and cohesiveness

MATERIALS

Chalkboard or easel pad

Speaker Power Object *(optional)*

Whole-class displays of the steps in "Listening Position" (Worksheet 5.1.1) and "Respectful Listening" (Worksheet 5.1.2)

Poster board and markers

PREPARATION

Decide on the location and physical layout of the Sharing Circle and, at the start of this lesson, have the students arrange themselves into the pattern you have chosen. The Sharing Circle will be used as the format for conducting formal SDM/SPS lessons and class problem-solving discussions.

NOTE

After the group has compiled a list of rules, have students write them on a sheet of poster board and display them in the classroom. Change the list as rules are refined and new rules are added.

INSTRUCTIONAL ACTIVITIES

1. Introduce the lessons.

Tell the students that they will be having lessons that will help them to work together as a problem-solving team. Knowing how to make good decisions, solve problems, and get along with other people is important in fifth grade and will also help them to be successful and healthy as they grow up.

2. Assess current skill level.

Ask if any students have had lessons like this before. Often, it is valuable to have students who have had SDM/SPS lessons in the past explain in their own way what they have learned. School conditions change from year to year, and this exercise provides an opportunity to assess prior knowledge and skills and to structure students' expectations of what you actually plan to do this year. If you are working in a district with an established scope and sequence of skills for grade levels, it is a good idea to ask students to describe and demonstrate skills they already know to help gauge the need for review.

3. Establish rules and agreements.

Tell the class that to work as a problem-solving team you will first have to establish some rules to follow so the meetings will go well. Ask the students to volunteer rules that would help make everyone feel good about being a member of this team. Keep a list on the chalkboard or easel pad. Ask the students to think about what would make them feel good about sharing their ideas and how they would like to be treated. Then ask them to list some things that might make them not feel good on this team.

Usually, most of the student suggestions fall into general categories that overlap nicely with skills that will be covered during upcoming lessons and later given a label, skill prompt, or cue. Therefore, when just getting started, team rules should be brief and positive, leaving room for more explicit phrasing to be added later.

Let the students know that as they learn about specific ideas that can help the team work well, the rules can be updated. It is valuable to post some initial ideas to get started. Here are some common rules to begin with:

- Listen to each other without interrupting.
- Respect each other in words and what we do.
- Remember that behavior outside the rules has consequences.

4. Introduce the idea of a Sharing Circle.

Explain that the first activity is called a *Sharing Circle*. To participate, everyone (children, teachers, visitors in the room) in turn will at least say their name and answer a Sharing Circle question.

If the maturity of the group seems to warrant it, you can skip the Speaker Power activity and move straight to Listening Position. Come back to Speaker Power if your students are having difficulty taking turns speaking or respecting listeners.

5. Introduce Speaker Power.

If you wish, select an object (magic wand, stuffed animal, ball, ruler, pen . . .) that will be passed to the person speaking to designate a turn to talk. Say:

> *A Speaker Power object helps remind us to respect the person who is speaking, and the job of the other team members at that time is to listen carefully without interrupting.*

Explain that everyone will have a chance to have *Speaker Power*—either by receiving the object as it gets passed around the group or by raising a hand to ask for it.

Remind students that as the teacher you always have a kind of invisible Speaker Power. You will ask for the object when it fits into the lesson to do so, but it's your job to speak whenever you regard it as necessary.

6. Introduce Listening Position.

Explain that this lesson will also help the class explore what listening is and how to go about doing it better. To be a good listener it is necessary to pay attention. Establish the behavioral components of *Listening Position:*

1. Sit or stand straight.

2. Face the speaker or source of sound.

3. Look toward the speaker or source of sound.

7. Introduce Respectful Listening.

Explain that a new listening skill introduced today is a way to be sure you understand what you have listened to. Say:

> *To be sure that you have actively paid attention and are right about what you heard, you can repeat what you think you heard. You might say, "I heard you say that . . . " and say back to the other person what you heard them say. And then you ask*

if you are right, by saying something like "Did I understand you?" When you do this, you also show respect for the people talking. You show them that you are trying to listen carefully and that what they are saying is important to you.

Display the components of *Respectful Listening:*

1. Use Listening Position.

2. Pay attention to what the person is saying.

3. Repeat what the other person said.

4. Check to see if you are right.

8. Conduct a Sharing Circle.

Begin by asking a simple and nonthreatening question that will allow everyone in the group to have a turn. Let them know that there are no right or wrong answers and they can share with the group anything that comes to mind as long as it addresses the question. During the initial Sharing Circle, it would be a good idea to set the tone for further circles. Remind students that they don't have to agree with everything that is being said; they can agree or disagree with someone's statement but still respect the person.

When first getting started, it can also be helpful for you to go first and model what is expected. Students often enjoy learning things about their teachers, and this helps generate interest in what other people feel and think about a similar question.

Here are some questions that are useful for introducing the Sharing Circle:

- What has happened to you lately that made you feel amazed?
- What is your favorite cartoon or animated character?
- If you could be an explorer for one day and go anywhere, where would you like to explore?

As time permits, ask the students two or three additional questions that will gradually reveal something new about them to their classmates. After each additional question, have four or five students answer, then move on to the next question.

The following questions have been found to be quite useful for an initial group-building exercise:

- What is your favorite food? (Why?)
- What is your favorite sport or hobby? (Why?)
- If you were going to be the star of a television show, what show would you pick? (Why?)
- If you could spend one hour talking to anyone you wanted to, who would you pick? (Why)?

9. Introduce a Reflective Summary.

As outlined in the Introduction, ask students to reflect on the question "What did you learn from today's lesson?" Reinforce key themes, then go over any follow-up work.

10. Follow up.

The following steps will help make sure that the students have a chance to continue working with the new concepts.

Assignment

Ask students if they can think of some times when it would be a good idea to check and be sure that they are listening well to what other people say. Generate a list of ideas, such as when someone is explaining something to do, when someone is telling you why they think doing something is a good or bad idea, and when a teacher is giving instructions for or reminders about homework. Have students pick one of these ideas to try and to write it on their homework list.

Take-Home

Distribute a letter to parents or guardians like the one presented in the Introduction at this time (if it hasn't been sent home earlier or distributed at Back to School Night), to introduce the Social Decision Making/Social Problem Solving skill-building lessons to the students' families.

Plans to Promote Transfer and Generalization of Skill

Plan ahead to provide opportunities for students to practice using Sharing Circle, Speaker Power, Listening Position, and Respectful Listening as part of an academic lesson or class discussion.

Tips for Teachers

1. Review the first five items in the Grade 4 "Tips For Teachers" for Topic 1.

2. Fifth graders often like to create their own name for the format of problem-solving meetings, rather than using "Sharing Circle"—which may seem childish to them. Encourage them to do this to give them a greater sense of ownership and involvement. Some names students have used include "Team Huddle," "Morning Meeting Circle," "Team Time," and "Group and Share Time." Some classrooms have changed names monthly or each marking period. Keep in mind that the process is more important than the name.

3. It is helpful to identify situations and subject content areas where the practice of SDM/SPS skills would fortify existing objectives. It is also useful to document these plans and monitor the opportunities students have to practice and generalize the skill they are learning to academic and real-life situations. This effort helps ensure that teaching practices remain faithful to the instructional design that led to research-validated outcomes. It also helps teachers—in their role as adult learners—to integrate new skills within the complex repertoire of existing teaching practice.

4. Active listening skills help students learn to summarize and paraphrase instructions and information provided to them and to check for listening comprehension. Active listening skills are also considered foundation skills for conflict resolution.

Listening Position

1. Sit or stand straight.

2. Face the speaker or source of sound.

3. Look toward the speaker or source of sound.

From *Social Decision Making/Social Problem Solving: A Curriculum for Academic, Social, and Emotional Learning (Grades 4–5)*.
Copyright © 2005 by Maurice J. Elias and Linda Bruene Butler. Research Press (800-519-2707; www.researchpress.com)

Worksheet 5.1.1

Respectful Listening

1. Use Listening Position.

2. Pay attention to what the other person is saying.

3. Repeat what the other person said.

4. Check to see if you are right.

From *Social Decision Making/Social Problem Solving: A Curriculum for Academic, Social, and Emotional Learning (Grades 4–5)*.
Copyright © 2005 by Maurice J. Elias and Linda Bruene Butler. Research Press (800-519-2707; www.researchpress.com)

Worksheet 5.1.2

2   Introduction to FIG TESPN

OBJECTIVES
- To help students recognize the cognitive process underlying problem solving
- To help students discover the links between emotions and problem solving
- To establish *FIG TESPN* as a skill prompt and shared language

MATERIALS

Poster board or chart paper, markers, tape

Whole-class display of the steps in "FIG TESPN" (Worksheet 5.2.1)

INSTRUCTIONAL ACTIVITIES

1. Conduct a brief review.

Go over the skills introduced in Topic 1, emphasizing Respectful Listening.

2. Introduce the idea of using a strategy for decision making.

Explain to students that today they are going to work as a team to learn (or review, for those students familiar with this approach) a way to further develop their problem-solving and decision-making skills. Say something along these lines:

We take many steps in the course of solving a problem. Today we will learn a consistent strategy for problem solving with the ultimate goal of being able to call on it during a crisis. This problem-solving strategy is called FIG TESPN, after the first letter of each step in the strategy.

3. Conduct a practice activity.

Tape two pieces of paper to the wall. On the first paper write the heading "Problems and Decisions I Faced in K–4," and on the other paper write "Future Problems and Decisions."

Divide the class into two groups and assign each group to begin at one of the posters. Have students brainstorm a list for their heading.

After a few minutes, have each group switch to the other poster. Have each group read the list and then brainstorm more ideas to add to it.

After the brainstorming, ask students about the feelings and emotions associated with the problems and decisions that they listed. (Emphasize how an emotional component is inherent in nearly all problems, using specific examples from the student-generated lists.)

Some teachers call this activity "The Carousel" because of the way the students move around the room.

4. Introduce skill components.

Say:

Now we all know that decisions and problems can be emotional, and one thing about emotion is that it can make it harder to think clearly. Today, we are going to learn a strategy to guide us in thinking through a problem or decision, so it'll be there for us when we need it.

Let students know that the framework is called FIG TESPN and that FIG TESPN is the skill prompt and cue to describe this strategy for decision making and problem solving. The letters stand for the following ideas:

F —Find the Feelings

I —Identify the Problem

G —Guide Yourself with a Goal

T —Think of Many Possible Solutions

E —Envision Consequences

S —Select the Best Solution

P —Plan and Be Prepared for Pitfalls

N —Notice What Happened (Now What?)

Conclude by saying:

In the next few weeks, we will be discovering and practicing each of the steps to help us become better problem solvers.

5. Introduce a Reflective Summary.

As outlined in the Introduction, ask students to reflect on the question "What did you learn from today's lesson?" Reinforce key themes, then go over any follow-up work.

6. Follow up.

The following steps will help make sure that the students have a chance to continue working with the new concepts.

Assignment

Think about a time when you had trouble solving a problem or making a decision. Be prepared to share your situation at the next class meeting.

Take-Home

Students should inform their parents that their class will be working on problem solving.

TIPS FOR TEACHERS

1. Consider asking students what the word *strategy* means. Ask them to generate examples of times they use strategies, in school and out of school. Make this point:

   A strategy is a way to do things, usually a series of steps that help you get at what you have to do over and over. Strategies make it easier for you and make you more successful. Strategies are especially helpful when you are too tired or stressed and emotionally upset to want to stop and figure out what to do.

   Ask the class how this idea applies to problem solving and FIG TESPN, and encourage the students to come up with ideas for places and situations where they could use the technique.

2. Each of the eight FIG TESPN steps taught in this curriculum is a complex skill that must be addressed individually to be fully understood and used in the decision-making process.

3. It is most effective to teach the FIG TESPN model through the use of facilitative questioning—that is, through turning each of the eight steps into questions designed to guide students through the FIG TESPN process. This approach will allow you to move from being the solver of your students' problems to becoming the facilitator of your students' own thinking and decision-making skills—and that is the heart of a teacher's mission. You can find guidelines and examples for building students' problem-solving skills in the Introduction, especially in the section titled "The Facilitative Approach of Open-Ended Questioning."

4. An important aspect of these lessons is the consecutive building of one step upon another. Although students may already have memorized the steps from preceding years, the material should still be presented:

   - One step at a time
   - Consecutively, in the order given in this volume
   - With the preceding skills reviewed cumulatively as each new skill is presented

5. To ensure transfer and generalization of these skills, which is the point of teaching them, they must be *overtaught,* using repetition and as much practice of each skill as possible. Teachers must look for opportunities within content areas and the life of the school to generate social problem solving and social decision making practice, enlarging upon the curriculum as individual classes and circumstances allow. These lessons should be considered the jumping-off point for a creative process of planning to find numerous, regular, and visible opportunities for students to use their problem-solving and decision-making skills (that is, FIG TESPN, supported by all of the skills previously learned for team building and emotional regulation) throughout the school day. This approach will work best when coordinated with other teachers in your grade, as well as with all school support staff and administration.

FIG TESPN

F — Find the Feelings

I — Identify the Problem

G — Guide Yourself with a Goal

T — Think of Many Possible Solutions

E — Envision Consequences

S — Select the Best Solution

P — Plan and Be Prepared for Pitfalls

N — Notice What Happened (Now What?)

Worksheet 5.2.1

3 Feelings Identification

OBJECTIVE
- To help students become more sensitive to personal feelings and the feelings of others by learning to recognize and verbalize those feelings

MATERIALS   None

INSTRUCTIONAL ACTIVITIES

1. Conduct a brief review.

Go over the basic FIG TESPN steps and their importance to the class. Discuss the results of the preceding assignment.

2. Introduce the idea that solving problems requires detecting feelings.

Say:

> *Good problem solvers are "Feelings Detectives." What do you think that means?*

Draw analogies between problem solving and detective work—especially looking for subtle clues, in this case of how people feel. Make a list of feelings clues (the nonverbal messages that people send through their facial expressions and posture: a raised eyebrow indicating doubt or surprise, a slumping back indicating tiredness or boredom). Say:

> *Good detectives—who are also good problem solvers—recognize when they have strong feelings themselves and learn to tell others accurately what those feelings are.*

3. Review skill components.

Ask students how they will be able to detect what others are feeling. Possible responses:

- By *looking* at facial expressions and how people act
- By *listening* to what people say and how they say it

- By *asking*, "How are you feeling?"

4. Discuss examples.

Ask students to think of a time when they were in a bad mood (over-tired, cranky, irritated, or angry) and someone approached them to ask a favor (for example, "Can I borrow your CD player?" or "Can I use your science book?") Ask what happened. Have the class discuss how mood affects a situation like that.

Two important points can be made:

- The person in the irritated mood should recognize being in this mood and be able to express it—for example, "Look, I'm sort of angry right now. Maybe we could talk about this later." Things will be much less irritating down the line if the person responds this way rather than with an angry outburst such as "No way! I'll never lend you anything."
- The person doing the asking should be able to read the other person's feelings, which would be a sign to wait until another time to ask.

5. Conduct a practice activity.

Describe a situation, or use one of the samples given here, and ask several different students how they would feel if this happened to them. (Or insert hypothetical names and ask how they think that person would feel.)

Sample situations:

- You had been doing well in math, but lately your grades have started slipping.
- Your poem or drawing has been selected for display on a special bulletin board.
- The people you want to sit with at lunch won't let you join them.
- Your teacher just reprimanded you for not paying attention.

Encourage clarification by asking why they might feel that way. Also, you may ask how the other person might be feeling.

Choose from these feelings:

enraged	*proud*	*excited*
shocked	*annoyed*	*embarrassed*
frustrated	*joyful*	*curious*
elated	*horrified*	*worried*
dejected	*amazed*	*suspicious*
intimidated	*distressed*	*confident*

If you prefer, you can add your own feelings words to the list and choose those appropriate for your students.

6. Additional practice: Feelings Detective Story.

Prepare students by telling them that they will hear a story about an older and younger boy who are good friends but run into a problem with each other. Students should use their Feelings Detective skills and pay attention to signs of different feelings in each boy.

Pressure on the School Bus

It was Friday afternoon, and Kelvin was sitting on the bus next to his friend Brad. They were riding home from school together, just as they always did. Brad was a few years older than Kelvin, but they were good friends just the same.

Brad was moving around in his seat a lot and seemed different to Kelvin for some reason. As the bus driver steered the bus out of the parking lot and onto the street, Brad quietly took a small bottle out of his pocket and showed it to Kelvin.

"Look, Kelvin," he said, "it's a little bottle of some stuff that I found in my brother's room last night. Here, have a sip."

Kelvin coughed a bit, then looked at Brad and said, "What is it?"

"It's some kind of wine or liquor or something. Are you going to have some or not?" Brad said impatiently.

Kelvin hesitated, then said, "No . . . no, thanks."

Brad's face wrinkled up a little, and he said, "C'mon, I've already had some. Are you a baby or what?"

Kelvin's face started to feel a little tight, and he said in a strong voice, "No . . . and put that away!"

Ask the following questions:

- When did Kelvin first notice that something different might be happening on this bus ride?
- What are some possible feelings Brad could have had:
     When he found the bottle the night before?
     When he first offered the bottle to Kelvin?
     When Kelvin refused the bottle the first time?
     When Kelvin refused the bottle the second time?
- How would you be feeling if you were Kelvin:
     And you first noticed Brad moving around in his seat so much?
     When Brad first offered you the bottle?
     When Brad insisted and tried again to make you take a sip?

Remind students that one reason Kelvin was so strong and refused to do something wrong was that he was able to recognize upset feelings inside himself. He expressed his feelings by saying, "No . . . and put that away!" He also may have felt angry at being pressured by his friend.

7. Introduce a Reflective Summary.

As outlined in the Introduction, ask students to reflect on the question "What did you learn from today's lesson?" Reinforce key themes, then go over any follow-up work.

8. Follow up.

The following steps will help make sure that the students have a chance to continue working with the new concepts.

Assignment

Tell students to look for signs of different feelings, both internally and in their classmates. Have them keep a list and be prepared to discuss it during a future lesson.

Plans to Promote Transfer and Generalization of Skill

Language Arts and Social Studies

Students can practice recognizing feelings in stories and videos and then discussing them. Before reading aloud, having students read, or showing a video, prepare students by reminding them to be thinking about (and watching for) signs of feelings. Stop to ask about feelings with questions like these:

- What was the character feeling? How do you know?
- What did the character say or do that let you know they were feeling that way?
- How would you feel in that situation? Have you ever felt that way?

Social Studies

Have students go through magazines to find pictures of leaders in government, health, education, sports, and entertainment and locate at least eight different individuals showing signs of feelings that students can identify. Students should identify the feeling and the physical signs that lead them to believe that a certain feeling is being expressed. You can have the class share these observations as a group or use them to create a bulletin board or other display.

TIPS FOR TEACHERS

1. Students who are less verbal or have similar difficulties can use feelings flashcards (to provide a word bank of feelings words) during the practice activities. Alternatively, they may draw pictures of people exhibiting the feelings being discussed.

2. Students enjoy these activities and benefit greatly from the practice, so consider spending more than one lesson on this topic or working in practice activities when brief periods of time present themselves during a school day.

4 Trigger Situations and Physical Signs of Stress

OBJECTIVES

- To help students become aware that some situations elicit or trigger strong emotions *(Trigger Situations)*
- To increase students' awareness of the unique way strong feelings manifest themselves in the body *(Feelings Fingerprints)*
- To teach students about fight-or-flight reactions and how strong feelings impair the ability to think clearly
- To introduce the importance of taking responsibility to use Feelings Fingerprints as signs of the need to calm down before thinking and acting

MATERIALS

Chalkboard or easel pad

Notebooks or journals

INSTRUCTIONAL ACTIVITIES

1. Conduct a brief review.

Go over the vocabulary of feelings and the detective skills discussed in Topic 3. Discuss the results of the feelings identification assignment.

2. Introduce the concept of Trigger Situations.

Point out that everyone at one time or another has a problem that needs to be solved. These can be problems with parents, teachers, brothers, sisters, or friends. Remind students of prior lessons in which they identified how feelings are associated with problems. Say:

Sometimes we jump right in and try to solve a problem before we are ready. If this happens, nothing gets accomplished because we are too upset and our emotions get in the way of being able to think clearly. To make a good decision and begin to solve a problem, we need to be able to use all of our brain to think about what we can or want to do.

Point out that everyone has certain kinds of events or situations that are especially likely to make them get upset, and those are called *Trigger Situations*. When faced with a Trigger Situation, we experience feelings such as anger, nervousness, fear, and so on.

It will help the class to discuss their own triggers if you can provide some personal examples, such as giving a speech, getting into an argument, and so on. Brainstorm a variety of common Trigger Situations with the group, and post the results on the chalkboard or easel pad.

3. Introduce the concept of Feelings Fingerprints.

Tell students that emotions are called *feelings* because people really *feel* them; emotions cause changes in the body that are predictable for any one person but differ from one person to the next. Explain that human bodies are equipped to respond to upsetting situations with a "fight or flight" response: What happens in a Trigger Situation is that the body makes a chemical called adrenaline, which causes various physical reactions and provides a lot of energy. When people have strong feelings, it is a lot easier for them to get angry (fight) or run away (flight) than to think because adrenaline also makes it hard to use the thinking part of the brain.

4. Identify personal Feelings Fingerprints.

Point out that people experience physical signs of stress in different ways. Have the class brainstorm their own Feelings Fingerprints, or physical signs of stress, by sharing what they experience when faced with Trigger Situations. (As noted, this will work best if you lead and model the activity, talking about your own experience when under stress.) The list may include headache, increased heart rate, jittery stomach, sweaty palms, tense shoulders, rapid breathing, shaking knees, and so on.

You could say something along these lines:

> *Let me give you an example: Do any of you watch sports?*

Give an example of an athlete (use a name likely to be familiar to the students) who gets nervous before a competition:

> *Athletes feel many different physical signs of stress, what we're calling Feelings Fingerprints. For example, they get butterflies in their stomachs, their hands get sweaty, or their shoulders tense up. Just as athletes experience pressure to perform, you can also be under a lot of stress. The ability to recognize physical signs of stress is an important first step in learning to stay calm and to think clearly in Trigger Situations that may lead to more problems.*

5. Match situations and feelings.

Have the students generate examples of situations where they have felt nervous, restless and unable to concentrate, or about to lose their temper.

You may suggest that they close their eyes and try to remember how they felt in that situation. Ask them to try to visualize the experience and feel how their bodies felt at the time.

Then ask the class:

> *Are there any ways you can think of to get self-control when there is a problem?*

Give the class a few minutes to come up with suggestions.

6. Emphasize the importance of self-awareness.

Repeat the point that sometimes people jump ahead and try to solve a problem before they are ready or able to do so. If this happens, nothing gets accomplished because they are too upset and out of control to think about what they might be able to do.

Say:

> *It is important to be aware of your triggers and how they affect your body. Try to notice where you feel the stress. This physical sign of stress is the clue that the fight-or-flight response may happen. By being aware of your triggers and Feelings Fingerprints you can take deliberate steps to regain control and have access to your thinking skills.*

Tie the discussion back to the biology of stress and show how people can use their brains to control some of their fight-or-flight responses. Say that in the next lesson the students will have a chance to practice an exercise called "Keep Calm" that will let them take control of their reactions.

7. Introduce a Reflective Summary.

As outlined in the Introduction, ask students to reflect on the question "What did you learn from today's lesson?" Reinforce key themes, then go over any follow-up work.

8. Follow up.

The following steps will help make sure that the students have a chance to continue working with the new concepts.

Assignment

Have students record Trigger Situations and the corresponding Feelings Fingerprints in journal format. Keep papers on hand for future practice.

Present students with potential Trigger Situations by staging role-plays, acting out a situation yourself, or showing a video or pictures and then having students add examples of their own to those presented. Try these situations:

- Giving a presentation or oral report
- Not having your homework ready when the teacher collects it
- Making the last out in a game

Take-Home

Encourage students to begin to notice other people's triggers and Feelings Fingerprints, on television, at the mall, on the bus, at school, and so on. Encourage students to record their observations in a notebook or journal, without naming specific people.

Plans to Promote Transfer and Generalization of Skill

Social Studies

Have students identify current events from newspapers and magazines, broadcast media, or Internet sources in which individuals encountered Trigger Situations. Instruct students to identify the Trigger Situation and the resultant actions.

TIPS FOR TEACHERS

Modeling and calling the students' attention to your own triggers and physiological responses to stress is an effective teaching tool at this point. Likewise, calling attention to the triggers and Feelings Fingerprints of characters in literature and on screen is another means of developing children's awareness of these situations.

T O P I C

5   Keep Calm

OBJECTIVES
- To point out problem situations in which students can use self-control to calm down before reacting
- To teach students to regulate their emotions and maintain control in problem situations
- To practice a deep-breathing exercise called *Keep Calm*

MATERIALS
Chalkboard or easel pad

Whole-class display of the steps in "Keep Calm" (Worksheet 5.5.1)

INSTRUCTIONAL ACTIVITIES

1. Conduct a brief review.

Go over the vocabulary from Topic 4, with a focus on Trigger Situations and Feelings Fingerprints (physical signs of stress). Give students a chance to share their own Trigger Situations and corresponding Feelings Fingerprints.

2. Introduce Keep Calm.

Explain that today's topic is the importance of keeping calm. Ask if students know the prompt *Keep Calm*. If most do not, then use the lesson for Grade 4, Topic 10, to introduce the strategy and provide practice. In either case, refer students to the whole-class display of the steps in the skill:

1. Tell yourself to STOP.

2. Tell yourself to KEEP CALM.

3. Slow down your breathing with two long, deep breaths.

4. Praise yourself on a job well done.

If most students do know Keep Calm but some do not, group students in triads (two who know Keep Calm, one who does not). Have your veterans talk to their classmates about the steps of Keep Calm and times when it is helpful to use it, and then role-play and practice Keep Calm. Walk among the groups and assist as needed.

3. Discuss uses for the exercise.

Open up a general discussion about using Keep Calm. Ask students to name upcoming situations when it may help them to use the strategy. Record their responses on the chalkboard or easel pad.

Encourage students to find a time when they can use Keep Calm and try it. Let them know that you will expect an example of how they used Keep Calm at the next lesson.

4. Introduce a Reflective Summary.

As outlined in the Introduction, ask students to reflect on the question "What did you learn from today's lesson?" Reinforce key themes, then go over any follow-up work.

5. Follow up.

The following steps will help make sure that the students have a chance to continue working with the new concepts.

Assignment

Present students with situations by staging role-plays, acting out a situation yourself, or showing a video or pictures and then having them add examples of their own to those presented. Try these situations:

- Your parent or guardian says to do your homework, but you want to talk on the phone.
- You are going to a new school or new place.
- You're competing in a sporting event.
- You get blamed for something you didn't do.
- You get caught doing something wrong.

Plans to Promote Transfer and Generalization of Skill

Social and Current Events

Instruct students to seek examples of people taking deep breaths before performing certain tasks. Encourage students to observe athletes, politicians, surgeons, or others in life or on TV. Have students keep track of observations of deep breathing used for calming.

Language Arts

Instruct students to identify points in books during which a character could use Keep Calm. Have students predict what might have happened if the character had used Keep Calm and how that might differ from what did occur in the story.

TIPS FOR TEACHERS

1. Some children may need a real-life example of what it's like to be nervous or antsy, or to lose their temper. This can be illustrated in several ways. Use a mirror to show differences in physical appearances before and after using Keep Calm. Jogging in place to increase breathing can also be used to show the contrast before and after Keep Calm.

2. During problem situations that come up during the week, encourage children to use Keep Calm techniques before discussing the situation with a teacher or classmates.

3. Focus on helping students use Keep Calm just prior to and during exams and quizzes throughout the school year. Follow through with reminders before exams. This strategy can be especially helpful before and during standardized tests.

4. It may be a good idea to remind children about Keep Calm before potentially stressful situations such as a mainstreamed class or a special subject like art, music, physical education, and playground period.

5. Some students will learn to use their Feelings Fingerprints as a sign to use Keep Calm. Others will be prompted by Trigger Situations or other sets of cues. Regardless, the lesson is designed to introduce the concept. The skill will be learned to the extent that students are prompted and reminded to use it in salient everyday situations, such as when moving from class to class, when released at recess, before a test, before an important meeting, or when they are upset at home—as well as in performance situations such as reading aloud, being in front of the class, being called on by the teacher, showing their work in music or art, or participating in sports activities.

6. Sample prompts to use when a student is upset or is beginning to lose control:

   Use your "Keep Calm" steps.

   Stop and think about what's happening.

   Let's "Keep Calm" and get focused.

   Let's take a look at what's going on. Tell me what you see (or what you saw, what happened, how you are feeling).

   Take a deep breath and Keep Calm—then we can talk about it.

7. Testimonials in which the use of Keep Calm is discussed and reinforced and in which feedback is given for future use of the strategy should be solicited regularly, as this will promote future use of self-control. Students should be encouraged to use Keep Calm to prepare themselves for possible Trigger Situations.

Keep Calm

1. Tell yourself to STOP.

2. Tell yourself to KEEP CALM.

3. Slow down your breathing with two long, deep breaths.

4. Praise yourself for a job well done.

Worksheet 5.5.1

TOPIC

6 Identify the Problem

OBJECTIVE
- To show students how to identify a problem and make a clear problem statement

MATERIALS
Chalkboard or easel pad

INSTRUCTIONAL ACTIVITIES

1. Review preceding lessons.

Remind the class that they are on their way to working together as a problem-solving team. Review all of FIG TESPN—especially the first step in the FIG TESPN process, feelings identification. Tie in more recent lessons on Trigger Situations, physical signs of stress, and Keep Calm as tools for learning how to regulate the strong emotions and feelings associated with a problem.

2. Introduce the concept of a problem.

Solicit student definitions of the term *problem,* remembering to encourage students to describe feelings associated with problems. (Suggested definition: something that happens to someone or between two people that usually makes one or both of them unhappy or uncomfortable.)

3. Introduce the skill components.

Ask students why it is sometimes difficult to tell yourself what the problem is. (Answers should include these points: Emotion gets in the way; the first or obvious problem is sometimes not the real problem; sometimes there are many problems or the problem is very complex; or the problem really belongs to another person.) Say:

> *After we have looked for signs of different feelings in ourselves and in others, we need to describe the problem in a specific way. We need to create a clear, concise problem statement. In this way, "I feel guilty" becomes "I feel guilty because I didn't invite my cousin to my party."*

Allow students to share examples of real or hypothetical problems.

Have students brainstorm things that might help them make a problem statement. Record their ideas on the chalkboard or easel pad. Some examples:

> Look at feelings first, yours and others—they often point to a problem.

> Look at the facts—what is happening is often the problem.

> Consider other points of view—this helps clarify a problem.

Through their examples and others you generate, help them find an approach to help them put the problem into words. Tell students that one strategy is to say:

> *I feel _____ because (or when) _____.*

4. Conduct a practice activity.

Ask students to identify possible problems for the following openings:

- I feel angry because . . .
- I feel upset because . . .
- I feel worried when . . .
- I feel that I am ready to give up when . . .

Once the students have the idea of associating feelings and causes or events, read and discuss the story titled "Latisha's Problem."

Prepare students to hear a story by telling them that they will hear about a girl named Latisha. Tell students to think how people in the story might feel, notice different problems that people in the story have, and be prepared to discuss them.

Latisha's Problem

Latisha has been begging her mom to take her to a special salon to get her hair and nails done for weeks. As a reward for Latisha's improved behavior, her mom has arranged to take the afternoon off from work, to pick Latisha up after school, and spend a special mother-daughter afternoon at the salon.

Latisha is so excited about the special plans that she has a hard time paying attention in school that day. In the cafeteria, she accidentally cuts in front of a classmate, Denise, in the lunch line. Denise responds by shoving Latisha, who pushes her back. Suddenly, the cafeteria monitor has written both girls up for fighting in the cafeteria. They are sent to the office and receive mandatory after-school detention.

Ask the students to determine how each of the following characters is feeling:

Latisha

Denise

Latisha's mom

Cafeteria monitor

To practice the new skill, ask students to define a problem statement from each of the character's point of view.

Latisha

Denise

Latisha's mom

Cafeteria monitor

Ask first how the characters are feeling. Then have students tell what they think the problem is. Be careful that students do not confuse the problem with a goal or possible solution. The problem can often be a simple statement of what happened.

Spend enough time on this step for students to practice clearly defining the problem.

5. Introduce a Reflective Summary.

As outlined in the Introduction, ask students to reflect on the question "What did you learn from today's lesson?" Reinforce key themes, then go over any follow-up work.

6. Follow up.

The following steps will help make sure that the students have a chance to continue working with the new concepts.

Assignment

Over the next week, ask students to watch for problem situations in which someone has been involved in a joke or experienced an embarrassing or teasing remark. They could look on TV for similar situations. They should write brief problem descriptions and hand them in.

Take-Home

Send a note home to parents, suggesting the following activity.

Problems in the News

The news is filled with problems. Read a newspaper or magazine story with your child. Discuss the problems related in the article. Ask your child to create a clear problem statement for each of the problems discussed in the article. You may want to discuss how these problems affect the different people involved in the news item.

Note: Television or radio news items are often not as useful for this activity because these stories are so brief that they usually define the problem for viewers and listeners.

Plans to Promote Transfer and Generalization of Skill

Language Arts and Social Studies

To reinforce identification of problems, ask students what a character's feelings and problem are as stories are read, videos seen, history lessons presented, school-based situations encountered, and so on.

Language Arts and Creative Writing

Have the class use one of these as the opening sentence of a short story or journal entry.

- Carmen felt disappointed because . . .
- The policeman felt confused because . . .
- "Overjoyed" was the best way to describe Robert when . . .
- The baseball player felt thrilled because . . .
- The Johnson family felt very pleased when . . .

Social Applications

Have students describe some common classroom, hallway, cafeteria, and playground problems by creating clear problem statements that can be used with later lessons. Have students decide if there might be several problem statements that can arise from a single situation or incident.

TIPS FOR TEACHERS

1. The use of the concept of a *problem* has special value. It encourages students to describe social matters with the same familiar language that is used in math or science. In addition, placing a social difficulty into a problem context suggests optimistically that it may be solvable.

2. Another important aspect of this skill is that if students can put what is bothering them into words, a seemingly overwhelming situation becomes manageable. "I feel sad" becomes "I feel sad because I forgot to feed the dog."

T O P I C

7   Trigger Journals

OBJECTIVE
- To provide students with practice in monitoring triggers and dealing with conflicts and criticism through the use of Keep Calm and Be Your BEST

MATERIALS   Copies of the "Trigger Journal" (Worksheet 5.7.1)

INSTRUCTIONAL ACTIVITIES

1. Conduct a brief review.

Go over the concepts of Trigger Situations and problems. Then, as part of the opening Sharing Circle question, ask the students to share a recent Trigger Situation that ended unhappily.

2. Introduce the new activity.

Tell the students that today they will learn to use Trigger Journals, which will help them deal with difficult Trigger Situations, especially ones that occur frequently.

Distribute the Trigger Journals and have students take turns reading the questions aloud to ensure that everyone is clear on how they should be completed.

3. Complete a retrospective journal page.

Have the students complete their worksheets, using a Trigger Situation from a time when they were younger. Tell the students that they will be reading their Trigger Journals to the class, so they should use a situation that they are comfortable sharing. Have students pay special attention to whether they remembered to use Keep Calm and Be Your BEST skills in the incident they're describing. Also have them pay attention to the last question, the one that requires them to create a positive alternative solution that they could try if a similar situation arises.

When the students have completed their Trigger Journals, have them take turns reading in front of the class or from their desks. Remind students to use Keep Calm if they become nervous.

4. Conduct a practice activity.

After all the students have had a turn to read, choose situations that seem particularly relevant to use for role-playing. Discuss each situation with the class, emphasizing the question "What is something else you could have done to handle the situation?"

Have the students role-play the situation as it happened, then have them role-play using the positive alternative solution that was presented at the end of the journal page. Divide the class and have each group watch for a specific component in the role-play. Have the class analyze the role-play and talk about how well the positive alternative solution might have worked.

Have students create additional solutions that might work and have them practice these role-plays, as time permits.

5. Conclude the lesson.

Discuss your expectations for how the students will continue using the Trigger Journals throughout the year, whenever a situation arises where the systematic approach would help reach a satisfactory resolution.

6. Introduce a Reflective Summary.

As outlined in the Introduction, ask students to reflect on the question "What did you learn from today's lesson?" Reinforce key themes, then go over any follow-up work.

7. Follow up.

The following steps will help make sure that the students have a chance to continue working with the new concepts.

Assignment

Distribute copies of the Trigger Journal and have students complete them for homework, using a situation that arises during the upcoming week. Have the students bring them to the next meeting and repeat the practice activity by having the students share their completed Trigger Journals. Again, role-play the situations that you feel are most relevant to your students. Emphasize that there is always more than one way to handle a difficult situation. This activity is getting the students ready for more advanced problem solving and decision making.

Take-Home

The Trigger Journal is a tool that can be used by teachers and other school staff when working with parents and guardians around difficult Trigger Situations. Reviewing Trigger Journals with responsible adults provides good examples of situations that the child has faced in school and can be used during conferences or disciplinary meetings, allowing for joint planning to approach these issues in the future. Parents and guardians can also use this tool to help their children deal with Trigger Situations at home.

Plans to Promote Transfer and Generalization of Skill

Academic Application

Have the students pretend that they are a character in a story and complete the Trigger Journal from that character's point of view. Have the students share their completed journals during a language arts lesson.

TIPS FOR TEACHERS

1. The practice opportunities presented in this Topic are essential for solid skill building. Often, this Topic will take two or even three class sessions to complete.

2. This Topic gives children an opportunity to practice using Keep Calm in class. The Trigger Journal gives students a way to encourage their use of these skills outside the formal lesson context. Teachers can then use Trigger Journals in an ongoing manner as a way to help students think through problem situations that occur during the week and also to recall the situations for discussion during SDM/SPS lessons.

3. Some children have difficulty with writing, and provisions can be made for them to talk to an aide, teacher, counselor, or a helpful peer who can help them complete the worksheet.

4. There is much benefit to reviewing the use of the Trigger Journals several times throughout the week. The Trigger Journal reviews all the important skills in this phase of the curriculum. Have students complete Trigger Journals regularly at times you feel that it is important for them to self-monitor.

5. Sometimes it is difficult for students to share actual examples of Trigger Situations with the group because the class lacks the cohesiveness and trust to support the activity, or some or all of the students are not sufficiently mature to handle it. If you have such a group, you can collect the completed Trigger Journals in advance and create anonymous, hypothetical Trigger Journals based on the real-life situations presented by students. It can be beneficial to actually complete a Trigger Journal and present it in a whole-class format so the entire class can see it and work on it together.

Student _____ Date _____

1. **Briefly describe a difficult Trigger Situation that you were involved in this week.**

   What happened? _____

   _____

   _____

   Who was involved? _____ (peer/adult)(*Circle one.*)

   When and where did this happen?_____

2. **How did you feel?**

3. **What did you say and do?**

4. **What happened in the end?**

5. **How calm and under control were you before you said or did something?** *(Circle one.)*

1	2	3	4	5
Under control	Mostly calm	So-so	Tense and upset	Out of control

6. **How satisfied were you with what you did?** *(Circle one.)*

1	2	3	4	5
Not at all	Only a little	So-so	Pretty satisfied	Very, very satisfied

7. **What did you like about what you did?**

8. **What didn't you like about what you did?**

9. **What is something else you could have done to handle the situation?**

8 Guide Yourself with a Goal

OBJECTIVE	▪ To help students figure out how to decide what they or another person would like to have happen in a problem situation
MATERIALS	Chalkboard or easel pad
	Copies of "My Goals" (Worksheet 5.8.1)

INSTRUCTIONAL ACTIVITIES

1. Review past lessons.

Explain that earlier topics covered the "F" and "I" of FIG TESPN, and today the class will be working on the "G": Guide Yourself with a Goal. (When discussing goals, in this session or whenever goals are a factor in problem solving, always begin by addressing feelings and problem definitions. You may state them or elicit them from students.)

2. Ask students to define "goal."

Look for responses that include how you would like things to end or what you would like to see happen. Emphasize the relationship of goal to problem: The goal is the resolution of the problem. Some students find the image of a bull's-eye or a finish line helpful in grasping the concept of a goal and working toward it.

Explain that young people or adults who do not set goals for themselves often wind up working toward a goal that someone else has set for them. Have them imagine that a group of students are waiting for class to begin. The teacher is not in the room. If no one has a goal in mind, such as getting ready for class or preparing some schoolwork, then whoever first comes up with something amusing will control what the group does. What might that be? Is that the best situation?

3. Present a working definition.

Explain to students that the goal is often the opposite of the problem. For example, if the problem is "Someone is bullying me," the goal might be "I don't want to be bullied." Students should begin a goal statement with "One goal is that . . . "

4. Give some examples.

It is important that students understand that a given situation can pose several problems and that different people can have different goals. Also, goals are easily confused with solutions. For example, "I am upset *(feeling)* because I did not do well on the test *(problem)*."

Goal statements:

Good examples: "One goal is that I do better on tests" or "One goal is that I raise this grade."

Poor examples: "One goal is that I study harder" or "One goal is that I take better notes." (These statements confuse goals with solutions.)

Model your own goal-setting practice by saying things like:

- My goal is to see us finish this work early so we can play a game.
- I'd like to see everyone sitting quietly—that's my goal.

Put the good and poor examples on the chalkboard or easel pad. Ask:

Where might each of these guide you?

What goal is most likely to guide you to where you most want to end up?

5. Conduct a practice activity.

Have students share what their goal is in the following situations:

- Going to sports or hobby practice
- Helping a neighbor
- Studying for a test
- Putting money in a bank account
- Getting good grades

Discuss realistic and unrealistic goal setting. Propose the following goals, and for each, ask:

Is that a realistic goal? Why or why not?

- Anna wants to become a professional athlete.
- Simone wants to buy a diamond necklace for her mother.
- Tyrell wants to have his comic strip published in the school newspaper.
- Luis wants to become a lawyer.

Students may add circumstances to these scenarios to support their claim that the goal is realistic or unrealistic. This "what-if" thinking is OK and adds to the discussion. It also helps students to sort out their own goals.

6. Introduce the idea of the time frame for a goal.

People can have both *long-term goals* and *short-term goals*. Long-term goals will take time to achieve and will need to have some short-term goals met first. Ask students to identify these as long-term or short-term goals:

- Becoming a doctor
- Buying a bike
- Going to Mike's house
- Winning an Olympic medal in the marathon

Ask students to give a short-term goal for becoming a doctor (studying in school) and winning an Olympic medal in the marathon (begin running short distances).

Have students discuss some short-term and long-term goals they might have.

7. Introduce a Reflective Summary.

As outlined in the Introduction, ask students to reflect on the question "What did you learn from today's lesson?" Reinforce key themes, then go over any follow-up work.

8. Follow up.

The following steps will help make sure that the students have a chance to continue working with the new concepts.

Assignment

Distribute copies of Worksheet 5.8.1 and ask students to identify something they feel needs work in each of the categories (in other words, identify the problem). They can then name the feeling associated with these issues and create short-term goals to work toward in each case. Students will need these worksheets again in Topic 10.

Take-Home

The following activity can be sent home with a note or can be done in the classroom.

Ad Attack

Television and magazines assault us with cleverly constructed attempts to influence our actions. Ad Attack is a simple activity that can help break the spell. When a commercial comes on television, ask your child what the makers of the commercial are trying to get us to do.

All advertisers have a goal in mind, such as getting people to buy something or go someplace. By doing this activity, children see what commercials are up to, and unmasking advertisements in this way makes them become less real and less magical.

Other questions to consider: "How do they make [the product] look so good?" "What makes [the product] something you would want to buy?" It is also important to note that by keeping advertisers' goals and tactics in mind, we become smarter consumers of goods and services. This activity can also be used with radio, newspaper, and other kinds of ads.

Plans to Promote Transfer and Generalization of Skill

Language Arts

When reading a story or book, have students discuss the author's goal in writing the story. What did the author want to have happen?

Go to www.lawsoflife.org and look at the Laws of Life Essay Contest. Use the ideas here to have your class write an essay on their Laws of Life, Goals of Life, or Purpose in Life. Consider involving your school in the contest, starting with Grade 5.

Social Application

Where appropriate, ask students to set personal goals, classroom goals, community and state goals, national goals, and worldwide goals for a variety of issues.

TIPS FOR TEACHERS

1. Problems and goals are often confused. Remember that the goal is the reverse of the problem. This will help students clarify the difference. It is also important for students to realize that a given situation can pose several problems and that different people can have different goals.

2. Goals and solutions are also commonly confused. Goals are end states, not actions. They also should be under your control and be structured more toward "I want" than "So-and-so will." Have students practice deciding if something is how they want things to end up or what they'll do to get there.

Student _____ **Date** _____

Classwork Goal

Feeling _____

Identify the problem _____

Goal _____

Behavior Goal

Feeling _____

Identify the problem _____

Goal _____

Relationship Goal

Feeling _____

Identify the problem _____

Goal _____

9

Understanding Different Points of View

OBJECTIVES
- To introduce the concept of different points of view
- To practice Respectful Listening and FIG
- To practice taking different points of view to resolve conflicts

MATERIALS
Chalkboard or easel pad
Colored construction paper and scissors
Bell or whistle to signal change of view *(optional)*

INSTRUCTIONAL ACTIVITIES

1. Review the first three steps of FIG TESPN.

F — Find the Feelings
I — Identify the Problem
G — Guide Yourself with a Goal

2. Introduce the new skill.

Explain that everyone has a different point of view:

The way we see things can make a difference when we are tying to work out a problem. For example, when I look out at our classroom, I see a group of students facing me. When you look out at our classroom, you see me and the backs of the students in front of you, unless you're in the front row. (Modify as appropriate to your classroom arrangement.) Because I am the teacher, I have a different point of view.

Explain that sometimes when people have different points of view, they disagree on how to resolve problems. But they can all use FIG to express their own point of view.

3. Conduct a practice activity.

Explore the concept of different points of view by using a relevant situation—for example, classmates:

How many of you have classmates who sometimes like to use or borrow things that are yours?

What is your point of view? How do you feel? How would you describe this situation from your point of view?

What about your classmates? How do you think it feels from their point of view?

Now, illustrate the example, using FIG:

Say what you see and feel (F).

Give a reason why you do not like it—that is, identify the problem (I).

Tell what you want instead—your goal (G).

Example:

I feel frustrated . . .(F)

. . . when you touch things on my desk. (I)

I want you to stop so nothing gets ruined. (G)

Then consider the classmate's point of view:

I feel jealous . . .(F)

. . . when you have everything you need, all neat and organized. (I)

I want to have what I need for class when I need it. (G)

Ask students if they can think of any other examples of times when people had different points of view. Prompt for both academic (history, language arts, social studies) and real-life situations.

Examples may include things like these:

- The settlers wanted to move West, but the Native Americans did not want the settlers taking over their territory.
- Differences in the points of view of two characters in a piece of literature that your class is using.
- My brother and I want to watch different TV shows.
- I was blamed for something I did not do.

4. Role-play the process.

Have student pairs act out a situation based on two characters under study in history, social studies, or language arts, or an example of a current problem from the classroom or the playground. Talk about each situation, using some of the questions from Step 3. As you present the situation, include elements of motivation on both sides, as in the following example:

Ashley and Alex are having a misunderstanding. Ashley feels hurt because Alex said Ashley's new shoes were "different." Ashley likes the shoes and wants to wear them all the time. Alex didn't mean to hurt Ashley's feelings. He just thinks the shoes might be too fancy for their camping trip.

5. Introduce the "Footsteps" activity.

Tell students that they will learn more about different points of view when they play an activity called Footsteps. Pass out the art supplies, and have each student make a set of paper feet big enough to stand on.

Display the following three steps, explaining that the idea is to finish each statement that ends in three dots:

Step 1: Use Speaker Power

I feel . . .

I think . . .

I want . . .

Step 2: Use Respectful Listening

I think I understand what you said.

You feel . . .

You think . . .

You want . . .

Is that right?

Step 3: Think of ways to solve the problem

"How about if . . . ?" or "How can we . . . ?"

Point to the three steps and explain that these steps will be used in an activity to practice taking different points of view by standing in different places. That is, the idea is to literally move across the floor so each person stands right where the other one started out for the second set of statements, then goes back to the original place for the third. Use your example to demonstrate the process.

Select two students to demonstrate the steps, using the following scenario while you read the viewpoints and step prompts. They should use the sample dialogue as a guide.

Kevin wants the class to put on a show for the school and thinks that his class should be the only performers.

Donna is in Kevin's class and wants to put on a show, too, but she thinks they should invite other classrooms to be a part of the show.

Stage directions:

Step 1: Each actor stands on a pair of paper footprints and explains one of the two points of view using "I" sentences, such as "I think," "I want," or "I feel."

After both have spoken, the students switch places so each stands in the other's footsteps. You should tell them to wait for your signal to switch places so the one who spoke first isn't tempted to move too soon.

Step 2: Each person explains the other person's point of view as well as possible, using statements like these: "I think I understand what you said. You feel . . . " "You think . . . " or "You want . . ." Follow up each sentence with the question "Is that right?" or "Is that how you think or feel?" or "Is that what you want?"

After both have spoken, the students switch places so each stands in their original footsteps. You should tell them to wait for your signal to switch places, so the one who spoke first isn't tempted to move too soon.

Step 3: Pairs think of ways to work out the problem, taking both points of view into account, using sentences that start with: "How about if . . . ?" or "How can we . . . ?" For example:

Kevin: How about if we let our class figure out what kind of show we want to do.

Donna: We could try that, but how about if we come up with the kinds of acts, too, and see if there is any extra time for other classes.

Kevin: That's a good idea.

Donna: All right, I'll ask the teacher for a class meeting about the show.

The actors should then ask the class:

What "I sentences" did you hear us use?

How about "you" sentences?

What were our "How about it . . . " suggestions?

Did we agree on a solution? What was it?

Explain that students will use the same three steps to act out a problem you will give them.

6. Conduct another practice activity.

Divide your group into pairs. Assign parts—one is Student A and one is Student B—in each pair. Have the pairs take their places around the room, facing each other on their footsteps.

Read the following problem aloud:

A and B both want the last two pieces of blue construction paper for their book report covers. The students playing "A" want the blue paper because blue is their favorite color, and the ones playing "B" want the blue paper because their book report is on the oceans of the world.

Give students about one minute for each step, with all pairs acting out the situation at the same time. Remind them to take turns talking.

Walk around the room and listen to what students are doing. If necessary, help with suggestions.

7. Call the large group back together.

Choose one pair to act out the situation for the group. Ask everyone the following questions:

- What else could each student have said to explain their point of view?
- Did they seem to understand each other's points of view? What misunderstandings did you see?
- What was the solution they came up with? Would both people reach their goal?
- What are some other solutions they could try?

8. Introduce a Reflective Summary.

As outlined in the Introduction, ask students to reflect on the question "What did you learn from today's lesson?" Reinforce key themes, then go over any follow-up work.

9. Follow up.

The following steps will help make sure that the students have a chance to continue working with the new concepts.

Assignment

Have students practice using FIG and the Footsteps activity, either at home or at school, when disagreements arise out of people's different points of view.

Plans to Promote Transfer and Generalization of Skill

Language Arts and Social Studies

Stop at critical points of a story in language arts, social studies, and so on and ask students to role-play—using Footsteps—the different points of view.

Social Applications

When conflicts occur on the playground, prompt students to use Keep Calm and then try using Footsteps to help them think of a way that they could solve their problem.

Here are some additional conflict situations to use for practice:

- One student calls another a name in a humorous way, but the other sees nothing funny in it.
- Two students want to read the same book. One student says he needs it for a report. The other says it is his favorite book and he wants to read it again.
- Two students are arguing over a very fancy pen. One says that it looks like the one she bought with her allowance. The other says that it looks like the one given to her by her favorite aunt.

TIPS FOR TEACHERS

1. The Footsteps activity can also be combined with FIG, especially if students have a hard time taking others' points of view.

2. Keep two sets of laminated footsteps available to use whenever students are involved in a conflict. Doing so will let you establish "Drop the Feet" as a prompt, directing the students to literally drop the feet and stand on them to carry out the Footsteps procedure. This can also be done at a critical point in a story, asking two students to play the role of two characters who encounter a conflict.

10 Think of Many Solutions and Envision Consequences

OBJECTIVES
- To help students think flexibly and creatively and consider a variety of alternative responses to a given situation
- To teach students to think ahead to two or three consequences that might follow each alternative

MATERIALS

Chalkboard or easel pad

Whole-class display of "What Could This Be?" (Worksheet 5.10.1)

Whole-class display and copies of "FIG TESPN: Eight Steps for Social Decision Making and Social Problem Solving" (Worksheet 5.10.2)

NOTE

After this Topic, Worksheet 5.10.2 is referred to as the "FIG TESPN steps worksheet." Keep the whole-class version of the worksheet posted for future reference.

INSTRUCTIONAL ACTIVITIES

1. Review accomplishments to date.

In particular, go over the FIG problem-solving steps (that is, FIG TESPN Steps 1, 2, and 3).

2. Introduce new skills.

Ask students to define the terms *brainstorming, alternative solutions,* and *consequences.*

Define *alternative solutions* as all the ways that a problem could be solved. Define *brainstorming* as the process of coming up with alternative solutions by listing as many as possible. Define *consequences* as feelings or actions that follow or happen after something else.

Explain that considering consequences encourages students to forecast or predict what is going to occur.

The following questions help elicit consequences:

- What might happen if you try _____?

- What do you think might happen?
- Anyone else have some ideas?
- How would you feel if _____ were tried?
- If you try _____, what else might happen?
- Is that what you want to happen?
- What else could you try?

Encourage a balance, where appropriate, of anticipating positive and negative consequences.

Discuss the way students think about consequences. What factors influence what they think might happen? Possibilities include:

- Past experience
- Knowledge of persons involved
- Rules, regulations, and laws

There may be others, depending on the experience of the class. Ask which kinds of consequences most influence their choice of a solution.

Have students discuss the difference between short-term and long-term consequences; what might happen now and a while from now.

Explain that when people brainstorm many solutions to a problem, they sometimes get excited and rush ahead, acting on a solution without thinking about the consequences. Ask what can happen when people do this.

Draw from your own experience and offer an example of how anticipating consequences was very helpful for you (buying a used or new car, deciding which books or materials to use with your class, choosing which means of transportation to use on a trip).

3. Establish skill prompts.

Explain to the class that you'll be saying, "Think of as many possible solutions to the problem as you can" to remind them not to stop brainstorming too soon. To help them think clearly about each solution, you'll be saying, "Envision the consequences."

4. Conduct a practice activity.

Refer students to one of the drawings on Worksheet 5.10.1 and have them list as many answers as possible to the question "What could this be?"

When they have finished, have everyone share their lists. Make a master list on the chalkboard or easel pad.

Ask if the group had more ideas than any one person. Discuss the benefits of brainstorming in a group.

5. Conduct another practice activity.

Have students discuss the possible consequences (What might happen if . . .) of this situation:

You find a book you need in the library for a report. You put it down, and another student picks it up and goes to check it out.

Use the whole-class display of the FIG TESPN steps worksheet to answer these questions:

- How do you feel?
- What is the problem?
- What do you want to have happen? Your goal?
- What can you do? What are some possible solutions?
- What would the consequences be for each solution, positive and negative?

Solutions	Possible Consequences
1. Grab the book back.	You check the book out.
	You tear the book.
	The other student grabs it back from you.
2. Explain the situation to the student.	The student gives you the book.
	The student refuses to give you the book.

As an extra practice activity, ask students to work with this situation:

You see two students at recess picking on a classmate of yours.

6. Introduce a Reflective Summary.

As outlined in the Introduction, ask students to reflect on the question "What did you learn from today's lesson?" Reinforce key themes, then go over any follow-up work.

7. Follow up.

The following steps will help make sure that the students have a chance to continue working with the new concepts.

Assignment

Distribute copies of the FIG TESPN steps worksheet, and then refer students to the worksheet titled "My Goals" (Worksheet 5.8.1), which they completed as an assignment in Topic 8. Have them choose one situation from this worksheet and transfer the "FIG" portion to the

FIG TESPN steps worksheet. Ask students to brainstorm as many solutions to that problem as they can. Encourage students to consider both positive and negative consequences for the solutions they choose. Students will need these worksheets again in Topic 13.

Note: If students do not have any examples or feel their examples are too personal, they may choose a more neutral or hypothetical situation.

Take-Home

Send a note home to parents and guardians with this idea.

Alternative Alternatives

Try this game with your child the next time you go for a ride or walk. Ask your child to brainstorm as many items as possible for each of the following questions:

- How many kinds of soda can you think of?

    (Orange, grape, ginger ale, cream, cherry, cola . . .)

- What are all of the games that you can play with a ball?

    (Football, soccer, pinball, baseball, polo . . .)

- What are different ways that you could use a shoe box?

    (House for a pet, as snowshoes, as a hat . . .)

- How many ways can you think of to prepare eggs?

    (Poached, scrambled, fried, as eggnog, an omelet . . .)

- What are different ways that you could use the cardboard tube from a roll of paper towels?

    (Telescope, microphone, pet's toy . . .)

Plans to Promote Transfer and Generalization of Skill

Social Studies

Have students think of the potential consequences of these and other developments:

- The United States had a king or queen rather than a president.
- Children were allowed to vote.

Science

Have students discuss the possible consequences of different combinations of weather patterns (front systems, pressure areas, wind speeds and directions, atmospheric conditions, and so on), short- and long-term forecasting, and accurate versus inaccurate forecasts.

Social Application

When a class problem comes up, have students focus on the long- and short-term consequences of these actions and the effect these might have on themselves and others. You may use situations relevant to your class and phrase them hypothetically, if necessary. Situations involving peer pressure, breaking rules or laws, and getting along with others provide an endless supply of problem-solving opportunities.

TIPS FOR TEACHERS

1. It is important that students be encouraged to respond with as many ideas as possible in this step. Remember the basic principles of brainstorming:

   - Defer judgment (verbal or nonverbal).
   - Allow original, off-beat responses.
   - Go for quantity—the more ideas the better.
   - Expand on ideas as they come up—nobody owns a brainstorming idea.

2. Here are some words and phrases that will stimulate students' thinking and promote expansion of ideas:

   - What else is like this? What other idea does this suggest? What could I copy? Whom could I emulate?
   - How about a blend, assortment, ensemble of ideas? Combine purposes, ideas?
   - What if you look at it from different angles, perspectives?

3. When a student gives an unrealistic or inappropriate consequence, encourage more appropriate thinking. Here are several ways to get the student back on track:

   - Asking what the most likely consequence would be.
   - Asking, "How would you react or feel if the proposed solution were tried on you?"
   - Bringing other children into the discussion by saying, "OK, let's hear what some other people think. Are there things that are more likely to happen?"

1. __ ___ ___ ___

      ___ ___

 ___ ___ ___ ___

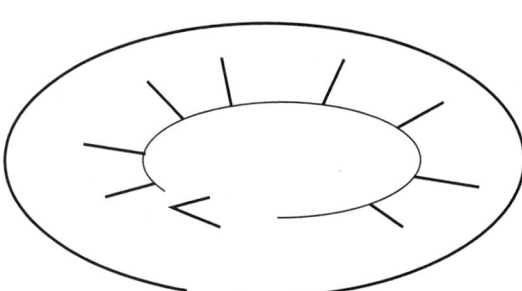

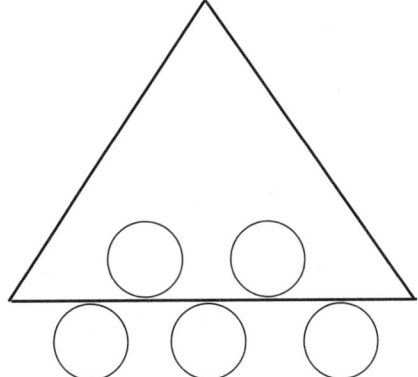

FIG TESPN: Eight Steps for Social Decision Making and Social Problem Solving

Student _____ Date _____

1. **Feelings** _____

2. **Problem** _____

3. **Goal** _____

4. **Think of many solutions.**   5. **Envision consequences.**

A. _____ _____ (+)

_____ (−)

B. _____ _____ (+)

_____ (−)

C. _____ _____ (+)

_____ (−)

D. _____ _____ (+)

_____ (−)

6. **Select the best solution:** _____

7. **Plan and be prepared for pitfalls.**

   In your plan, consider who, what, when, where, and how.

8. **Notice what happened. (Now what?)**

11

Practice Thinking of Solutions and Envisioning Consequences

OBJECTIVES
- To help students learn to think flexibly and creatively and consider a variety of alternative responses to a given situation
- To help students think ahead to consequences that might follow each alternative

MATERIALS   Copies of the FIG TESPN steps worksheet (Worksheet 5.10.2)

INSTRUCTIONAL ACTIVITIES

1. Conduct a brief review.

Go over FIG TESPN problem-solving Steps 1 through 5.

2. Introduce skill components.

Remind students that many people who have not learned decision making and problem solving rush right into a solution without stopping to think about the consequences of the solution or about other possible solutions. Sometimes the first solution that comes to mind may not be the best one.

Ask students what can happen when a person decides on a solution without envisioning, or picturing, the consequences.

3. Conduct a practice activity.

Read the following situation:

Reggie and Karen are the president and vice president of their class. They have planned a meeting of the student government for Thursday after school. On Wednesday, Reggie's friend Komal calls to say that he has tickets for a sporting event on Thursday night.

Reggie says, "I have a meeting that won't be over until late."

Komal says, "Just cancel it; you're the president. It will be an unbelievable game, and I have great seats."

On Wednesday night, Karen calls Reggie and asks, "What room is the meeting in? A few people have called to ask me." Reggie realizes that he has a problem.

Divide the class into problem-solving teams and distribute FIG TESPN steps worksheets.

Have the teams complete problem-solving Steps 1 through 5, in that order.

Reconvene the class to compare solutions and consequences that were generated by the teams. Discuss similarities and differences in each of the steps, feelings, goals, and so on. Focus in particular on solutions and corresponding consequences. Be sure to help students see the difference between long-term and short-term consequences and consequences for themselves and for others.

4. Introduce a Reflective Summary.

As outlined in the Introduction, ask students to reflect on the question "What did you learn from today's lesson?" Reinforce key themes, then go over any follow-up work.

5. Follow up.

The following steps will help make sure that the students have a chance to continue working with the new concepts.

Assignment

As students encounter problems and decisions, have them brainstorm solutions and envision consequences that can be discussed during their next lesson. This can be done individually or in teams. Have them use the worksheet to help them.

Take-Home

Send a note home to parents and guardians explaining this activity.

What-If Game

This game is one of the best ways to help children anticipate consequences, as well as encourage alternative thinking. Simply ask children these "What-if" questions and let them generate as many answers as they can to each one. The first two questions have some sample answers to illustrate the kinds of things children often say, but each child should be encouraged to come up with individual answers; there's no right or wrong here.

- What if you could read minds?

    I'd be surprised at what people think.

    I could rule the world.

    I'd be really smart.

    I'd have too much on my mind.

- What if you found a thousand dollars?

    I'd play videogames all day.

    I'd put it in the bank.

    I'd find out whose it was.

    I'd buy presents for all my friends.

Here are some more examples.

- What if . . .

    You could breathe underwater?

    You could jump as high as a horse?

    You had your own car?

    You could run as fast as a deer?

    It snowed every day all year?

    Birds could talk to us?

    You met someone from outer space?

    You had your own TV show?

    You were the president?

    The New York Yankees wanted you to play for them?

    It rained roses?

Plans to Promote Transfer and Generalization of Skill

Language Arts and Social Studies

As the opportunity arises in stories, videos, and materials from various content areas, stop when a problem is presented and encourage students to brainstorm ideas and envision consequences. For example, suppose you are showing the video *Johnny Tremain,* in which the colonists are outraged over taxes imposed by the king, especially the new one on tea. Stop the video at an appropriate place. Ask students what feelings the colonists are expressing. What is the problem and the colonists' goal? Now have students brainstorm solutions. What could the colonists do to reach their goal? What ideas do you have? What consequences can you envision for each idea? Resume the movie to see what idea the colonists chose.

Social Applications

When a class problem comes up, have students focus on the long- and short-term consequences of different actions and the effect these might have on themselves and others. You may use situations relevant to your class and phrase them hypothetically if necessary. Situations involving peer pressure, breaking rules or laws, and getting along with others provide an endless supply of problem-solving opportunities.

TIPS FOR TEACHERS

1. The first five steps of the FIG TESPN eight-step framework should be practiced as often as possible in both academic and social situations. The more often the students repeat and practice the steps, the sooner they will begin to call upon the skills automatically during times of stress.

2. Use the FIG TESPN steps worksheets to help structure academic and nonacademic problem-solving activities.

TOPIC

12   Your BEST Chance for Success

OBJECTIVES
- To present or reinforce the BEST strategy of effective communication, including the differences in the passive, aggressive, and assertive styles of communication
- To provide an opportunity for students to practice the assertive style, as shown by their body posture, eye contact, spoken words, and tone of voice
- To have the chance to apply BEST in advocating a position about a topic relating to citizenship and democracy

MATERIALS

Whole-class display of the steps in "Be Your BEST" (Worksheet 5.12.1)

Whole-class display and copies of the "Be Your BEST Grid" (Worksheet 5.12.2)

NOTE

A copy of the BEST grid, including sample student responses, is given as Worksheet 4.5.3.

INSTRUCTIONAL ACTIVITIES

1. Introduce the basic concepts.

In a Sharing Circle, ask students what the word *citizenship* means to them. Ask what it means to be a good citizen.

Next, talk about *democracy*. Ask students what this word means. Talk to them about our form of government and link to social studies and civics to the extent possible. Indicate that part of being a citizen involves being part of groups, going to meetings, and communicating clearly. An important skill for clear communication is "Be Your BEST."

Ask students if they have ever heard of the "Be Your BEST" exercise. With the help of the class, define the components of BEST. Elicit from the students a definition of each of these components.

B stands for Body Posture.

E stands for Eye Contact.

S stands for Speech. (Say something nice.)

T stands for Tone of Voice.

2. Review material from prior years as needed.

If most students are unfamiliar with BEST, teach Grade 4, Topic 5, before proceeding with this topic. If most are familiar, move straight to the practice activity.

3. Conduct a practice activity.

This activity is designed to practice using BEST while advocating a position. Have students work in groups of six. In each group, randomly choose two students to be in Group A, two in Group B, and two in Group C. Explain the roles as follows:

For the issue I'm about to present, Group A will be For, Group B will be Against, and Group C will give feedback on BEST.

The issue: Should high school students be allowed to vote in national, state, and local elections? Each group will have ten minutes to prepare their ideas and then present their position along with two or three reasons. Group C will plan how they will monitor the techniques involved in "Be Your BEST" and give feedback. (You can use the BEST grid, if it will be helpful.)

As time allows, switch roles—that is, have Group A be Against, Group B give feedback about BEST, and Group C be For. Introduce a second issue, such as "Should a person be able to be president for more than two four-year terms in a row?"

Close with a discussion about what the different groups felt went well and what was the most difficult. Review the "Be Your BEST" skills and talk about all the different times students are in groups or meetings where being their BEST—assertive, not passive or aggressive—will help them be better citizens.

4. Introduce a Reflective Summary.

As outlined in the Introduction, ask students to reflect on the question "What did you learn from today's lesson?" Reinforce key themes, then go over any follow-up work.

5. Follow up.

The following steps will help make sure that the students have a chance to continue working with the new concepts.

Assignment

Since Be Your BEST is a very difficult skill to learn and one that may not meet with much success in an aggressive environment, teachers should provide follow-up and discussion, especially as this effort relates to improving school climate. Give students the assignment to try to use their BEST skills during disagreements with their peers, both in school and in extracurricular and social situations. Have the students write a brief description of the situation, without using any names of those involved. Tell students that they will be sharing their experiences and how well their attempts worked or did not work during the next lesson.

During the next lesson, have students share their experiences, with the focus on the situations and not the names of the people involved. Have the students practice doing more role-plays using these situations and have a class discussion regarding how the students can be assertive and influence others to act assertively rather than passively or aggressively.

Take-Home

Send home a copy of the BEST grid worksheet and these suggested activities.

BEST on Television

Have a discussion with your child regarding the assertive, aggressive, and passive behaviors shown in movies, videos, and television programs that you watch together. Also, discuss the impact of one character's assertive, aggressive, or passive behaviors on the other characters on the show.

Assert Your Beliefs

Help your child think of ways to take a personal stand instead of going along with the crowd because it is easier. Initially, have the child practice being assertive with seemingly inconsequential issues. This builds skills for the times when tougher issues arise.

Plans to Promote Transfer and Generalization of Skill

Have students find a character in a story (in language arts, social studies, or health lessons) who acts aggressively or passively and discuss the consequences of that behavior. Discuss how the story or situation might have been different if the character had acted assertively. Have students write a different ending to the story, based on the character's assertive behavior. Another option is to have the students create a role-play showing the character acting assertively rather than passively or aggressively and have students change the story to reflect the impact that the assertive behavior would have had.

TIPS FOR TEACHERS

1. Educators should keep in mind that behavior in the BEST areas strongly influences impressions in social interactions but that there are cultural differences in how and when certain of those behaviors should be displayed (Banks, 1991, 1992; Banks & McGee, 1989). For example, some children may be less likely to make eye contact with adult males, out of respect.

2. It is usually helpful to state explicitly that everyone uses passive, aggressive, and assertive behaviors at times. The Topic is not about different types of people, but about different styles of behavior.

3. When discussing bullying, talk about the role of bystanders and how their passivity affects the situation. Have the children practice being assertive when they are bullied and when they see others being bullied. Use the following role-plays and conversation topics list as needed.

Role-Plays

- Sara is a fifth grader, and a group of her classmates are spreading rumors that she is going out with several boys in the middle school. They write notes that say embarrassing things about her and show them to the rest of the class. Now everyone in class is against Sara, and no one wants to be her friend.

- Jacob is a boy in the fifth grade. He is having problems with reading and needs to go to the resource room every day during reading time. Several of the boys in his class call him "stupid" or "idiot." Every morning, they tease him about not being able to read the simplest "baby stories."

- A group of fifth-grade girls jump rope every day at recess, but they will not let Emma play with them. Emma gets tired of just standing there, so she goes over to Tina, and they start a four-square game with two other kids. One of the girls jumping rope walks over to Tina and says loudly, "Why are you letting Emma play? Nobody likes her."

Conversation Topics

- Ways that you can help a friend
- How you can include a new child in your games at recess
- How you can help a child who is being picked on
- What you can do when another child picks on you
- What makes a good friend

Be Your BEST

B —Body Posture

E — Eye Contact

S — Speech (Say something nice.)

T — Tone of Voice

	AGGRESSIVE	ASSERTIVE (BEST)	PASSIVE
Body Posture			
Eye Contact			
Speech			
Tone of Voice			

13 Select the Best Solution, Then Plan and Prepare for Pitfalls

OBJECTIVE
- To show students how to consider different solutions and consequences and decide which solution is best for them in their situation

MATERIALS
The FIG TESPN steps worksheet that students began in Topic 10 (Worksheet 5.10.1)

INSTRUCTIONAL ACTIVITIES

1. Conduct a brief review.

Go over FIG TESPN problem-solving Steps 1 through 5.

2. Introduce skill components.

Have students discuss "selecting your best solution." Begin by brainstorming synonyms for *select*. Ask if they recognize that different people make different decisions based on different knowledge and perspectives (recall the lesson on different points of view, Topic 9) and that making a good decision is a special, personal act. Discuss "making up your own mind."

When selecting their best solution, students should consider:

- Will that choice help you reach your goal?
- Will it harm anyone?
- What will your choice mean now and how will you feel about it later?
- How will that choice affect others?

It is critical to remind students to link goal and solution throughout this lesson.

3. Discuss making a choice among possible solutions.

Offer an example or two from your own experience of how you arrived at a "best solution" or "best decision" for you or a member of your family (for example, where to go on vacation, how to deal with a difficult friend or relative, how to select activities for the class to do). Say:

Now think about a problem that you have solved. How did you decide which solution to choose?

Elicit information on the FIG TE steps and then focus on the new skill, choosing a solution. When students answer, ask them:

What makes that the best solution?

Tell students that now they have learned how to find their best solution. Ask them what they think the next step would be.

4. Move on to planning and reviewing plans.

Define a *plan* as the detailed steps necessary to carry out a solution: the how, when, where, with whom, and so on.

When planning, have students consider:

- Timing
- Tone of voice
- The right people to help
- Past experiences that may be useful now

Point out that it's necessary to take a long, careful look at a plan before carrying it out—that is, to do a *final check* of it. Define this step as thinking of possible obstacles to carrying out the plan and planning for those possibilities. The key prompt and question is "What will you do if . . . ?"

Ask students to describe and help define the word *obstacle*. Explain that sometimes even good solutions won't work. Ask these questions:

- How do you feel when you stop and think of a good solution, try it, and things still don't get better—the problem is still there?
- Can anyone give me an example of a problem they tried a good solution for, but it didn't work? How did you feel?
- If you think of a good solution, will it always solve your problem?
- How can you be ready, just in case your first solution doesn't work?

The idea is to think about obstacles ahead of time and plan to have another solution ready in case the first one doesn't work.

Establish "Select the best solution" and "Prepare for pitfalls" as skill prompts.

5. Conduct a practice activity.

Have students discuss plans for the following decision:

You have decided to have a surprise party for your best friend's birthday. What do you need to think about to make it work? What is the first thing you should do? Next? Then what?

Give the class a few minutes to work on this, then ask:

What would you do if . . .

You didn't have enough money for the party?

Your friend canceled the plans you made to join you at your house that night?

When students answer, ask them:

What makes that the best solution?

6. Expand the activity.

Using another sample situation, have students problem solve, using the FIG TESP steps.

Present a situation. For example:

Ganesh wants to try out for the school band as a drummer. He is afraid to try out because he's worried he might get rejected by the band director, Mr. Claxton.

Lead a discussion using these or similar questions:

- How do you think Ganesh is feeling?
- Can someone tell us what they think Ganesh's problem is?
- What could Ganesh's goal be in this situation?
- What are some possible solutions for Ganesh's problem?

Encourage the class to generate at least four to six possible solutions. Have the class envision consequences for each solution:

Considering all the thinking we have done, which solution is the best one?

Select the class's two best solutions and have students role-play each one. This will allow them to see that there may be more than one workable solution and that it is OK to disagree with classmates about which one is "best," based on individual choice.

Next have the class plan how to carry out the solution and prepare for obstacles to carrying out the plan. Allow role-plays to continue through the SP steps.

7. Take on a specific project.

Have students brainstorm what could happen if, without planning, they decided to ask the principal if they can sponsor an environmental cleanup day. (Answers may include: It would be a bad time to ask, everyone would talk at once, no one would know what to say, and so on.)

Ask students to work in groups and use the FIG TESPN steps worksheet to plan a meeting with the principal to talk about sponsoring an environmental cleanup day. Include what they could do to plan this meeting. Elicit who will speak and what will be said. Decide when, where, how to make an appointment, and so on. Have groups share their plans with the class.

Now have students think of what could happen to block the plan (the principal is absent, gets called out during the meeting, just says no). Students should think of a new plan that includes what they will do if each of the projected obstacles occur.

Have the groups role-play. First, set up a role-play that will not be successful. Have actors use poor timing, tone of voice, and so on. Elicit observers' reactions. Then, using Be Your BEST guidelines, have students practice talking to the principal until they are satisfied with their performance. You may interject an unexpected obstacle so the students can practice what has been discussed.

8. Introduce a Reflective Summary.

As outlined in the Introduction, ask students to reflect on the question "What did you learn from today's lesson?" Reinforce key themes, then go over any follow-up work.

9. Follow up.

The following steps will help make sure that the students have a chance to continue working with the new concepts.

Assignment

Refer students to the copy of the FIG TESPN steps worksheet that they began to fill out in Topic 10. In that Topic, students completed the FIG TE portion of the strategy. Encourage them now to complete the S (select the best solution) and P (plan and be prepared for pitfalls) steps. Let them know that they will need this worksheet again in Topic 14, to record what happens when they carry out their plans.

Plans to Promote Transfer and Generalization of Skill

Language Arts and Social Studies

This activity should be repeated often, using a variety of situations, both hypothetical and real. Use situations and content areas that are complex enough to demand problem solving, extensive and ongoing planning, and some degree of persistent rethinking.

Here are some examples:

- Choosing an environmental issue that will become a project for the class
- Instituting a United Nations day in your school
- Starting a peer-tutoring program
- Publishing a classroom newsletter
- Fund-raising for a class trip

Health

Have students make cartoon strips showing themselves in one of the following situations. (Be sure that the last cartoon block clearly shows the decision made.)

- Being offered drugs or alcohol
- Being asked to smoke
- Being asked to cheat on a test
- Being asked to take something that doesn't belong to them

Social Studies

Have students bring in and discuss newspaper or magazine articles in which leaders in government have made important decisions. Students should be prepared to explain what the decision was about. Discussion may follow on how that decision was made, whether students consider it to be a good one, what decision they might have made instead, and how that decision could have been planned and carried out.

Science

Have students consider the obstacles that must be overcome to solve various problems (ensuring clean water, finding a cure for AIDS, making travel to Mars possible, and so on).

Social Applications

When a class problem comes up, have students decide what their best solution to the problem would be. Have students focus on the effect their decision might have on themselves and others. Then have students formulate a plan, consider obstacles, and formulate a backup plan.

TIPS FOR TEACHERS

1. When having the class choose a solution, you may sometimes call for a vote. It can be helpful to review the consequences to help students clarify which solution is associated with positive or negative consequences.

2. Sometimes you may want to have students individually choose a solution in order to practice independent thinking.

3. Ask students to share what they do to give themselves the confidence it takes to choose a best solution, even if it means going against the crowd. Encourage them to choose their own best solutions and not be followers. It can help to say something along these lines:

   There are no right or wrong answers. Everyone has their own perspective on the time and energy they will expend to reach a certain goal. It is important to know when to walk away from a problem. However, it is also important to develop persistence so that you can reach important goals.

4. The use of hypothetical situations is helpful until the students become familiar with the framework and are comfortable using it. Role-playing provides an important link in the transfer and generalization of the skills from the hypothetical to real life.

14 Notice What Happened (Now What?)

OBJECTIVES
- To help students learn to enact a plan
- To help students learn to evaluate a plan's success and, using the problem-solving process, decide what to do next time
- To help students learn to solve problems using the full FIG TESPN process

MATERIALS
Students' FIG TESPN steps worksheets, continued from Topic 13 (Worksheet 5.10.1)

INSTRUCTIONAL ACTIVITIES

1. Conduct a brief review.

Go over FIG TESPN problem-solving Steps 1 through 7. Say:

Today we are going to learn about the final step in FIG TESPN.

2. Introduce skill components.

Read Step 8—Notice What Happened (Now What?)—and ask students what they think it means and how it might help them. Point out that getting things done, enjoying ourselves, and accomplishing goals involve this eighth step—trying out our plans and then rethinking what we did to learn from the situation. Discuss with students whether they think trying out a plan is risky. Why or why not? (It might not work, people might laugh, you might not get what you want, and so on.)

3. Set up the background for a practice activity.

Ask the class to propose some goals that are worth rethinking if the first solution doesn't work. Some examples might be:

- Getting a better grade
- Trying to make the basketball team
- Trying to end water pollution

Then present the following situation:

In two weeks, it will be Tommy's sister's birthday, and he doesn't know what to get her for a gift. One day they are watching television at home and Tommy notices that she sees a new videogame that she really seems to like. Tommy considers lots of alternatives and consequences, and he decides that he will get it for her.

Have the students apply FIG TESPN problem-solving Steps 1 through 7 to Tommy's situation as a review. Do this as either a whole class or in groups, using the FIG TESPN steps worksheets.

4. Practice the new skill.

Go on to say:

Thinking about a good solution is important, but there are a lot of things that Tommy still has to think about to make the solution work.

What does Tommy need to think about to make the solution work?

Have students list at least six things, such as where to get the videogame, how much it costs, when the store is open, how to get the money, how to get to the store, and how to find the game.

What is the first thing that you would have Tommy do? What next? Then what?

Be sure that the children get an appreciation of the order and sequence and the many steps involved. Encourage them to be specific in their suggestions—that is, to create clear and concrete plans.

Build in obstacles to show the importance of planning and being persistent, but be sure that the obstacles are not insurmountable so that the students will not be discouraged.

For example:

- What could Tommy do if they didn't have the game in stock in the two stores he called? What if the game was not in any store in town?
- What if his mother wouldn't lend him any money?
- What if his parents couldn't give him a ride to the store?

After the students have worked through the obstacles, continue along these lines:

Let's say Tommy finally found a gift—two days late and not the exact new videogame that he was looking for. What if his sister isn't excited when he gives her the gift? If Tommy looks back on what happened, what could he learn for next time?

Generate a list and role-play as time allows. Then ask:

What if she really likes the gift? What could Tommy still learn from looking back at his problem solving?

Be sure students understand the value of looking back on and learning from their problem-solving experiences, even when things have gone well.

In discussion, reinforce these points:

- It is important to plan the steps needed to make a solution work.
- When you meet an obstacle, persisting in rethinking ways to solve the problem can be helpful.

As time permits, have students role-play several of the steps that Tommy must take and several obstacles that he encounters. Have the students change roles frequently.

5. Introduce a Reflective Summary.

As outlined in the Introduction, ask students to reflect on the question "What did you learn from today's lesson?" Reinforce key themes, then go over any follow-up work.

6. Follow up.

The following steps will help make sure that the students have a chance to continue working with the new concepts.

Assignment

At this point, have a Sharing Circle and invite students to talk about what happened when they put the plans they identified on Worksheet 5.10.2 into effect, if they have had a chance to do so. Encourage them to discuss what they learned, even if their plans didn't solve the problems they identified. What did they learn that they could use another time? How has going through the FIG TESPN steps helped them? If students have not had the opportunity to carry out these specific plans, they can speak about another situation in which they learned something they could use in the future. (If you wish, you can have students first write stories about the outcomes of their plans, then discuss them in the Sharing Circle.)

Take-Home

Share this idea with parents and guardians as the opportunity arises.

Decision Making in the Family

Model the eight-step decision-making process for children, as this will help them apply the process to decisions that they must make. Whenever possible, include children in family decisions that affect them. Give children a chance to express their feelings and opinions when making these decisions. Encourage children to use problem-solving and decision-making skills when they participate in community activities. Finally, praise children when you see them using the FIG TESPN skills—this will encourage them to use these important skills often.

Plans to Promote Transfer and Generalization of Skill

Language Arts or Social Studies

Have students find characters in a story or real-life people in history or in current events who have used social problem solving and social decision making skills. Have students write and discuss what these people did in the "Notice What Happened (Now What?)" phase of their problem solving and decision making. What lessons could they have learned from what happened?

Social Applications

Have students choose a role model—someone in their family, neighborhood, or school whom they know and admire because of this person's ability to overcome obstacles and achieve a goal. Have them interview this person and write about what they had to overcome and what they had to do to achieve their goal.

Use "What did you learn about that for next time?" as a skill prompt. Help students rethink problem-solving strategies that worked and did not work so they can learn how to build this skill.

TIPS FOR TEACHERS

1. An important aspect of the final step of the decision-making and problem-solving framework is the review process. Constructively reviewing decisions and actions can be difficult for some people, but it is essential—without it, decision making cannot improve.

2. Persistence is the major theme of the final step in the framework. Students need to see decision making and problem solving as a process that they can cycle through until they are able to reach their goal. By practicing the process in academic and social situations, students will gain the confidence they need to persist in solving their own problems and making the decisions they need to make.

15 Problem Solving: Using All the FIG TESPN Steps

OBJECTIVES
- To demonstrate students' understanding of FIG TESPN
- To provide an opportunity for students to systematically apply FIG TESPN to a variety of situations

MATERIALS
Copies of the FIG TESPN steps worksheet (Worksheet 5.10.1) and "Personal Problem-Solving Planner" (Worksheet 5.15.1)

INSTRUCTIONAL ACTIVITIES

1. Conduct a brief review.

Go over the full list of FIG TESPN problem-solving steps.

2. Introduce skill components.

Explain that being a good problem solver and decision maker is a habit and that practice helps people develop their habits. Tell the class that today students will use all the FIG TESPN steps to practice solving some challenging problems.

3. Conduct a practice activity.

Read the following story. Instruct the class to think about the FIG TESPN steps as they are listening to the details.

Keyshawn's Friday

Keyshawn's parents are divorced, and Keyshawn lives with his mother. Because his mother works full time as a secretary, she asks Keyshawn to help with the chores around the house.

It was Friday, and Keyshawn had forgotten that he had promised his mother that he would clean the house on Friday afternoon because they were expecting company on Friday evening. Instead, he agreed to bring his broken bike over to his friend Alex's house because Alex's father said that he would show

Keyshawn how to fix it. As Keyshawn was just about to call his mother to tell her about his plans to go to Alex's, he remembered his promise to her.

Review and practice the problem-solving skills. Lead a discussion using these and related questions:

- Who can express some of what Keyshawn may be feeling?
- Could someone put Keyshawn's problem into words?
- What should his goal be?
- What are some of the things that he could consider doing about this problem? What's another thing he might try?
- Who can try to envision the outcomes and say what might happen?

Look for long-term and short-term outcomes, and for outcomes that relate to Keyshawn and to others:

Which solution would Keyshawn pick? Why?

Plan the solution with the class.

4. Test out the proposed solution.

Select students to role-play to see if the problem is resolved by using their solution or if they need to rethink the solution and try it again. Afterward, make the point that a situation such as the one described in "Keyshawn's Friday" indicates how a real social problem can feel (for instance, you may be caught between what different people want from you, such as your parents, teachers, and friends). Reinforce the use of role-playing as a clear way of practicing a solution ahead of time and then rethinking it once it is done. After they try out a solution, encourage the students to review it so that they can do an even better job next time.

5. Extend the lesson.

For added practice, have students generate hypothetical stories (which can be based on real situations) either now or earlier in the week. Have students use their Personal Problem-Solving Planners in groups to apply FIG TESPN. Be sure that all groups are working on the same problem or at least that two groups are working on the same problem so there can be an opportunity to share ideas and role-play different possibilities. Think about obstacles and allow a chance for students to rethink and replan their ideas.

6. Introduce a Reflective Summary.

As outlined in the Introduction, ask students to reflect on the question "What did you learn from today's lesson?" Reinforce key themes, then go over any follow-up work.

7. Follow up.

The following steps will help make sure that the students have a chance to continue working with the new concepts.

Assignment

Provide students with another copy of the FIG TESPN steps worksheet and tell them to use it during the week with an academic or personal problem or decision. Have students share their worksheets during the next class meeting.

Plans to Promote Transfer and Generalization of Skill

Language Arts

Have students select three different characters from stories that they have read this year. Ask them to imagine what might be each character's best FIG TESPN problem-solving step and why.

Health

Have students use one or several of the FIG TESPN problem-solving steps as a basis for discussing or writing about how to persuade another student not to smoke or use drugs or alcohol. Students can also use FIG TESPN to address a wide range of issues in the health curriculum, such as the use of bicycle helmets, how to react when approached by a stranger, and healthful eating, personal hygiene, and other lifestyle choices.

Social Activity

Distribute copies of the Personal Problem-Solving Planner and encourage students to use them as they confront or approach you with difficult choices or problems. Offer to review the planner with them or encourage them to share it with a counselor or other concerned adult.

TIPS FOR TEACHERS

1. As class, grade-level, or schoolwide situations arise, create hypothetical scenarios and have subgroups of students use the Personal Problem-Solving Planner to do problem solving and compare ideas, as in this Topic's role-playing sessions.

2. Learning students' problem-solving strengths helps pave the way for you to prompt their use of the eight FIG TESPN steps outside the formal lesson. For example, you may have only a few minutes to help a student (or group) resolve a recess-time problem. In that case, it might be helpful for you to call attention to one or two steps that are each child's strengths as well as to any that you feel would be particularly relevant. (For example, if you were talking to an impulsive child, you may want to request a list of solutions and consequences. With an overly intellectual child, you may want to emphasize recognition of feelings as an important and motivating first step.)

Student _____ **Date** _____

1. I am feeling _____

   _____.

2. My problem is _____

   _____.

3. My goal is _____

   _____.

4. I am going to stop and think of as many solutions as I can and think about their consequences.

   Solutions I might try: If I try this, these consequences might happen:

   _____   _____

   _____   _____

   _____   _____

   _____   _____

   _____   _____

5. My plan for solving my problem is _____

   _____.

6. *(Wait awhile and recheck your plan.)* Here is how I think it will work:

   a. Very well   b. OK   c. Not so well   d. Terribly

7. What I think I'll change is _____

   _____.

8. What actually happens when you try your plan? _____

   _____.

PUTTING IT ALL TOGETHER

Topics 16–26

16/17 Using FIG TESPN with Literature

OBJECTIVES
- To demonstrate understanding of FIG TESPN
- To systematically apply FIG TESPN using problems and situations that are presented in literary works

MATERIALS Copies of the "Literature Discussion Guide" (Worksheet 5.16/17.1)

PREPARATION Select stories or chapters from books for the students to work with.

NOTE This topic ideally runs at least two weeks, giving the students a chance to practice with several different problems from literature.

INSTRUCTIONAL ACTIVITIES

1. Conduct a Sharing Circle.

Have the students talk about their favorite books and why they are their favorites. Encourage them to exchange favorite books with each other to read at school.

2. Introduce the skill components.

Explain that it is often possible to practice social decision making and social problem solving skills by using materials from academic subjects and that it can be especially fun to use these skills with literature. Tell the class that today students will use all eight steps to practice solving some challenging problems that characters face in a story.

3. Present a story to read for practice.

Select a short story in which one of the characters faces a problem toward the middle of the story. Select a critical point, or stopping point, at which the character's problem has been introduced but before the character does any problem solving or decision making.

Distribute a copy of the story or instruct students to open their textbooks to the selected story. Ask the students to keep the following questions in mind as they read the story:

- What is the author's goal?
- Why did the author write this story?

Have students read the story aloud or silently to themselves, warning them to stop reading when they reach the preselected critical point in the story.

4. Distribute the Literature Discussion Guide.

Lead the class in a discussion of the problem faced by the character, using the Literature Discussion Guide through Question 6.

After Question 6, have students continue reading the rest of the story.

After students are done reading, discuss the last three questions on the Literature Discussion Guide as they pertain to the story.

5. Repeat the exercise.

The process can be used with another short story or a different section within a chapter book.

6. Introduce a Reflective Summary.

As outlined in the Introduction, ask students to reflect on the question "What did you learn from today's lesson?" Reinforce key themes, then go over any follow-up work.

7. Follow up.

The following steps will help make sure that the students have a chance to continue working with the new concepts.

Assignment

Provide students with another copy of the Literature Discussion Guide and tell them to complete it, using a short story of their choosing or one you assign to them. Tell students that they will be sharing their worksheets during the next meeting.

Plans to Promote Transfer and Generalization of Skill

1. The Literature Discussion Guide can be infused into the academic curriculum and used with many stories in the fifth-grade language arts curriculum.

2. Use the "FIG TESPN as a Book Report Guide" (Worksheet 4.30.1 in the Grade 4 curriculum) with full books.

TIPS FOR TEACHERS

1. This area is so important that it benefits from being structured as two Topics. This way, teachers have the time to do two full examples of applying FIG TESPN to literature and drawing out practice opportunities and applications that arise.

2. After this introduction, the application of FIG TESPN to literature can be continued across multiple lessons, especially if students work in pairs or small groups. Even a single use of the discussion guide might take more than one class period.

3. This Topic enables students to see that most pieces of literature focus on characters who deal with problems in both positive and negative ways.

4. Stories and books for students this age include the following.

Short Stories

It's Our World Too: Stories of Young People Who Are Making a Difference, by Phillip Hoose

The Witch of Fourth Street, by Myron Levoy

Fiction

Holes, by Louis Sachar

Tuck Everlasting, by Natalie Babbitt

Number the Stars, by Lois Lowry

From the Mixed up Files of Mrs. Basil E. Frankweiler, by E.L. Konigsburg

Felita, by Nicholosa Mohr

Maniac Magee, by Jerry Spinelli

Historical Fiction/Biography

Freedom Crossing, by Margaret Goff Clark

The Hundred Dresses, by Wanda Petronski

Amelia Earhart: Courage in the Sky, by Mona Kerby

Eleanor Roosevelt: First Lady of the World, by Doris Faber

Thank You, Jackie Robinson, by Barbara Cohen

Kokopelli's Flute, by Will Hobbs

Student(s) _____ **Date** _____

Before starting the story, keep the following questions in mind: What is the author's GOAL? Why did the author write this?

When you reach a point where one of the main characters faces a problem, stop reading. (Your teacher will tell you where to stop if you're doing a group exercise.) Ask the following questions.

1. How do you FEEL about what you've read so far?

2. In one or two sentences, tell what the story is about up to this point. What is the

    PROBLEM that _____ faces?
                     (main character)

3. How does _____ FEEL about the problem?
          (main character)

4. What is _____'s GOAL? What does that character want to happen?
        (main character)

5. If you were _____, what are the different SOLUTIONS to the problem
           (main character)
   that you would think of?

6. What are the possible CONSEQUENCES that you can envision for each solution?

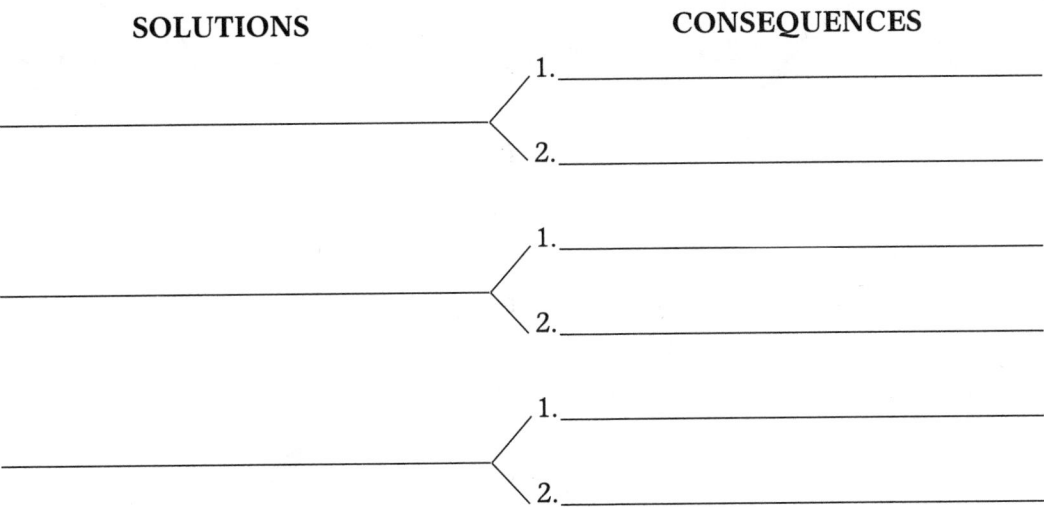

| SOLUTIONS | CONSEQUENCES |

Now return to the story and see what _____ decides to do. After you finish the
                                        (main character)
story, consider these follow-up questions.

7. What was the SOLUTION that _____ chose to solve the problem?
                              (main character)

8. How well did it work?

9. Now that you've learned what happened, would you have handled this situation
   any differently? If so, what would you have done?

18 Using FIG TESPN for Creative Writing

OBJECTIVES
- To show students how to use FIG TESPN to organize their thinking before beginning a creative writing assignment
- To show students how to use FIG TESPN to review their own work and that of classmates
- To show students how to study a story or chapter assigned as part of a reading or language arts assignment

MATERIALS
Copies of "Creative Thinking for Creative Writing" (Worksheet 5.18.1) and "Using Decision Making to Examine Your Writing" (Worksheet 5.18.2)

NOTE
The process described in this Topic can be repeated several times to improve students' writing process.

INSTRUCTIONAL ACTIVITIES

1. Conduct a brief review.

Use a Sharing Circle to review the preceding lesson by having students share their latest Literature Discussion Guides.

2. Introduce the new techniques.

Present the lesson as part of a creative writing assignment. Indicate that figuring out what to write and how to write it is an example of problem solving. Then distribute and review the "Creative Thinking for Creative Writing" worksheet. Give the assignment and ask students to fill out the first five questions and show them to you for feedback before proceeding to the sixth question. After your approval, have them complete the sixth question and begin a rough draft of their creative writing assignment, continuing as time allows.

3. Have students conference on their writing.

When students have completed their drafts, either at this meeting or at another time, instruct them to pair up and give each pair two copies of the "Using Decision Making to Examine Your Writing" worksheet. Students exchange stories and review each other's work by answering the first four questions. They then return the drafts and worksheets, and the author of the story completes the questions on the worksheet and revises the story on the basis of the reviewer's comments. (You may want to choose a student and story and model this type of feedback before asking students to proceed on their own.)

4. Introduce a Reflective Summary.

As outlined in the Introduction, ask students to reflect on the question "What did you learn from today's lesson?" Reinforce key themes, then go over any follow-up work.

5. Follow up.

The following steps will help make sure that the students have a chance to continue working with the new concepts.

Assignment

Have students finish their rough drafts, if they have not already completed them, and prepare a final draft of their creative writing assignment to share at the next meeting.

Plans to Promote Transfer and Generalization of Skill

This writing and editing process can be used whenever students are assigned writing assignments in language arts and in other academic subjects. Students should be assigned writing assignments on a regular basis. The various writing assignments can be kept in a creative writing notebook and can include copies of the "Creative Thinking for Creative Writing" and the "Using Decision Making to Examine Your Writing" worksheets. The notebooks can be reviewed periodically during teacher-student conferences.

TIPS FOR TEACHERS

1. This Topic may be spread over several class periods to allow time for students to thoroughly finish their writing. Parts of the work may be begun in class and completed at home.

2. This Topic provides students with important tools for reflecting on their work and on that of their classmates and for working to make their good work even better. The worksheets included in this lesson will help students learn whether others understand the meaning and intention of their work. As stories are shared, attention can also be paid to linking the written stories to everyday events and helping the students consider alternative plots, changes in story details, and different approaches to the assignment. Doing so will reinforce the range of situations in which FIG TESPN can be usefully applied.

3. When students use FIG TESPN to improve story logic, you can either tell them that the situations that they write about can be whatever they choose, or you can provide boundaries: for example, the story must involve students, it must take place in a school, it must involve learning to cope with differences among people, or the like. It is useful to provide an example or allow someone in the class to provide one and to discuss it in terms of the ways in which problem-solving steps (such as looking for signs of different feelings and thinking of many possible solutions) were made parts of the plot. You may find it useful with some groups to create and distribute a brief sample to help students get started. Some teachers have also found it useful to provide page limits, particularly a minimum, for the stories. Others have had students include obstacles to solutions as part of the story.

Student _____ **Date** _____

1. How do you feel about this assignment?

2. State the goal of this assignment.

3. What is your first idea about what to write?

4. State two or three different ways in which you could write the assignment. Think about things such as different characters, ideas, and the time and place you will be writing about.

5. Decide what you will write about. State the main idea in one or two sentences.

6. Plan and prepare. Think about your main idea, characters, time, and place. Write down your ideas. Think about things that will help you do the assignment, such as when and where you will do it and books or materials that you might need. Then try it, and make a final check before you hand it in!

Reviewer's name _____ **Date** _____

1. How did you feel about what you read?

2. In one or two sentences, tell what the story is about.

3. Why do you think the writer wrote this? What was the goal?

4. What else could be written to help you understand the story better? Think about the characters and the time and place of the story.

Writer's name _____ **Date** _____

5. Plan some changes that you might make in your story and list them here.

6. Think about how you could make your story even better next time. Write down things that you might do differently.

19 Using FIG TESPN to Critically Examine Stories and Media Reports

OBJECTIVES
- To use FIG TESPN to examine the parts of a televised (or other) story
- To show students how to use FIG TESPN to practice critical home viewing

MATERIALS
Copies of "What's in a Story?" (Worksheet 5.19.1) and "Media Literacy Assignment" (Worksheet 5.19.2)

Chalkboard or easel pad

INSTRUCTIONAL ACTIVITIES

1. Conduct a Sharing Circle.

Ask students what they think about when they hear the term *the media*. What does this mean? What does it include? Help students understand that *a medium* is a technology used to communicate ideas and tell stories, and *the media* collectively refers to all the companies and organizations in the business of presenting ideas. Be sure students identify books, videos, television, newspapers, magazines, billboards, and the Internet as media. Also be sure they understand that painting, sculpture, dance, poetry, music, theater, and opera are also kinds of media.

Next, ask students what *literacy* means. The point to make here is that literacy refers to the ability to understand a certain kind of communication. Note that people with handicaps sometimes are unable to be literate in one area but are literate in others (ask for examples, such as deafness, blindness, paralysis, and dyslexia).

Finally, ask what the term *media literacy* means. Be sure students understand that it refers to the ability to understand ideas and stories communicated in certain ways. Tell students that the focus for the next two Topics will be television, first programs and then commercials.

2. Introduce the lesson.

Distribute the "What's in a Story?" worksheet. The worksheet explains some of the major components of stories and contains room for the homework assignment. Explain that the class will learn about the parts of a story by thinking about television programs that most people have seen.

3. Select an example.

Ask students to name some television series they watch often or a recent special that they remember well. Create a list on the chalkboard or easel pad. Try to maintain a balance between generally positive stations, like PBS, Nickelodeon, Disney, Hallmark, and the Discovery Channel, and network and related cable stations that have much more mixed content (ABC, CBS, Fox, NBC, UPN, WB, TNT, TBS, and USA).

Choose one show as the focus of discussion (or if no shows are familiar enough to most students, have students work in two, three, or four subgroups focused on shows with which they are familiar). Review each story part by asking students:

What questions would you want to ask yourself so that you could understand more about this part of the story?

Be sure that the students give specific examples from the programs that most of them have seen.

4. Analyze the examples.

Once the class has discussed each story part, divide the class into five groups. Assign each group one of the five story parts (flow is excluded), and tell the students to think about some details so that their part could be put into the script of a television story. For example, the Characters group can create one or more characters to be involved in the story. This group determines the ages, appearances, and other attributes of the characters. The Settings group decides which location or locations will be involved. Each group has its own domain, but each works independently.

After about fifteen minutes, reconvene the class. Ask each group to report their work and to put together the story. List the story outline on the chalkboard or easel pad. (This often leads to quite a bit of fun.) Ask the class to provide the Flow and suggest different creative ideas about how to link these unrelated story parts together.

5. Replay the exercise.

Repeat the process with a different kind of program. Afterward, ask students to talk about how they feel about the different programs and what kind of problem solving they see in each kind of program. Alert them to how watching violent solutions makes it harder to use FIG TESPN and easier to solve problems through violence.

6. Introduce a Reflective Summary.

As outlined in the Introduction, ask students to reflect on the question "What did you learn from today's lesson?" Reinforce key themes, then go over any follow-up work.

7. Follow up.

The following steps will help make sure that the students have a chance to continue working with the new concepts.

Assignment

Refer students to the "Media Literacy Assignment" worksheet. With the class, decide which one or two programs most students will watch as part of their assignment. Have students write the names of and why they watch these programs on the worksheet. Have students complete the other two parts as their homework assignment.

Take-Home

It is advisable to send information home to parents and guardians about this subject matter. Let them know the importance of media literacy and the need to help children think critically and carefully about media messages, including advertisements, and how to analyze them.

Send home the "What's in a Story?" worksheet and encourage parents and guardians to watch the programs discussed as part of the homework assignment with their child. They can help their child by discussing and reviewing the ideas that their child will include in the writing assignment.

Plans to Promote Transfer and Generalization of Skill

1. This assignment can be repeated regularly to build students' understanding of the grammar and methods of television and the existence of alternatives.

2. Many teachers find it highly effective to adapt the activities described here to health subject matter and the creation of public service messages by students. The students both learn the logic of persuasive messages and persuade themselves of the truth of the messages they present, which makes the points much more powerful than they would be if the teacher simply spelled them out.

3. The media examination assignment can be adapted to plays, short stories, poems, and other storytelling media.

TIPS FOR TEACHERS

1. Media literacy can be a very controversial topic, and teachers must keep community norms in mind and adapt lessons as necessary. Some teachers find print ads from magazines, including those for children, are easier to work with than television commercials, at least as a starting point.

2. You may want to record the shows on video or DVD for those students who are unable to watch the shows at home and also to use for future reference.

3. In the sharing discussion, focus on eliciting answers to each question. Be sure to emphasize the link between actions and consequences and the nonviolent alternatives to the story line.

4. Allow students to view acceptable programs other than those selected in the class brainstorming session if they are unable to watch the assigned shows.

Student(s) _____ Date _____

Stories have many parts that must fit together carefully. The list below contains some of the most important parts of a story. It also has some questions that you can ask yourself that will help you think about how these parts fit together. Use them as you read, watch, or listen to a story.

Story Part	Questions to Ask Yourself
Characters	What are the names of the most important people in the show? How old is each of these people? Where do they come from? What else do you know about them?
Setting	Where does the story take place? When? What are the most important settings? What words can you use to describe them?
Problem	What are the characters doing? How are they feeling? Do they disagree or have some difficulty? What decisions do they have to make?
Story Line	What is the order of events or actions in the story? Where did people go? What did they do? How? How well did the story hold your interest? What events had the strongest effect on how you felt?
Main Idea	What did the authors want you to learn from the story? Put their message into one or two sentences.
Flow	How well were the events or actions connected to each other? What consequences did different actions have? Were they realistic? Did they make sense to you? Is this how real-life events happen? How is real life different?

Student _____ **Date** _____

1. What program will you watch or listen to?

2. Why do you watch or listen to this program?

3. Write a short paragraph about how each of the first five story parts applies to your program. Then write one paragraph about the Flow of the story. Then write at least three different ways in which the Story Line could have been presented so that you would have understood the Main Idea. Do not use any violent alternatives.

4. Below, make a list of some better things that you could do instead of watching a television program. Place a check mark next to the two things that you might try doing instead of watching television.

   ❐ _____   ❐ _____

   ❐ _____   ❐ _____

   ❐ _____   ❐ _____

TOPIC

20 Using FIG TESPN to Critically Examine Advertising

OBJECTIVE
- To use FIG TESPN to examine the parts of a televised (or other) advertisement

MATERIALS
Copies of "Commercial Analysis" (Worksheet 5.20.1)

A video or DVD of a variety of commercials

Sample ads from newspapers or magazines

INSTRUCTIONAL ACTIVITIES

1. Conduct a Sharing Circle.

Ask students to think of their favorite television commercial—specifically, why the commercial attracts them and how it makes them feel. Go around the room and have the students share their responses to these questions. Ask students if they have a favorite brand of sneaker or clothing. After you go around in the circle, ask students to tell you why that brand is their favorite. Ask them what they know about how it is different from other brands that other students have mentioned. Help them to notice that they have come to believe that some brands are "cooler" than others but that they probably don't have good reason to think so other than "cool" people use or wear them.

2. Introduce the main topic.

Ask students what a *commercial* is. Then ask them what *advertising* is. Be sure they understand that commercials are a kind of advertising and that, in general, commercials and advertisements are created to try to persuade us to buy products or to think in certain ways—and that many of us are not even aware that they are trying to do this. Ask students if they think that the people they see in commercials and ads really use the products or if they are paid to say that they do. Be sure the students get the point that, from the ads, one can't tell. The people on commercials may use the products, or they may be paid to tell you that they do. Go back and ask students if they are still as sure about why the brands of sneakers or clothes they like are really as different or special as they first thought.

3. Generate examples.

Ask students, as a class or in subgroups, to generate a list of the techniques and approaches advertisers use to persuade consumers to do what they would like. Ask them how people who create commercials and other forms of advertisement try to get people to believe what they have to say. This goes back to the Sharing Circle question, but now students are likely to have more ideas about how it is that commercials "work" to influence people. Generate a list of advertising appeals commonly used by producers of commercials and advertisements. Here are some that students may or may not mention but can be added to keep the list more complete:

Bandwagon: Everyone is doing it.

Bargain: This product is the cheapest or the best buy.

Change your life: This product will make you better looking, rich, smart, thin, strong, and so forth.

Excitement: This product will make your life exciting.

Lasting joy: This product will bring you happiness.

Manly (or womanly): This product will make you more of a man (woman).

Science: Scientist or doctor uses charts, lab coat, fancy office, serious tone and posture, big words to sell product.

Testimonial: Famous person says he or she uses the product.

True love: This product will bring you true love.

4. Conduct a practice activity.

Show video clips of one or two commercials. Begin with a full-group discussion. Identify and discuss the advertising appeals used in the commercials, the feelings that the commercials evoke, and what it is like to be an active viewer. Ask if anyone saw something new in the commercials that they had not seen before. Continue by showing additional clips and allowing students to carry out small-group discussions based on the worksheet and then to report back to the large group.

Use Worksheet 5.20.1, "Commercial Analysis," as a guide. You may want to use it as an outline for discussing the commercials, or it may serve as a worksheet for students to fill out as they watch the commercials. In the latter case, you will probably need to show the clip more than once for students to get all of the information. Regardless, it is recommended to go through the worksheet once with the entire class prior to having students work in subgroups, pairs, or individually.

Ask students how FIG TESPN is related to the worksheet and what changes they would make to the worksheet, if any, based on the FIG TESPN steps.

Repeat with other television commercials and print or radio ads as time and interest allow.

5. Introduce a Reflective Summary.

As outlined in the Introduction, ask students to reflect on the question "What did you learn from today's lesson?" Reinforce key themes, then go over any follow-up work.

6. Follow up.

The following steps will help make sure that the students have a chance to continue working with the new concepts.

Assignment

Give students two copies of the worksheet. Ask them to fill it out for two television commercials or other types of ads they see at home over the next few days and to bring the completed forms for you to look at. You may want to send a note home explaining that you have given this assignment but are not requiring students to watch commercial television to complete it. (Explaining this assignment also is enlightening for many parents and guardians.)

Take-Home

Copy the final list of advertising strategies and give students a copy for future reference and to take home and discuss with their families.

Plans to Promote Transfer and Generalization of Skill

1. This assignment can be repeated regularly to build students' understanding of the pervasive nature of advertising and how it operates on them.

2. Many teachers find it highly effective to adapt the activities described here to health subject matter and public service messages about drug, alcohol, and tobacco use; HIV and other sexually transmitted diseases; weapons; and bullying and other forms of peer harassment. Students cannot only analyze these messages but can also use the "What's in a Story?" (Worksheet 5.19.1) and the FIG TESPN steps worksheet (Worksheet 5.10.2) to plan what they believe will be more effective ways to deliver these important health messages.

TIPS FOR TEACHERS

1. When choosing commercials and programs, it is important to remain sensitive to students' ethnic and cultural backgrounds. The idea of promoting cultural diversity should help to guide one's decisions, and whenever possible a variety of races and cultures should be represented in examples chosen. Commercials that portray characters in stereotyped roles and those that exploit certain groups of people are not appropriate for use as material you introduce in class unless proper context is provided and issues of prejudice, stereotyping, and bias are an explicit focus of class curricula. In that case, analyzing commercials can and should be used to teach students how harmful stereotypes and exploitative attitudes are taught and reinforced through commercials and other advertising.

2. Videotapes of public service announcements often can be obtained from local television or cable television stations and from such groups as the Advertising Council and the National Clearinghouse on Alcohol and Drug Information. Your librarian or media/technology specialist may be able to help you locate print versions of public service ads. A further adaptation of this topic can be made to radio advertising.

3. Be sure to help students use BEST when viewing media ads involving people. This will help to further sharpen their social analysis skills.

Student _____ **Date** _____

1. Type of product: _____

2. Name of product: _____

3. To whom does the product appeal?

4. What advertising appeals did you notice in the commercial?

5. What feelings did you experience while viewing the commercial?

6. Would you consider buying this product?

7. If you were remaking the commercial, what would you do differently? Here are some questions you may find it useful to answer:

   a. Is the name of the product a catchy one? Do you remember it easily?

   b. Would you choose to appeal to a different group of buyers? Why or why not?

   c. Would you choose alternative advertising appeals? What would be the consequences of those changes?

21 Using FIG TESPN to Solve Problems in Science

OBJECTIVES
- To help students use FIG TESPN to examine issues and problems related to science
- To help students actively learn about science-related current events

MATERIALS
A whole-class display and copies of "Using Science to Solve Problems" (Worksheet 5.21.1)

Sample science article

INSTRUCTIONAL ACTIVITIES

1. Conduct a brief review.

Discuss the way FIG TESPN helps students and other citizens evaluate media presentations and other written material.

2. Introduce the lesson.

Distribute the "Using Science to Solve Problems" worksheet and explain that this is a new kind of science assignment.

Read over the worksheet with the class. Answer any questions that the students may have.

3. Present the selected science article.

Distribute copies of the sample article and either give the class time to read it or have students read it aloud.

Complete the worksheet as a class, having students provide answers verbally for the sample article. As answers are given, it is helpful to write them on a whole-class version of the worksheet.

4. Introduce a Reflective Summary.

As outlined in the Introduction, ask students to reflect on the question "What did you learn from today's lesson?" Reinforce key themes, then go over any follow-up work.

5. Follow up.

The following steps will help make sure that the students have a chance to continue working with the new concepts.

Assignment

Distribute an article related to science or guide students to find an article from newspapers, magazines, or the Internet about a science-related problem. Have students complete the worksheet using their article as a homework assignment or as part of a science class.

Plans to Promote Transfer and Generalization of Skill

1. This activity can be repeated regularly throughout the year and can be used as a "current events" activity.

2. This activity is an ideal way for students to see how problem-solving and decision-making skills are directly linked to and necessary for scientists' work when dealing with problems and issues in science.

3. A related application is to help students use FIG TESPN to understand the process of scientific discovery and invention (that is, actions by individuals or groups in response to problems).

TIPS FOR TEACHERS

Initially, the students may need extra help in getting used to using this worksheet as a learning tool. If so, the following procedures will be helpful: Distribute copies of another sample article. Have the students complete the worksheet with this article in class. Review the article and the worksheet together as a class, using a whole-class display. Discuss the difficulties students had answering the worksheet questions.

Student _____ **Date** _____

Instructions

A. Find a newspaper article about a science-related problem somewhere in the world.

B. Attach the article to this worksheet.

C. Read the article and answer the following questions:

1. What is the topic of the article? _____

_____

_____

_____

2. When and where is the scientific event happening? _____

_____

_____

_____

3. Put the topic into words: What is the problem? _____

_____

_____

_____

4. What people or groups are involved in the problem? _____

_____

_____

_____

5. What are their different feelings and points of view about the problem?

_____

_____

_____

6. If you were involved in the problem, what would be one of your goals?

_____

_____

_____

7. What do you know about science that might help solve the problem (for example, how to conduct an experiment, how to think of hypotheses)?

_____

_____

_____

8. Name some different solutions to the problem that you think would help you reach your goal.

_____

_____

_____

9. For each solution you list, think of at least two things that might happen next. Think about short-term and long-term consequences.

SOLUTIONS   **CONSEQUENCES**

1._____

2._____

1._____

2._____

1._____

2._____

10. What do you think the final solution should be? _____

_____

_____

_____

22 Using FIG TESPN to Examine Problems in History

OBJECTIVE	▪ To help students use FIG TESPN to examine issues and problems related to history
MATERIALS	Copies of "Events in History" (Worksheet 5.22.1)

INSTRUCTIONAL ACTIVITIES

1. Conduct a brief review.

In a Sharing Circle, review the previous lesson by having students share their science-related current events article with the class.

2. Introduce the lesson.

Distribute the "Events in History" worksheet to students. Present a topic that the class has studied in the past—picking one that could benefit from review as students practice completing this new worksheet.

3. Conduct a practice activity.

Using the worksheet, help the students put the events into words as a problem and define the people or groups that were involved in the historical topic that they studied.

Help students take the perspective of each person or group and identify the goals of each group.

Have students generate solutions that follow from each point of view and then have students envision consequences for each solution.

Continue eliciting ideas about the rest of the questions on the worksheet.

4. Introduce a Reflective Summary.

As outlined in the Introduction, ask students to reflect on the question "What did you learn from today's lesson?" Reinforce key themes, then go over any follow-up work.

5. Follow up.

The following steps will help make sure that the students have a chance to continue working with the new concepts.

Assignment

Distribute another copy of the "Events in History" worksheet and have students complete the worksheet for a topic that the class is currently studying in history. Have students follow the same procedure they used with the class activity. It is often valuable to have students work in groups of four, all groups dealing with the same starting point. At the conclusion, the class can compare and contrast the groups' plans and analyses of obstacles.

Take-Home

Be on the lookout for opportunities for students to interview parents, grandparents, or other family members about historical events that they might have experienced. It is probably best to work with students to create an interview guide tailored to the particular situation being explored.

Plans to Promote Transfer and Generalization of Skill

1. The worksheet can be used in a relatively brief group discussion format, as the basis for a more extended lesson or as the basis for class activities that cover a longer period of time, including the entire school year. Once introduced as part of SDM/SPS, it can be applied during social studies class time.

2. Students could be asked to do some additional reading on given topics. The worksheet can be helpful to the students in processing this additional information.

3. The worksheet can also be used by the students when writing book reports about historical events or famous persons.

TIPS FOR TEACHERS

1. On the worksheet, Question 5 acquaints students with ideas about political decision making. Question 6 allows students to learn and think about the historical facts in as much detail as the teacher feels is appropriate. Question 7 attempts to have the students think through their own views about the events and integrate the other points.

2. Another useful way to use the worksheet is to have several groups of students read different assignments that reflect different points

of view on the same topic. The lesson based on the readings can follow the worksheet.

3. Other adaptations of the worksheet to the study of historical events can be made with the focus remaining on understanding the alternative perspectives, goals, and solutions surrounding what is most often portrayed as fact.

Student _____ **Date** _____

1. What is the event that you are thinking about? When and where did it happen? Put the event into words as a problem.

2. What people or groups were involved in the problem? What were their different feelings and points of view about the problem? Try to put their goals into words.

3. For each group, name some different decisions or solutions to the problem that they thought might help them reach their goals.

4. For each solution, envision all the things that might have happened next. Envision both short-term and long-term consequences.

5. What were the final decisions? How were they made? Who made them? Why? Do you agree or disagree? Why?

6. How was the solution carried out? What was the plan? What obstacles were met? How well was the problem solved? Why?

7. Rethink the event. What would you have chosen to do? Why?

23 Using FIG TESPN to Think About Fairness and Prejudice

OBJECTIVES

- To make students aware of the subtle and not-so-subtle stereotypes and prejudices they hold
- To teach students to use their problem-solving skills when thinking about other people, with a focus on considering alternative solutions and checking them out before making decisions or forming opinions
- To foster tolerance, understanding, and respect for others
- To promote empathy by providing an opportunity for students to consider what it feels like to be discriminated against

MATERIALS

Copies of "Complete the Sentences" (Worksheet 5.23.1) and "Being Fair to Others" (Worksheet 5.23.2)

INSTRUCTIONAL ACTIVITIES

1. Dive in.

This topic is best carried out without introduction or preparation. To get students into a problem-solving way of thinking, ask:

Before we begin, who would like to share a time in the past week when you used FIG TESPN to help you in any way? It could be at school or home, with friends or schoolwork . . .

Take about four or five responses and then praise the class for being such good problem solvers.

2. Begin the lesson itself.

Distribute the "Complete the Sentences" worksheet. Have students complete the worksheet without discussing it with anyone.

When students have completed the worksheet, divide the class into two groups: the Challengers and the Thinkers. Explain that good decision makers and problem solvers think clearly and can defend their ideas and listen to and consider new ones. When they believe something, good problem solvers and decision makers make sure that they have good reasons and are willing to listen and learn on a daily basis. It is important to think carefully about ideas. A good problem solver asks for reasons or proof that someone's ideas or beliefs are true.

3. Conduct a practice activity.

Pick a set of opposites (for example, men-women, boys-girls, young-old or should–should not) and ask the Thinkers to share their ideas. After some sharing, have the Challengers ask questions. List the following criteria on the chalkboard or easel pad to help guide what Challengers say:

Challengers' statements should . . .

Take the form of a question.

Not be directed at any particular Thinker.

Not be a question with a yes-or-no answer.

Be related to the sentences on the worksheet.

For example, Challengers might ask, "How can it be all right for boys to be tough and also be kind?" or "How did you learn that Hispanic people [show whatever quality the Thinkers described]?" or "How can you prove that old people should not walk long distances?"

It might be helpful to begin by modeling some Challenger statements and to help Challengers by rephrasing their statements to conform to the rules until children understand them.

After several challenges, have students switch roles. Note that those who began as Challengers may be hesitant to share their answers. Pick a different set of items and encourage the new Thinkers to speak up. Help the new Challengers as before.

4. Introduce the idea of stereotypes.

Once it becomes clear that many Thinkers are having difficulty defending their beliefs, introduce the idea of stereotyping by saying:

Sometimes when we think about other people, we are not really being good problem solvers. Instead, we use stereotypes or prejudices.

Ask the children to define the words *stereotype* and *prejudice*. List the students' ideas on the board and then look up and read the dictionary definitions.

Explain that stereotypes are ways in which people try to make things easier for themselves. Instead of thinking about everyone they meet as a unique individual, people can put other people in a category. Say:

When we put another person in a category, we think we know about the person, but in reality, we have not collected enough information to have an informed opinion.

Remind students of a few examples that came up when students had to answer questions asked by Challengers. Try to think of examples that demonstrate that sometimes stereotypes might be right, but much of the time they can be wrong. A good social decision maker and problem solver stops to learn about another person before making assumptions about what the person is like.

5. Conduct another practice activity.

Continue the lesson by distributing the "Being Fair to Others" worksheet. Explain that the next part of the lesson is about how to be fair to others and not stereotype them.

Ask students to answer the first question about how it would feel to be on the receiving end of a stereotype. Encourage them to take the other person's perspective. Then have them fill out the worksheet.

Lead a group discussion, having students share their ideas. Reinforce the importance of considering the consequences of stereotypes and prejudices. Discuss different ways in which a person can think and act so that others are treated in a fair way.

End the lesson by having children plan ways to help each other monitor and avoid stereotyping.

6. Introduce a Reflective Summary.

As outlined in the Introduction, ask students to reflect on the question "What did you learn from today's lesson?" Reinforce key themes, then go over any follow-up work.

7. Follow up.

The following steps will help make sure that the students have a chance to continue working with the new concepts.

Assignment

Have students look and listen for examples of situations in the news (on television, in the newspaper, on the Internet) or in the movies where problems occur because of prejudice or stereotyping. Have students write several examples that they can share during the next lesson.

Plans to Promote Transfer and Generalization of Skill

Current Events

Scan newspapers for articles that describe ways that individuals or groups appear in the news because of conflicts or different points of view. Share these via display, distributing copies, or reading aloud, and have students identify the stereotyping. Have students discuss the consequences of stereotyping and prejudice, especially when it leads to violence.

Social Studies

Infuse questions about stereotyping, the feelings and consequences it evokes, and ideas about what could have happened that would have been more fair during lessons that explore issues such as the Civil War, the Spanish-American War, immigration, civil rights, women's rights, or the rights of the elderly.

Real-Life Application

Let students know that you will be looking for any incidents of prejudice and stereotyping among them and will be using FIG TESPN to address these problems.

TIPS FOR TEACHERS

1. Some students have difficulty being Challengers, and you may need to model this to help them. The rules, however, will help keep a focus on how different people have different beliefs and how any of them might be true or false in any one case.

2. Use the roles of Thinkers and Challengers as students have prejudice- and stereotype-related conflicts with each other. Integrating "Footsteps" (from Topic 9) with this discussion can also help focus students and calm strong emotions.

3. Throughout the school day, use the prompt "Are you being fair?" as a way to challenge students to avoid or question stereotypes and prejudices.

Student _____ **Date** _____

For each of the following, try to give three answers that will complete the sentence. There are no right or wrong answers—just what you think.

1. I think that old people should:

    a. _____

    b. _____

    c. _____

2. I think that men should not:

    a. _____

    b. _____

    c. _____

3. I think that girls should:

    a. _____

    b. _____

    c. _____

4. I think that young people should not:

    a. _____

    b. _____

    c. _____

5. I think that women should:

    a. _____

    b. _____

    c. _____

6. I think that boys should not:

    a. _____

    b. _____

    c. _____

7. I think that girls should not:

    a. _____

    b. _____

    c. _____

8. I think that old people should not:

   a. _____

   b. _____

   c. _____

9. I think that boys should:

   a. _____

   b. _____

   c. _____

10. I think that Black people are:

   a. _____

   b. _____

   c. _____

11. I think that White people are:

   a. _____

   b. _____

   d. _____

12. I think that Hispanic people are:

   a. _____

   b. _____

   c. _____

13. I think that Asian people are:

   a. _____

   b. _____

   c. _____

14. I think that people in wheelchairs cannot:

   a. _____

   b. _____

   c. _____

Student _____ **Date** _____

To answer the first question, you must pretend that you are the kind of person listed and that others are prejudiced against you. That means that they are treating you as a stereotype and not as a person.

1. How does it feel to be prejudiced against and to be:

   a. Black?

   b. White?

   c. Hispanic?

   d. Arab?

   e. A member of the opposite sex?

   f. Elderly?

   g. Someone with a physical disability or learning problem?

2. What kinds of things would people say and do to you that would tell you that they are being unfair to you?

3. What are some consequences of thinking that stereotypes and prejudices are true about someone?

4. When you see someone or meet someone you do not know, say to yourself, "There are lots of things that this person could be. I will have to think, check, and see."

   a. Write at least three things that you could think about to help you be fair and not use a stereotype.

   b. Write at least three things that you could say or do to show that you are being fair to someone and not treating the person according to a stereotype.

24 Using FIG TESPN to Make Decisions and Solve Problems in Our Lives

OBJECTIVE
- To help students use FIG TESPN to make personal social decisions

MATERIALS
Copies of the "Personal Problem-Solving Planner" (Worksheet 5.15.1)
Journals or notebooks *(optional)*

INSTRUCTIONAL ACTIVITIES

1. Conduct a Sharing Circle.

Review Topic 23 by having students share the examples of stereotyping and prejudice that they have seen in the media or movies.

2. Introduce the idea of solving personal problems in an orderly way.

Distribute the "Personal-Problem Solving Planners." Discuss the worksheet elements with the class. Point out the benefits of writing down and learning from attempts to solve problems, whether or not they are successful.

Ask students to complete the worksheet on their own, describing a problem situation that they encountered recently. Say that you plan to ask for volunteers to share parts of their worksheet for class role-plays, so students should try to use problems they wouldn't mind talking about with the class.

Offer students individual help as necessary.

3. Share the results.

After students have completed their worksheets, ask for a volunteer to share a problem and solution with the class. Set up the role-play to emphasize planning or reacting to obstacles. This will help reinforce the integration of the various problem-solving steps.

As time permits, have other volunteers share their problems and solutions and do role-plays. Make the point that students can use their classmates as a problem-solving team. When a situation comes up that they feel is a problem, or if they get stuck on a particular step, they can ask someone for advice or suggest that the matter be discussed at a class meeting.

4. Introduce a Reflective Summary.

As outlined in the Introduction, ask students to reflect on the question "What did you learn from today's lesson?" Reinforce key themes, then go over any follow-up work.

5. Follow up.

The following steps will help make sure that the students have a chance to continue working with the new concepts.

Assignment

Distribute another copy of the Personal Problem-Solving Planner and have students complete it, using a problem that they encounter and try to solve during the week. Have students bring their completed worksheets to the next lesson. Inform students that they will be asked to share parts of their worksheet, so the problem they choose should be appropriate to discuss with the class.

Plans to Promote Transfer and Generalization of Skill

Language Arts

Encourage the students to keep a Personal Problem-Solving Journal to record problems and decisions that they are experiencing. In the future, when faced with a similar problem, students can review their past entries to help them think through the current problem. In addition, a journal will allow for review of skill improvement.

Social Application

Establish a Problem-Solving Corner in a specific area of the room. Have copies of the FIG TESPN steps worksheet (Worksheet 5.10.1) and the Personal Problem-Solving Planner (Worksheet 5.15.1) available for student use.

TIPS FOR TEACHERS

1. Learning children's problem-solving strengths helps pave the way for you to prompt their use of FIG TESPN outside the formal lesson. For example, you may have only a few minutes to help a stu-

dent (or group) resolve a recess-time problem. In that case, it might be helpful for you to call attention to one or two steps that are each child's strengths as well as to any that you feel would be particularly relevant. (For example, if you were talking to an anxious child, you may want to focus on setting a positive goal. With a shy or depressed child, you may want to emphasize recognition of feelings and then help with brainstorming many options.)

25 Using FIG TESPN to Prepare for a Test

OBJECTIVES
- To show students that a test can be considered a problem that can be solved
- To help students apply their problem-solving knowledge to develop strategies to cope with upcoming tests

MATERIALS
Copies of "Testing Feelings" (Worksheet 5.25.1) and the FIG TESPN steps worksheet (Worksheet 5.10.1)

Chalkboard or easel pad

INSTRUCTIONAL ACTIVITIES

1. Conduct a Sharing Circle.

Review Topic 24 by having students share parts of their Personal Problem-Solving Planners.

2. Introduce the new subject matter.

Ask the students to describe their feelings about tests and quizzes, especially standardized tests. Encourage them to mention the Feelings Fingerprints that they notice when thinking about tests. As usual, elicit a range of feelings in a nonjudgmental manner.

Distribute the "Testing Feelings" worksheet to help the students analyze their feelings (see Topic 4). Remind students of the many skills that they have learned that could help them with test taking. Have students think about which FIG TESPN skills they will need to use as they prepare for and take tests, and ask them to explain why the skills would be helpful.

3. Frame the problem.

Ask different students to put the problem into words. Encourage them to use the format "I feel _____ because _____" or "I feel _____ when _____." Put the most important problem statements on the chalkboard or easel pad; then, under each, have the children state a goal (such as "know what to do").

4. Make an action plan.

Divide the students into subgroups, and for each goal stated in the discussion of the worksheet have a different subgroup of the class work together to brainstorm as many ways as they can to reach the goal, keeping a list as they go.

Have each subgroup envision the consequences for each of their solutions. Give them a fixed time for discussion, and have each subgroup give you their two best solutions. Put these on the board under the goals.

5. Act out the plans.

Assign a subgroup other than the one suggesting a particular solution to plan the steps to make the solution work. When and where can it be done? Who should be involved? How should it be done? Have the students create a role-play.

Ask each subgroup to role-play their plan and have the other students provide feedback in preparation for pitfalls. Then, under each solution, write the plan that the class (and you) feel will help make a solution work best.

6. Make a record.

Have the students copy these problem-goal-solution-plan sequences in some form that they are likely to keep.

7. Introduce a Reflective Summary.

As outlined in the Introduction, ask students to reflect on the question "What did you learn from today's lesson?" Reinforce key themes, then go over any follow-up work.

8. Follow up.

The following steps will help make sure that the students have a chance to continue working with the new concepts.

Assignment

Encourage students to review and use their FIG TESPN skills in the future as they prepare for and take all exams and quizzes.

Take-Home

The Plan Sequences can be sent home with a brief cover note asking parents or guardians to save them and to review the options with the children before tests. Parents and guardians should encourage children to review and use their FIG TESPN skills in the future when they have exams or quizzes or difficult projects.

Plans to Promote Transfer and Generalization of Skill

Social Application

Encourage students to use their FIG TESPN skills when faced with change, problems, and decisions.

TIPS FOR TEACHERS

A useful adjunct to using FIG TESPN is for students to use Keep Calm right before, as well as during, tests and quizzes. You will need to prompt this often. In addition to counting, it can also be useful for students to add positive self-talk messages, such as "I know I can do it," "Keep breathing deeply," "Picture what you studied," and "Read the question carefully."

Student _____ **Date** _____

Put a check mark in the box that best shows how you feel about the words in each pair (Sad-Happy and so on).

Regular Class Tests

	Very	Sort of	Just a little	In the middle	Just a little	Sort of	Very	
Sad	☐	☐	☐	☐	☐	☐	☐	Happy
Calm	☐	☐	☐	☐	☐	☐	☐	Worried
Unsure	☐	☐	☐	☐	☐	☐	☐	Sure
Lazy	☐	☐	☐	☐	☐	☐	☐	Persistent
Unfriendly	☐	☐	☐	☐	☐	☐	☐	Friendly
Safe	☐	☐	☐	☐	☐	☐	☐	In danger
Helpful	☐	☐	☐	☐	☐	☐	☐	Unhelpful

Standardized Tests

	Very	Sort of	Just a little	In the middle	Just a little	Sort of	Very	
Sad	☐	☐	☐	☐	☐	☐	☐	Happy
Calm	☐	☐	☐	☐	☐	☐	☐	Worried
Unsure	☐	☐	☐	☐	☐	☐	☐	Sure
Lazy	☐	☐	☐	☐	☐	☐	☐	Persistent
Unfriendly	☐	☐	☐	☐	☐	☐	☐	Friendly
Safe	☐	☐	☐	☐	☐	☐	☐	In danger
Helpful	☐	☐	☐	☐	☐	☐	☐	Unhelpful

26 Review SDM/SPS Skills and Celebrate Our Strengths

OBJECTIVES
- To help students use the social problem solving and social decision making process to plan an event
- To acknowledge and celebrate student successes and to help students recognize the importance of this type of celebration

MATERIALS
Chalkboard or easel pad

Whole-class display of "SDM/SPS Skills: Grade 5" (Worksheet 5.26.1)

Copies of the following worksheets:

FIG TESPN steps (5.10.1)

"Certificate of Achievement" (5.26.2)

"SDM/SPS Student Progress Report" (5.26.3)

"SDM/SPS Summary and Recommendations (5.26.4)

INSTRUCTIONAL ACTIVITIES

1. Conduct a Sharing Circle

Referring to the whole-class display of SDM/SPS skills, encourage students to go around the circle and say which skill or concept they found to be most helpful. If you wish, you can ask them to name two or three skills or concepts they found helpful.

The SDM/SPS skills concepts for this grade level, and the topics in which they were introduced, are as follows:

- Sharing Circle; Speaker Power; Listening Position; Respectful Listening (Topic 1)
- Introduction to FIG TESPN (Topic 2)
- Trigger Situations; Feelings Fingerprints (Topic 4)
- Keep Calm (Topic 5)
- Trigger Journals (Topic 7)
- "Footsteps" (Understanding Different Points of View) (Topic 9)
- FIG TESPN Steps Worksheet (Topic 10)
- Be Your BEST; Be Your BEST Grid (Topic 12)

2. Discuss the importance of celebrations.

Tell students that people in various cultures throughout the world acknowledge their accomplishments and successes, and prepare for their transition to the next level or phase by holding a celebration.

Have students brainstorm a list of celebrations, especially those related to life transitions, that they are familiar with or have studied.

3. Decide on a celebration.

Begin by telling students that even though the word *problem* in Step 2 of FIG TESPN often has a negative connotation, the problem that they are about to solve will actually be fun. Tell students that they will be using FIG TESPN to create and carry out a celebration of their successes during the year.

Using the chalkboard or easel pad, work through the steps with the students as you and the class decide what kind of celebration you will hold.

4. Plan the details.

After the class decides on the kind of celebration to hold, discuss the planning process and make a list of all the things that need to be done to make the celebration a success—for example, deciding on the date and time, making arrangements regarding food, planning a ceremony and other activities, creating certificates or awards for the participants, and inviting guests.

Divide the class into groups and distribute copies of the FIG TESPN steps worksheet. Assign each group to brainstorm all the planning issues and work to produce a comprehensive overall plan.

When the groups are finished, have each group share their plans with the class. Acknowledge the hard work and strong feelings shown by each group. Help them look for commonalities in their suggestions and use FIG TESPN to solve the problem of disagreement. Once students arrive at a common goal and plan, discuss any potential pitfalls. Then rework the necessary details and finalize an overall plan for your celebration.

5. Have students follow through.

Based on the planning that the groups did, assign students to follow through on any tasks that need to be done to prepare for the celebration. Part of this process could be to create invitations or a flier listing the date and time so that everyone will know when their assignments or tasks are due. You may want to invite parents and guardians to participate in your celebration.

6. Celebrate students' participation in the program.

Hold the celebration that students planned. If you wish, give each student a Certificate of Achievement to honor participation.

7. Introduce a Reflective Summary.

As outlined in the Introduction, ask students to reflect on the question "What did you learn from today's lesson?" Reinforce key themes, then go over any follow-up work.

8. Follow up.

The following steps will help make sure that the students have a chance to continue working with the new concepts.

Take-Home

Send completed Student Progress Reports home to give parents and guardians a summary of student skill gains and recommendations for helping their children celebrate their achievements and continue building skills. Any portfolios or papers the students have completed can also be sent home at this time.

Plans to Promote Transfer and Generalization of Skill

The process that students use to plan their celebration can be applied to many different activities that occur both inside and outside school. This process can be helpful in planning class trips, grade-level picnics and parties, and other annual events. Often, adults do all the planning and problem solving for such events, missing a good opportunity to teach students essential social skills while also getting their input.

TIPS FOR TEACHERS

1. This lesson teaches children the importance of being responsible and following through on a task or assignment. In this respect, teachers may want to observe the progress of the group and do further problem solving if issues arise that could compromise the final outcome of the celebration.

2. Complete and distribute the SDM/SPS Summary and Recommendations. This form is designed for you, as the sending teacher, to let receiving teachers know what their incoming students have covered and provides recommendations for helping them maintain and continue to build skills.

SDM/SPS Skills: Grade 5

1. Sharing Circle

2. Speaker Power

3. Listening Position

4. Respectful Listening

5. FIG TESPN

6. Trigger Situations

7. Feelings Fingerprints

8. Keep Calm

9. Trigger Journals

10. "Footsteps" (Understanding Different Points of View)

11. FIG TESPN Steps Worksheet

12. Be Your BEST

SDM/SPS
Certificate of Achievement

_____

(Student)

Has successfully developed many Social Decision Making and Social Problem Solving skills

Sincerely,

_____   _____

(Teacher)   (Date)

Student Progress Report

 I appreciate your support and partnership as we have worked this year to help your child develop social decision making and social problem solving abilities. As the school year comes to a close, I would like to share my assessment of your child's progress and make some recommendations to you about ways that you can help to continue the development of these skills through the summer months.

Skill improvement

_____

_____

_____

Suggestions to help you reinforce and continue skill development

_____

_____

_____

Additional comments

_____

_____

_____

_____

Thank you!

_____

(Teacher signature)

- -

(Please sign and return this bottom section.)

Student _____ **Date** _____

We received the report. ☐ Yes ☐ No

Comments:

_____

(Signature of parent or guardian)

Teacher _____ **Date** _____

Students in my class worked on a Social Decision Making and Social Problem Solving (SDM/SPS) team this past year to develop a variety of skills. I have attached a copy of all of last year's SDM/SPS Topics we covered. The numbers of those we covered fully are checked; an *X* appears beside Topics we touched upon but that might need some review. In addition, I have noted below accomplishments and areas of focus for particular students:

1. **Students with general strengths in SDM/SPS:**

   _____   _____

   _____   _____

   _____   _____

2. **Students needing overall growth in SDM/SPS:**

   _____   _____

   _____   _____

   _____   _____

3. **Students with strengths in particular SDM/SPS areas:**

   Student   *Area*

   _____   _____

   _____   _____

   _____   _____

   _____   _____

4. **Students needing skill development in particular SDM/SPS areas:**

   Student   *Area*

   _____   _____

   _____   _____

   _____   _____

SDM/SPS Topics Covered

Social Decision Making and Social Problem Solving (Topics 1–15)

- ☐ 1. Introduction to Social Decision Making/Social Problem Solving (SDM/SPS) Lessons
- ☐ 2. Introduction to FIG TESPN
- ☐ 3. Feelings Identification
- ☐ 4. Trigger Situations and Physical Signs of Stress
- ☐ 5. Keep Calm
- ☐ 6. Identify the Problem
- ☐ 7. Trigger Journal
- ☐ 8. Guide Yourself with a Goal
- ☐ 9. Understanding Different Points of View
- ☐ 10. Think of Many Solutions and Envision Consequences
- ☐ 11. Practice Thinking of Solutions and Envisioning Consequences
- ☐ 12. Your BEST Chance for Success
- ☐ 13. Select the BEST Solution, Then Plan and Prepare for Pitfalls
- ☐ 14. Notice What Happened (Now What?)
- ☐ 15. Problem Solving: Using All the FIG TESPN Steps

Putting It All Together (Topics 16/17–26)

- ☐ 16/17. Using FIG TESPN with Literature
- ☐ 18. Using FIG TESPN for Creative Writing
- ☐ 19. Using FIG TESPN to Critically Examine Stories and Media Reports
- ☐ 20. Using FIG TESPN to Critically Examine Advertising
- ☐ 21. Using FIG TESPN to Solve Problems in Science
- ☐ 22. Using FIG TESPN to Examine Problems in History
- ☐ 23. Using FIG TESPN to Think About Fairness and Prejudice
- ☐ 24. Using FIG TESPN to Make Decisions and Solve Problems in Our Lives
- ☐ 25. Using FIG TESPN to Prepare for a Test
- ☐ 26. Review SDM/SPS Skills and Celebrate Our Strengths

Supplemental (Topics 27–29)

- ☐ 27. Using FIG TESPN to Change Target Behaviors
- ☐ 28. Using FIG TESPN in Student Government
- ☐ 29. Using FIG TESPN to Understand and Analyze Current Events

Topics 27–29

27 Using FIG TESPN to Change Target Behaviors

OBJECTIVES
- To help students recognize the negative consequences of inappropriate actions
- To help students consider alternative solutions and plan ways to improve their behavior and academic performance

MATERIALS
Copies of "Taking a Look at Myself" (Worksheet 5.27.1)

INSTRUCTIONAL ACTIVITIES

1. Conduct a Sharing Circle.

Have students name their favorite FIG TESPN skill and possibly describe a time when they used the FIG TESPN process recently. Have the class also take turns sharing positive experiences, favorite activities, and so on.

2. Launch the activity.

Distribute the "Taking a Look at Myself" worksheet. Have the students complete Part 1, which is a survey of their present behavior.

When students have completed Part 1, have them share ideas about it, encouraging them to discuss the questions in a general way so that they do not feel pressured to disclose their particular answers. For example, ask generalized questions like these:

- What are some things that make students your age proud?
- What kinds of things annoy students your age or make students your age upset?
- How do students your age look and sound when they lose control of their feelings and emotions?

3. Develop possible actions.

Have students continue deciding what they would like to change by completing the first four questions in Part 2 of the worksheet. This will help them select a behavior to change and consider alternative solutions.

When students have completed these four questions, ask them to share some behaviors that they intend to change.

Individually or in small groups, as you think appropriate, have students generate ideas to solve the problem and reach their goals. Have students get feedback from the group and then have each student complete the fifth question in Part 2, or just have students get feedback from you after they complete the question.

4. Introduce a Reflective Summary.

As outlined in the Introduction, ask students to reflect on the question "What did you learn from today's lesson?" Reinforce key themes, then go over any follow-up work.

5. Follow up.

The following steps will help make sure that the students have a chance to continue working with the new concepts.

Assignment

Have students complete Part 3 for homework as a two-day project. That is, have them do the first question in Part 3, and then get feedback from an adult, either from you or from a parent or guardian. After they have received some constructive criticism, have students do the second question in Part 3.

Take-Home

Send a note home to parents and guardians encouraging them to review the "Taking a Look at Myself" worksheet with their child. After students have completed the first question in Part 3, parents and guardians can provide constructive criticism on their child's plan.

Plans to Promote Transfer and Generalization of Skill

This activity is useful when students are having particular difficulty in a specific subject area. Students can complete the first two questions in Part 1 as they pertain to their success and shortcomings in a subject area. Using the example of mathematics, a student may learn new concepts quickly, but may be careless and make many calculation errors. The student can continue completing the worksheet and create a plan for how to improve performance in mathematics. The teacher can then follow up with the student to see how the plan is working and encourage successes or provide feedback if the grades do not improve.

TIPS FOR TEACHERS

1. Teachers can limit responses in Part 2 (about the behavior that students would like to change) to problems with study habits or open them up to include problems with other students or adults.

2. Some students are sensitive about sharing areas in need of improvement. It may be desirable to limit the use of group activities and sharing of individual responses. In any case, avoid pushing individuals to contribute if they are reluctant to do so.

Student _____ Date _____

Part 1: What are my strong and weak points?

1. Write several adjectives that tell about some of your strong points—things that you do well or things about your behavior that you or others are proud of.

2. Write several adjectives that tell about some of your weak points—things that you do not do well or things about your behavior that you or others are not proud of.

3. Write some things that you do that sometimes annoy other people. These are words or actions that make them upset at you, act unkindly toward you, ignore you, or keep away from you.

4. Write down anything that you say or do that sometimes gets you into trouble with your friends, teachers, or parents. Try to think of a time when you did get into trouble, and write it as an example.

Part 2: Finding a weak point that I want to change

Everyone has at least one weak point. Our weak points often get us into problem situations. Once we are in these situations, we have upset feelings. Sometimes, what we say or do has negative consequences. When this happens a few times, we should tell ourselves that we have a problem and try to think of as many ways as we can to solve the problem. If we do this, we will have better feelings and more positive consequences. In Part 1, you wrote some weak points that you have. Now complete Part 2.

1. Read over your weak points from Part 1. Which two or three things seem to get you into difficulty most often?

   a. _____

   b. _____

   c. _____

2. Which one of these weak points would you most like to change? Let's call this one your *target*. What will your goal be? How do you want things to be different?

   a. This is the target I want to change: _____

   b. My goal will be to _____

   _____.

3. Think of some times when your target got you into trouble or caused a problem. Write these examples below.

4. What are some things that you could have said or done differently so the problem would have been smaller or maybe not there at all? Write at least three different things.

5. Write what you think are the three best ways to solve your problem.

Part 3: Making a plan to change my target

1. You have picked a target, thought about some times when the target has caused a problem for you, and thought about things that you could say or do differently. Now make a plan that will help you change your target. How will you know when you are about to use your target? How can you stop yourself? How can you use your strong points to make things better? Who might help you? How can you say or do something that will not cause a problem for you? Write a paragraph and plan how you will change your target from a weak point to a strong point.

2. After you have received feedback on your plan, write the changes that you will make. If necessary, rewrite your plan.

28 Using FIG TESPN in Student Government

OBJECTIVE
- To produce a list of social problems common to the students in the school where FIG TESPN is being taught

MATERIALS
Copies of the "Student Government Survey" (Worksheet 5.28.1)

NOTE
This lesson is designed to take place at a meeting of the student council members from the grades in which FIG TESPN is being taught. If you wish, you can modify it to suit activities within a single class.

INSTRUCTIONAL ACTIVITIES

1. Introduce the topic.

Begin a student council meeting by discussing the fact that students run into many different social problems while they are in school. Ask if anyone can think of an example of a common problem that many students face at their school.

Tell students which classes have FIG TESPN lessons, and let them know that these lessons are meant to help students solve some of their problems.

2. Ask for help.

Tell the student council members that you are holding this meeting with them to use them as consultants. Tell them that you would like to find out some of the most common problems that students at their school are facing. Make sure that it is clear that you do not want to know what problems *they* have; you are interested in the problems that they see other students facing. For example, ask generalized questions like these:

- What are some things that bother students at this school?
- What kinds of things annoy students your age or make students your age upset?

3. Introduce the activity.

Distribute the "Student Government Survey" worksheet and ask the student council members to write several problems in each category.

Once the students have completed the survey, ask for volunteers to read a few of the problems from their sheets. For each problem mentioned, ask students to raise their hands if they wrote a similar problem. Ask students to continue sharing other problems they wrote that were different.

4. Introduce a Reflective Summary.

As outlined in the Introduction, ask students to reflect on the question "What did you learn from today's lesson?" Reinforce key themes, then go over any follow-up work.

Thank the student council members for their time and help. Collect the surveys. The meeting can either proceed to other business or adjourn.

5. Follow up.

The following steps will help make sure that the students have a chance to continue working with the new concepts.

Assignment

Distribute additional Student Government Surveys and have student council members do this same activity with whatever group they represent. This can be done during homeroom, at lunch, or at any other convenient time. Have the student council members compile their surveys into one general survey for each class that can be returned to the student council adviser.

Take-Home

Parents and guardians can be encouraged to become more actively involved in school problem solving and decision making by joining and participating in the school's Home-School Association, PTA, or PTO. This organization's primary focus is to encourage communication between the home and school and to provide parents and guardians with a way that they can actively participate in their children's education.

Plans to Promote Transfer and Generalization of Skill

School Government

The Student Government Surveys are a wonderful resource to use prior to discussing how FIG TESPN can be used and applied to everyday issues and problems that occur at your school. Students in various classes can work through the problems found in the surveys with the goal of creating a more positive school climate.

Language Arts and Social Studies

In language arts, students can write about ways to improve their school in a letter to the principal. In social studies, they can learn about citizenship and civics by solving real problems.

Art

Students can create posters and other artwork to encourage students to act in more positive ways.

Community Service

The problems listed in the surveys may also lead to school and community service activities and projects, using FIG TESPN to organize and plan for action.

TIPS FOR TEACHERS

In this lesson, students see how they can become more actively involved in their school, rather than being passive victims. They can also learn how to take more responsibility for changing what goes on around them, rather than depending on adults to do the problem solving and decision making.

FRIENDS	ACADEMICS	TEACHERS

29 Using FIG TESPN to Understand and Analyze Current Events

OBJECTIVE
- To help students use FIG TESPN to examine current events in history and social studies

MATERIALS
Sample news articles
Copies of "Current Events" (Worksheet 5.29.1)

PREPARATION
It is helpful to have the questions from the worksheet written in a whole-group format.

INSTRUCTIONAL ACTIVITIES

1. Introduce the lesson.

In your usual current events time, distribute the "Current Events" worksheet and explain that this is a new social studies assignment.

2. Conduct a practice activity.

Distribute copies of a sample news article and either give the class time to read it or have students read it out loud. Verbally complete the worksheet as a class for the sample article.

3. Introduce a Reflective Summary.

As outlined in the Introduction, ask students to reflect on the question "What did you learn from today's lesson?" Reinforce key themes, then go over any follow-up work.

4. Follow up.

The following steps will help make sure that the students have a chance to continue working with the new concepts.

Assignment

Assign a suitable article about a current problem in the news or have students find one from newspapers, magazines, or the Internet. Of particular value are local problems or local instances of general events, such as crime, unemployment, or community problems. Have students complete the worksheet, using their article as a class activity.

Have students meet in groups of two, three, or four to share ideas and complete a single worksheet. Encourage groups to share and compare ideas. Ask students what action steps they might want to take as an entire class as a follow-up.

Take-Home

Parents and guardians should be encouraged to help their child select an appropriate current events article from a newspaper, magazine, or the Internet. Parents and guardians can review and discuss the article with their child and help with any difficulties in completing the worksheet.

Plans to Promote Transfer and Generalization of Skill

1. This activity can be repeated regularly throughout the year as a format for teaching current events. Repeated use of this activity can help sharpen and organize students' thinking about events around them and also help them take the next step of actively and creatively attempting to find solutions to problems. Such thinking, if encouraged, can be an antidote to apathy.

2. This activity is ideal for helping students to see how problem-solving and decision-making skills are directly linked to everyday issues that all people face. It is also a powerful way to show students that how a person such as a politician or world leader handles a problem can affect thousands or even millions of other people.

TIPS FOR TEACHERS

1. Initially, the students may need extra help in getting accustomed to using this worksheet as a learning tool. If so, distribute copies of another article. Have the students complete the worksheet with this article in class. Repeat this process until students are able to fill out the worksheet without your assistance.

2. Students enjoy completing the worksheet in subgroups and then comparing perspectives. Some teachers start with Questions 1 and 2 as a whole class (others go from 1 to 5) and then let subgroups work out their own sorts of responses, share, and perhaps reach a consensus.

3. A valuable resource for helping students plan follow-up activities is *The Kid's Guide to Social Action,* by Barbara Lewis, published by Free Spirit. Lewis also has written several related books on the topic that will prove useful.

4. Note that some of the questions on the worksheet ask students to talk about their own individual ideas, which may or may not be the same as the ideas of the whole class or their subgroups.

Student _____ **Date** _____

1. What is the event that you are thinking about? When and where is it happening? Put the event into words as a problem.

2. What people or groups are involved in the problem? What are their different feelings and points of view about the problem? Try to put their goals into words.

3. For each group, name some different solutions to the problem that they think might help them reach their goals.

4. For each solution, envision all the things that might happen next. Picture clearly both short-term and long-term consequences.

5. What do you think the final decision should be? How should it be made? Who should make it? Why?

6. Think of a plan to help you carry out your solution. What could you do to make your solution work?

7. Make a final check. What might happen that could keep your solution from working? Who might disagree with you? Why? What else could you do?

8. If you were going to try to solve this problem, what would be your best solution? What plan would you make to help carry out your solution? What obstacles might occur to keep your solution from working? How could you overcome them? What else would you suggest?

Appendix A

The SDM/SPS Curriculum Approach: Evidence of Effectiveness

OUTCOME EVALUATIONS

The following is a summary of our evaluation data, which we have gathered over three decades. The data are organized around four claims of effectiveness. It is the research that produced this data that forms the basis for our program's being one of the few character education and social-emotional learning programs to have been validated as an Exemplary Program by the U.S. Department of Education's Program Effectiveness Panel. More recently, it has been granted Promising Program status by the Department of Education's Expert Panel on Safe and Drug Free Schools and the Character Education Partnership, and has also been designated as a Select SEL (empirically validated social-emotional learning) program by the Collaborative for Academic, Social, and Emotional Learning and as a Model Program by the New Jersey Center for Character Education (see Bruene Butler et al., 1997). (Note that these data are not exhaustive. For example, Thurston [1998] has studied the impact of SDM/SPS on special education populations, and Norris [1998] has evaluated the impact of SDM/SPS in a multicultural setting. Additional data are still being collected in urban implementation sites.)

Claim 1: Following training, teachers improve in their ability to facilitate children's social decision making and problem solving.

Fourth- and fifth-grade teachers from Middlesex, New Jersey, were given the Assessment of Responses of Teachers to Hypothetical Classroom Situations, a series of hypothetical school-based problem situations derived from the work of Irving Sigel and of George Spivack and Myrna Shure. Responses were classified according to a hierarchy ranging from *inhibitory* of children's representational competence (authoritarian responses) through *moderately facilitative* (providing consequences or alternatives to choose from) to *highly facilitative* of children's cognitive abilities (open-ended questions that encourage reflection on the possibilities and options). The results showed that, after training, teachers significantly increased their use of questioning strategies found to be highly facilitative of problem-solving thinking, with a significant difference ($p < .001$) between the experimental and untrained control groups. (The control group was later trained in the techniques as well.) Completing the instructional phase was associated with a significant reduction in the use of inhibitory responses (57 percent reduction by the experimental group; 61 percent by the control group after training) and a corresponding increase in the use of moderately to highly facilitative responses. Table 4 represents data from several further districts indicating gains in facilitative questioning by teachers. Teachers' inhibitory responses in these sites were reduced by a mean of 52 percent, while facilitative responses showed a mean increase of 58 percent.

Claim 2: Children receiving the program improve their social decision making and social problem solving skills relative to controls.

Self-Control and Social Awareness Phase

We have assessed the Readiness Phase of the curriculum by applying the measure "Getting Along With Others," using an expert rating scale we have developed and a scoring system that permits

Table 4   Summary of Change in Teachers' Inhibitory and Highly Facilitative Responses Following SDM/SPS Training

	N	Site*	Inhibitory			Facilitative		
			Pre	Post	-%	Pre	Post	+%
Center School	9	U U/S	17%	6%	-65%	46%	81%	+76%
Bartle School	7	U U/S	22%	9%	-59%	32%	52%	+63%
Clifton School	13	U/S	29%	14%	-52%	33%	46%	+39%
AK	16	R	20%	11%	-45%	52%	60%	+15%
OR	4	S	17%	8%	-53%	29%	63%	+117%
Mean			21%	10%	-52%	38%	60%	+58%

* Site: S = suburban; U/S = urban/suburban; U = urban; R = rural.

computerized statistical analysis. The measure yields scores for each of the eight questions that have been judged to reflect *average, competent,* or *at-risk* responses by a panel of experts in the field. For example, to be judged competent in response to the question "Name three things you do when someone is bugging you or bothering you," a child has to give at least two responses indicating either polite assertiveness (for example, "Ask them to please stop") or a means of finding a solution by talking it out. However, if any one of the child's responses refers to aggression (for example, "Punch them") or a display of anger or revenge, the child is coded as at-risk for this question. Other behaviors, such as telling someone rather than asking them to stop, physically leaving, or ignoring the person would be rated as average responses. These scores are then combined to provide a risk, average, and competence score for each child. We present three pretest/posttest, control group–design studies documenting the effectiveness of the Readiness Phase. In each case, there were no differences between the experimental and control groups at pretest. All data were analyzed using the nonparametric Wilcoxon rank-sum test for an approximate t-test result, using two-tailed tests. Interrater reliability exceeded 90 percent.

Study 1

Fourth-grade teachers at the Watsessing School in Bloomfield, New Jersey, were trained in February 1993. Bloomfield is an urban/suburban site, with a 41 percent minority student population at the Watsessing School. Thirty-two percent of the students qualify for free or reduced-price lunches. A control group ($n = 22$) was obtained from the Berkeley School in Bloomfield, which has comparable demographics.

From Table 5, it can be seen that the experimental group ($n = 46$) made a significant gain in competence by posttest in June 1994 ($p < .0001$), while the control group's competence score did not improve. By posttest, 54 percent of the experimental group were rated as low in risk and high in competence, based on their combined responses, while only 14 percent of the controls received that rating and 46 percent were in fact rated as high in risk and low in competence. For example, 74 percent of the experimental group could provide four characteristics that they look for in a friend, with over 60 percent providing qualities that result in reciprocal friendship or citing compatibility as an important characteristic, while 50 percent of the control group were unable to think of more than two qualities, with only 32 percent discussing reciprocity.

Study 2

In the Bartle School, Highland Park, New Jersey, the students of two trained third-grade teachers formed the experimental group ($n = 32$), with an in-school control of three classes of nontrained third-grade students ($n = 59$). Highland Park has the dual rating of urban and urban/suburban, with a 47 percent minority population, composed

Table 5   Summary of Mean Competence Scores and Statistics from the Three Studies of the Readiness Phase of the Curriculum

STUDY	GROUP	N	PRE MEAN (SD)	POST MEAN (SD)	Z	p <	Effect Size
Bloomfield, New Jersey	Experimental	46	1.64 (1.22)	3.17 (1.34)	5.08	.0001	1.25
	Control	22	1.85 (1.22)	1.68 (1.09)			
Highland Park, New Jersey	Experimental	32	1.95 (1.26)	3.50 (1.22)	4.56	.0001	1.23
	Control	59	1.77 (1.21)	2.20 (1.39)			
Litchfield, Arizona	Experimental	23	1.38 (1.17)	3.35 (1.15)	4.54	.0001	1.68
	Control	18	2.07 (1.21)	2.61 (1.46)			

ES = (Experimental posttest mean – Experimental pretest mean) / Experimental pretest SD. These effect sizes are considered to be significant in that for each study they exceeded one standard deviation.

primarily (28 percent) of African-American students. Fifteen percent of the third graders were eligible for free or reduced-price lunches.

Again, Table 5 shows that the experimental group's competence score improved significantly ($p < .0001$) by posttest in May 1994. By posttest, 78 percent were rated as low in risk and high in competence, compared with only 23 percent at pretest. At that time over 46 percent were actually rated high in risk and low in competence. This score was retained by only two experimental children (6 percent) at posttest. For example, at pretest, sixteen children from the experimental group are unable to identify a way of knowing when they are upset, and ten children had no strategy for talking to another person who was upset. By posttest, only three children were unable to provide ways of knowing when they are upset, and only one child had no strategy for approaching an upset person. Within the experimental group, at pretest, 20 percent were unable to name even one characteristic that they look for in a friend, and 46 percent could think of only two. By posttest, only one child (3 percent) was unable to list anything, and twenty-eight children (87.5 percent) could name, as requested, four characteristics that they look for in a friend. In contrast, at posttest, only 37 percent of the control group was rated as low in risk and high in competence, with twenty-one children (36 percent) scoring high in risk and low in competence.

Study 3

The fifth-grade teacher at Litchfield School, Arizona, became a certified trainer in June 1993, and agreed to conduct a Readiness Phase study with her students (n = 23) during the 1993–1994 academic year. The experimental site is rural, with a 39 percent minority population, composed mainly of Hispanic students (30 percent). The students are predominantly the children of enlisted personnel from a nearby air force base, and 40 percent qualify for reduced-price or free lunches. In this study, the control group (n = 18) represents a higher socioeconomic group, with fifth graders from a more affluent school that serves officers' children in a suburban district. Students' pretest scores were not statistically significantly different, although the controls' scores were higher. By posttest, in May, the experimental group outperformed the controls in terms of competence, despite the preexisting inequalities. At posttest, 74 percent of the experimental group scored low in risk and high in competence, compared with 28 percent of the control group.

For all three studies, at posttest, the experimental group differed significantly in competence from the control group (p < .0001, .0001, and .05, respectively). Table 5 also includes the effect size for each study, which was calculated using the formula ES = (experimental posttest mean – experimental pretest mean)/experimental pretest SD. These effect sizes are considered to be significant in that for each study they exceeded one standard deviation.

Instructional and Application Phases

The Group Social Problem Solving Assessment (GSPSA) was used to assess the Instructional and Application Phases of the curriculum. Summary data from the fourth grades of two districts (Clifton and Berkeley Heights, New Jersey) are included, and results by grade are available from an additional district (Bloomfield, New Jersey). Clifton is an urban/suburban district that introduced the program with the training of fourteen teachers and phased the program into all first-through fifth-grade classrooms, serving approximately three thousand children. The fourth grade has a 29 percent minority population, with 27 percent of the students qualifying for free or reduced-price meals. Berkeley Heights is a suburban district with a 15 percent minority population; it serves students from the upper middle class, with complete implementation of the program in the district for Grades 3 through 6. In Study 4, we present data from these two sites, using data from a control district (Middlesex, New Jersey) for comparison purposes because SDM is taught districtwide, and within-district controls could therefore not be obtained. (Middlesex is a blue-collar, multiethnic, but predominantly white town of about fifteen thousand in central New Jersey.) Scoring of this measure has not changed, and it is therefore a valid comparison. One hundred and forty-seven Clifton fourth graders and seventy-seven Berkeley Heights fourth graders completed the GSPSA pretest in September, prior to training in the Instructional Phase, and the posttest in May. The non-parametric Wilcoxon rank-sum test was again used to obtain approximate t-test results, with two-tailed tests, and interrater reliability exceeded 90 percent. The results presented in Table 6 indicate that children trained in SDM/SPS continue to make substantial gains in Interpersonal Sensitivity, Problem Analysis (which reflects a child's ability to examine a problem, define it, set goals, and consider alternative solutions), and Planning (which includes evaluating consequences and realistically assessing obstacles to problem resolution). In fact, the magnitude of effects for the current data exceeds that found in our original study.

A further study was conducted with fourth, fifth, and sixth graders in Bloomfield, New Jersey. Demographics for Bloomfield are presented under Study 1 in the Readiness section of this claim. As Table 7 shows, fourth graders again made significant gains in all three areas of social problem solving concepts, outperforming the original validation group (also shown in Table 7, for comparison). Following training, the fifth graders demonstrated significantly better knowledge of problem analysis and specificity of planning, while sixth graders demonstrated significant improvements in sensitivity to others' feelings and planning. Sixth graders' mean pretest score on problem analysis exceeded 14 points, which is the criterion for being rated highly skilled in this domain. While these students made gains in this skill by posttest, the nonsignificance of their result can be attributed to ceiling effects.

Table 6   Change in Fourth Graders' Mean Interpersonal Sensitivity (I.S.), Problem Analysis (P.A.), and Planning (PLAN) Scores Following Training in the Instructional Phase of SDM/SPS

	Middlesex (n = 120)			Clifton (n = 147)				Berkeley Heights (n = 77)			
	PRE	POST	ES	PRE	POST	Z	ES	PRE	POST	Z	ES
I.S. (sd)	9.89 2.20	10.29 1.54	.18	9.95 2.19	10.70 1.88	3.31*	.34	10.99 1.62	11.96 1.09	4.03**	.60
P.A. (sd)	10.37 3.62	12.47 3.72	.58	9.86 3.95	12.16 3.56	4.95**	.58	10.42 4.13	15.81 2.82	7.68**	1.3
PLAN (sd)	4.83 1.63	5.51 1.27	.42	5.55 2.08	6.56 1.91	4.06**	.49	6.20 1.76	7.61 1.72	4.65**	.80

$*p < .001$, $** p < .0001$; ES = Effect Size

Table 7   Change in Mean Scores for Interpersonal Sensitivity (I.S.), Problem Analysis (P.A.), and Planning (PLAN) by Grade: Bloomfield

	4th grade (n = 45)				5th grade (n = 25)				6th grade (n = 31)			
	PRE	POST	Z p <	ES	PRE	POST	Z p <	ES	PRE	POST	Z p <	ES
I.S. (sd)	10.10 (1.97)	11.22 (1.28)	3.00 .003	.57	10.55 (1.50)	10.96 (1.56)	n.s.		11.12 (1.51)	11.94 (1.00)	2.17 .033	.54
P.A. (sd)	8.31 (4.04)	12.84 (3.74)	4.80 .0001	1.12	11.35 (3.73)	13.84 (3.02)	2.75 .008	.67	14.47 (3.10)	15.55 (2.53)	n.s.	
PLAN (sd)	5.14 (2.33)	7.22 (1.88)	4.24 .0001	.89	6.68 (2.26)	7.88 (2.05)	2.02 .048	.53	7.15 (1.42)	8.06 (1.57)	2.19 .032	.64

ES = Effect Size

Claim 3: Students receiving the program in elementary school show more prosocial behavior in school and greater coping with stressors upon transition to middle school, when compared with controls.

Assessment of the generalizability of the program involved an examination of the impact of receiving full, partial (instructional only), or no exposure to the curriculum on reactions to stressors encountered upon transition to middle school. Elias et al. (1986) conducted a study involving 158 fifth-grade students (80 boys and 78 girls) in four elementary schools for whom parental permission was obtained (98 percent of the population). Academically, students averaged approximately one year above grade level on standardized academic tests. All fifth-grade teachers were involved in carrying out the program under a delayed control design. Within the larger project, it was agreed that sufficient quality control could not be maintained while beginning implementation in all fifth-grade classrooms simultaneously; it was decided to begin instruction in two schools and use the two other schools as a delayed comparison group, while simultaneously meeting the concerns of parents that their children receive a high-quality program before entering middle school. To examine the nature of adjustment among children who received no SDM training, a control group consisting of children entering middle school during the prior year was used. Thus there were three quasi-experimental conditions: (a) no training, (b) full training, and (c) partial training (Instructional Phase only).

For the purpose of this study, two primary assessments were made. The first involved assessment of children's transition to middle school. The instrument used, the Survey of Middle School Stressors, consists of twenty-eight commonly occurring situations in middle school identified through behavioral analytic procedures as leading to difficulty, distress, or upset feelings (Goldfried & D'Zurilla, 1969). Examples of these stressor situations range from logistical concerns such as forgetting a locker combination and learning the way around a larger new building to mastering new academic routines (having many different teachers, more homework, greater academic pressures) and new relationships with peers (being teased or asked to do things one does not want to do, being approached to smoke or drink, not being part of a desired group, undressing in a locker room). For each stressor, children were asked to rate that it was not a problem, a small problem, a medium problem, or a large problem for them since coming to middle school. In addition to patterns of response on the twenty-eight stressors, summary indices included Problem Frequency (number of stressors rated as a small, medium, or large problem) and Problem Intensity (number of stressors rated as a large problem). The present measure has an internal consistency coefficient greater than .90 across different samples and has been predictive of Piers-Harris Self-Concept scores (Piers & Harris, 1984), school attendance, and teacher ratings of school adjustment using the AML (Elias, Gara, & Ubriaco, 1985). In October of their first year in the sixth grade, all children who received social problem solving instruction were administered the survey. The preceding year, a comparison cohort entering the same middle school received the survey. The second primary assessment involved children's social problem solving skills. The instrument used was the GSPSA.

For the three groups of children, it was found that those entering without training were differentiated from those receiving at least some training in both the extent and severity of situations they considered to be problematic, with regression analyses significant at $p < .05$. Stressors such as peer pressure, academic demands, coping with authority figures, and pressure to become involved in behaviors such as smoking and substance abuse were felt to be significantly more difficult by children in the untrained group. Further, a significant discrimination could also be made between children with different amounts of training, in the expected direction, multivariate $F(282\ 107) = 1.62, p < .04$. Perhaps most important, a canonical analysis of the relationship of all children's social problem solving abilities to their responses to stressors indicated a significant inverse relationship of Problem Analysis and Action and Specificity of Planning with severity of stressors, multivariate $F(9, 326) = 2.00, p < .04$.

Overall, the results indicate a positive association between level of training and children's reports of coping with stressors and adjusting to middle school, and suggest that training in social decision making and social problem solving is an important aspect of this shared variance. These results cannot be accounted for by preexisting differences related to the children's elementary schools nor to marked differences in the degree of stressors encountered by students from one year to the next. Empirical support was found to suggest that a consistent mediating factor in children's responding to stressors was their social problem solving skills—most specifically, Problem Analysis and Action. These findings were obtained approximately four months after the conclusion of any formal training, including an intervening summer. None of the cues traditionally associated with the maintenance of an intervention (physical environment, prompts by a trained teacher, continued contact with the group within which training occurred) were available to the children. Furthermore, they were subjected to a transitional life event—middle school entry—with well-documented destabilizing influences on a "normal" population (Elias et al., 1985; Lipsitz, 1977; Toepfer & Marani, 1980).

Further, we have examined the function of explicit practice in SDM skills on the reduction of stress in the same situation, the transition to middle school, with the goal of exploring the difference between mere exposure to the social problem solving language, skills, and concepts, and systematic training in the use of those skills. We feel that the practice provided in the Application Phase, which is not included in many other problem-solving programs, is important in developing reflection and self-regulation, which ensure that the skill will be accessible in novel, real-life situations.

For this study, we chose a site, Clifton, where SDM/SPS is taught throughout the district. Half the students studied had formed an original control group for pilot studies and had never been explicitly trained. However, in a district of approximately three thousand first to fifth graders, which is thoroughly permeated with the program and language (including classroom posters of the problem-solving steps), it was unlikely that the sixth-grade control group would be oblivious to program concepts. We therefore decided to undertake an analysis of the strength of relations between knowledge of SDM skills and real-life outcomes, comparing sixth graders with exposure to problem-solving concepts and language with those who had received explicit training and opportunities to practice their skills. The staff hypothesized that by sixth grade there might be few differences between the two groups on a paper-and-pencil measure like the Group Social Problem Solving Assessment, but that real differences would emerge in terms of how well that knowledge would mediate stress or predict self-esteem. The new analysis, therefore, is in more depth, focusing on mediating factors.

All 623 sixth graders entering the two middle schools in the Clifton district completed the Survey of Middle School Stressors (which was used in our original validation study), the Piers-Harris Self-Concept Scale, and the Group Social Problem Solving Assessment (also used in the original study). Since Clifton is a district with a highly mobile population, the staff screened out students who had transferred into the district after third grade. This resulted in an experimental group of 175 students with three or more years of SDM/SPS training and a control group of 159 students who had been exposed to program concepts but had never been explicitly trained to use them.

As anticipated, the GSPSA did not discriminate between the two groups. Nor did their scores differ for the Survey of Middle School Stressors or the Piers-Harris. However, real differences emerged when we examined the strength of relationships within each group. The Survey of Middle School Stressors (SMSS) provides reliable subscales for stress arising from four different sources: conflicts with authority and older students, peer relationships, academic pressure, and substance abuse (alphas = .61 to .93). For the control group, there were no relationships between scores on the three GSPSA subscales (Interpersonal Sensitivity, Problem Analysis, and Planning) and scores on the SMSS subscales, with the exception of a counterintuitive positive relationship between Problem Analysis and stress from peer relationships ($r = .18$, $p < .03$). In contrast, as Table 8 shows, those sixth graders who had received three or more years of explicit SDM training had significant negative relationships between scores on both Interpersonal Sensitivity and Problem Analysis with stress from conflicts with authority and from academic pressure. Planning was also significantly negatively related to experiencing stress from academic pressure.

Similarly, when we examined the relations between self-esteem and social problem solving skills, a sharp distinction emerged between the two groups. The Piers-Harris contains eighty true-false items covering areas such as intellectual and school status, positive behavior, popularity, low anxiety, happiness, and physical attractiveness. A modified forty-four–item scale was used, in which all cross-loading items had been eliminated. The modified scale has an internal consistency of .85 and a six-month test-retest reliability of $r = .73$, and it has been used by other researchers in previous studies. Again, there were no relationships between the GSPSA subscales and the Piers-Harris score for the control group. However, as Table 8 shows, performance on all three GSPSA subscales related to the Piers-Harris Self-Concept score for the experimental group. A further examination of the relationships indicates that when children are explicitly trained in social problem solving skills, a good command of problem analysis predicts their sense of their intellectual and school status ($r = .30$, $p < .0001$), while planning skill is associated with positive behavior ($r = .21$, $p < .005$), low anxiety ($r = .16$, $p < .04$), and intellectual and school status ($r = .29$, $p < .0001$). Highly developed skills in interpersonal sensitivity are related to happiness

Table 8   Correlations Between GSPSA Subscales and Survey of Middle School Stressors and Piers-Harris Scores for the Experimental Group

	Interpersonal Sensitivity	Problem Analysis	Planning
SMSS: Conflicts with Authority	–.22**	–.18*	–.14
SMSS: Academic Pressure	–.23**	–.22**	–.31***
Piers-Harris	.43***	.25**	.29***

$* p < .05$, $** p < .005$, $*** p < .0001$

$(r = .29, p < .0002)$, low anxiety $(r = .17, p < .03)$, positive behavior $(r = .31, p < .0001)$, and intellectual and school status $(r = .42, p < .0001)$. Clearly, students who have highly developed interpersonal and problem-solving skills as a result of explicit training and practice are in a better position to cope with real-life stresses such as the transition to middle school, and they have improved self-esteem.

Claim 4: After receiving varying amounts of exposure to the program in elementary school, students followed up in high school showed high levels of positive, prosocial behavior and decreased antisocial, self-destructive, and socially disordered behavior, when compared with controls who did not receive instruction.

The design of the study (Elias et al., 1991) involved a comparison of three cohorts of students who received social decision making and social problem solving instruction in elementary school. Cohorts received different amounts or different levels of instructional fidelity to the program, according to the distribution shown in Table 9.

Children did not know the purpose of the study, and the participation rate exceeded 95 percent. The measures used were the National Youth Survey (NYS) of Antisocial and Delinquent Behaviors (Elliot et al., 1983) and the Youth Self-Report (YSR) Rating Scale (Achenbach & Edelbrock, 1987). Both are self-report, standardized, and have been validated against external behavioral indices. The NYS consists of forty-two items covering vandalism; theft; use of various illegal substances; aggressive behavior toward

Table 9   Experience of High School Follow-Up Group

Grade in High School at Time of Follow-Up[a]	Time Elapsed Since End of SDM Program (years)	Program Received[b] (years)	Components[c]
Grade 9	3	2 (H,P vs. C,W)	2R + 2I + A
Grade 10 (a)	4	2	R + 2I + A
Grade 10 (b)	4	1.5	2I + A
Grade 11 (a)	5	1	I + A
Grade 11 (b)	5	.5	I

[a] For grades 9–11, there was a no-treatment control.

[b] Of the four schools per grade (H, P, C, and W), implementation fidelity was consistently rated higher at two schools (H and P).

[c] R = Readiness, I = Instructional, A = Application; 2 = repeated in Grades 4 and 5.

parents, peers, and other adults; cheating at school; lying about one's age; facilitating others' lying about their age; and school-based discipline problems. The YSR taps six factors: depression, unpopularity, aggression, delinquency, somatic complaints, and thought disorders (an additional factor, self-destruction/identity problems, is scored for boys only). There is also a competence assessment, including overall social competence and positive social activity.

Results of analyses of variance indicated that, relative to ninth-grade controls, ninth-grade program students made significantly less use of alcoholic beverages; had fewer self-destructive/identity problems; had higher scores in overall social competence, membership, and participation in positive social organizations; a higher level of participation in nonsports activities; and a higher level of quality of on-the-job work. Tenth-grade control students were significantly higher than tenth-grade program students in vandalism against school property, attacking persons with intent to injure, hitting or threatening other students, self-destructive/identity problems, and unpopularity. They also showed lower scores in overall social competence. Eleventh-grade control students were significantly higher than eleventh-grade program students in vandalism against parental property, hitting or threatening parents, and use of chewing tobacco. Across grades, male controls significantly exceeded male program recipients in petty theft and in buying or providing alcohol for someone else. The overall pattern of findings also indicated that students receiving the higher-fidelity program implementation generally showed better goal attainment than those receiving lower-fidelity implementation. It should be noted that these results reflect generally low base rates, as well as no correction for attenuation and no program of follow-up in the middle school.

PROGRAM SATISFACTION QUESTIONNAIRES

From the inception of the program of research, students, teachers, parents, and administrators have been given our Program Satisfaction measures to complete. The general format of these surveys involves asking how much the lessons were liked and how much they should be used in the future. In addition, specific components of the program are listed and respondents are asked to rate the extent to which components are liked or seen as effective. Also, open-ended questions elicit nominations of which children are more or less affected (and why), and respondents are asked for suggestions regarding how the program can be improved.

Program Satisfaction measures are recommended for all first-year implementation efforts, along with measures to monitoring implementation. We also recommend that student outcome measures ideally be added to the battery in the second year of implementation rather than the first year (unless funding or other reasons make this impossible) due to a contamination in the first year of student skill gains with teacher professional skill gains. Program Satisfaction results, however, are very valuable in every phase of implementation, as important input to assess program effectiveness and to target areas in need of modification.

All district-level evaluations ever done since the start of our work in 1979 would be impossible to collect for this report, as many of those we collected are now archived or have remained in in-house district documents. In general, districts report that student and teacher satisfaction normally ranges over 95 percent in areas of enjoyment and recommendations to continue. In addition, more than 90 percent of teachers and students report using the skills that they have been learning to solve everyday life problems. These responses have been extremely valuable as face-valid data in presentations to the school board, parent groups, and funders. Teacher reports most often describe the use of skills to solve peer relationship problems, while student reports in the first year focus on the use of self-calming to avoid the escalation of a conflict with a sibling or peer.

ANECDOTAL EVIDENCE

Perhaps the most satisfying aspect of our work comes from the large numbers of stories staff members hear from those implementing SDM/SPS. As mentioned, the consumer satisfaction surveys provide great examples, ranging from a class coming together to share feelings and help one another cope with the death of a family member, classmate, or even a pet, or with a national tragedy such as that occurring at Columbine High School. Student anecdotes are heartwarming and describe coping with a difficult person, a stressful situation, or their own feelings. A third grader once reported using "Keep Calm" to help him in a baseball game when up to bat with two strikes. Besides reporting that his use of self-calming had helped him to make a hit, he added, "And so, when I am an all star hitter for the Yankees, I will always think back to the third grade when I learned Keep Calm."

Anecdotes just as often speak to how the procedures and methods help group functioning and productivity. A first-grade teacher reported how a small group of boys came in from the playground and told her that they needed to have a Sharing Circle. On their own they formed a circle of chairs in the back of the room, chose a Speaker Power object and took turns giving their point of view about something that had happened on the playground. She said she watched in awe. After about ten minutes of serious exchange the group brought their chairs back to their desks and let her know that they were finished. Just a few days later, a group of girls requested some time to have a circle, too. The teacher reported that the students had exceeded her expectations for taking responsibility for their own feelings and relationships once she had established the procedures and introduced the class to some tools.

A principal of a northern New Jersey school reported a variety of anecdotal indicators that she uses to monitor the effectiveness of programming in her building. "I'm not spending all my time dealing with uncomfortable situations, but instead spend more time working on improving the school, improving communications with parents by explaining what the child is doing in the area of social-emotional learning, and teaching them the program's language. Detention used to contain twenty kids before the program; now there are about two. It used to take fifteen to twenty minutes to calm everyone down enough after lunch to start class. Now, any bickering stops once they walk in the door. My Peer Peacemakers tell me there are fewer physical fights, not as many arguments, and the students are calmer."

"I can also see a difference in self-esteem," the same principal added. "Children aren't easily able to fall into peer pressure. They aren't afraid to speak out. There is better behavior at home. Children understand the common language and the expectations. The students use it every day in situations not just at school but on the playground and at home with siblings. They try to live up to it, and though they may not always do it, you can tell that they are trying. They feel a sense of responsibility. They feel a sense of community and pride for the school, the teachers, and other students. They even use it to help out the teachers. A teacher reported to me, 'I was getting upset, and one of the kids told me to Keep Calm. It does come back to you!'"

An independent site visitor (Elias et al., 1997) obtained the following interview report, which quotes a central New Jersey community's recreation director, as cited in a local newspaper article, regarding his participation in a community sharing circle of city officials including the mayor's office and town counsel and sixth-grade students. "Our town, like so many other communities, had been experiencing an increase in incidents of vandalism. Most vandals are early to mid-teenagers. I felt that getting sixth graders involved in controlling vandalism could raise their level of awareness and, hopefully, prevent them from turning into future vandals themselves."

The response of the school district, according to this recreation leader, "took his overture and turned it into a full-scale symphony." The sixth-grade students worked together over a course of the school year, using their social decision making skills to develop proposals to solve this problem, and their efforts culminated at the end of the year in a convocation where student representatives gave presentations of the proposals they had developed. After the presentations, the director said, "I was very impressed with the seriousness with which the students pursued this. I was overwhelmed with the response. I will provide a written report to the mayor and town council, and I believe they will approve these suggestions. I think that what the kids are learning through this process is far more significant than the proposals. I told them that what they are learning are life skills: Compromise, sharing, teamwork, seeking advice from peers" (Denker, 1999, p. 18).

Appendix B

Tools for Program-Level Assessment

SDM/SPS Curriculum Feedback

Teachers/leaders _____ **Date** _____

Class period and group worked with _____

1. General outline of lesson or class activities:

   _____

   _____

2. Student reactions to this session (for whom was it most or least effective):

   _____

   _____

3. Most effective or favorable aspects of this session:

   _____

   _____

4. Least effective or favorable aspects of this session:

   _____

   _____

5. Points to follow up in the next meeting:

   _____

   _____

6. Points to follow up in the following weeks outside group meetings (that is, in other class periods, other school settings, outside of school):

   _____

   _____

7. Suggested changes in this activity for the future:

   _____

   _____

Profile of Social Decision Making/Social Problem Solving Strengths

Student _____ Date _____

Observer _____ Title/position _____

Record your observation for each student by using this simple mastery rating, adjusted to appropriate age, grade, and ability expectations.

1 = Clearly does not demonstrate a satisfactory level

2 = Level in this area is uncertain

3 = Clearly demonstrates a satisfactory level

	To what extent can this child:	**Observation** *(circle one)*		
A. Readiness Area				
1. Self-control	1a. Listen carefully and accurately	1	2	3
	1b. Remember and follow directions	1	2	3
	1c. Concentrate and follow through on tasks	1	2	3
	1d. Calm himself or herself down	1	2	3
	1e. Carry on a conversation without upsetting or provoking others	1	2	3
2. Social Awareness	2a. Accept praise or approval	1	2	3
	2b. Choose praiseworthy and caring friends	1	2	3
	2c. Know when help is needed	1	2	3
	2d. Ask for help when needed	1	2	3
	2e. Work as part of a problem-solving team	1	2	3
B. Social Decision Making/Social Problem Solving Area				
1. Feelings	1a. Recognize signs of personal feelings	1	2	3
	1b. Recognize signs of feelings in others	1	2	3
	1c. Accurately describe a range of feelings	1	2	3
2. Problems	2a. Clearly put problems into words	1	2	3
3. Goals	3a. State realistic interpersonal goals	1	2	3
4. Alternatives	4a. Think of several ways to solve a problem or reach a goal	1	2	3
	4b. Think of different types of solutions	1	2	3
	4c. Do (a) and (b) for different types of problems	1	2	3

		To what extent can this child:	Observation *(circle one)*		
5. Consequences	5a.	Differentiate short- *and* long-term consequences	1	2	3
	5b.	Look at effects on self *and* others	1	2	3
	5c.	Keep positive *and* negative possibilities in mind	1	2	3
6. Choose	6a.	Select solutions that can reach goals	1	2	3
	6b.	Make choices that do not harm self or others	1	2	3
7. Plan and Check	7a.	Consider details before carrying out a solution (who, when, where, with whom, and so on)	1	2	3
	7b.	Anticipate obstacles	1	2	3
	7c.	Respond appropriately when plans are thwarted	1	2	3
8. Learn for Next Time	8a.	Try out ideas	1	2	3
	8b.	Learn from experience or from seeking input from adults and friends	1	2	3
	8c.	Use previous experience to help next time	1	2	3

References

Achenbach, T., & Edelbrock, C. (1987). *Manual for the Youth Self-Report and Profile*. Burlington: University of Vermont, Department of Psychiatry.

Bruene Butler, L., Hampson, J., Elias, M. J., Clabby, J. F., & Schuyler, T. (1997). The improving social awareness—social problem solving project. In G. Albee and T. Gullotta (Eds.), *Primary prevention works: Issues in children's and families' lives* (Vol. 6). Thousand Oaks, CA: Sage.

Denker, M. (1999, May 27). Vandalism as a learning tool. *Newark, New Jersey, Star Ledger*, p. 18.

Elias, M. J., Gara, M., Schuyler, T., Branden-Muller, L. R., & Sayette, M. A. (1991). The promotion of social competence: Longitudinal study of a preventive school-based program. *American Journal of Orthopsychiatry, 61*, 409–417.

Elias, M. J., Gara, M., & Ubriaco, M. (1985). Sources of stress and coping in children's transition to middle school: An empirical analysis. *Journal of Clinical Child Psychology, 14*, 112–118.

Elias, M. J., Gara, M., Ubriaco, M., Rothbaum, P. A., Clabby, J. F., & Schuyler, T. (1986). Impact of a preventive social problem solving intervention on children's coping with middle-school stressors. *American Journal of Community Psychology, 14*(3), 259–275.

Elias, M. J., Zins, J. E., Weissberg, R. P., Frey, K. S., Greenberg, M. T., Haynes, N. M., Kessler, R., Schwab-Stone, M. E., & Shriver, T. P. (1997). *Promoting social and emotional learning: Guidelines for educators*. Alexandria, VA: Association for Supervision and Curriculum Development.

Elliot, D. et al. (1983). *The prevalence and incidence of delinquent behavior: The National Youth Survey Report No. 26*. Boulder: Behavioral Research Institute.

Goldfried, M., & D'Zurilla, T. (1969). A behavioral-analytic model for assessing competence. In C. Spielberger (Ed.), *Current topics in clinical and community psychology*. New York: Academic Press.

Lipsitz, J. (1977). *Growing up forgotten: A review of research and programs concerning early adolescence*. Lexington, MA: Lexington Books.

Norris, J. A. (1998). *Promoting social competence and reducing violence and negative social interaction in a multicultural school setting*. Unpublished doctoral dissertation, Graduate School of Education, Rutgers University, New Brunswick, NJ.

Piers, E. V., & Harris, D. B. (1984). *Piers-Harris Children's Self-Concept Scale—Revised manual.* Los Angeles: Western Psychological Services.

Thurston, C. J. (1998). *A systems approach to the evaluation of a social and emotional development program for emotionally disturbed elementary school students in a private special education facility.* Unpublished doctoral dissertation, Graduate School of Applied and Professional Psychology, Rutgers University, New Brunswick, NJ.

Toepfer, C., & Marani, J. (1980). School-based research. In M. Johnson (Ed.), *Toward adolescence: The middle school years. Seventy-ninth yearbook of the National Society for the Study of Education.* University of Chicago Press.

About the Authors

MAURICE J. ELIAS, Ph.D., is professor, Department of Psychology, Rutgers University, and directs the Rutgers Social-Emotional Learning Lab. He is vice chair of the Leadership Team of the Collaborative for Academic, Social, and Emotional Learning (www.CASEL.org) and senior advisor for Research, Policy, and Practice to the New Jersey Center for Character Education. He devotes his research and writing to the area of emotional intelligence in children, schools, and families. His books for parents include *Emotionally Intelligent Parenting: How to Raise a Self-Disciplined, Responsible and Socially Skilled Child* (Three Rivers Press, 2000) and *Raising Emotionally Intelligent Teenagers: Guiding the Way for Compassionate, Committed, Courageous Adults* (Three Rivers Press, 2002), both published in several languages. His recent releases are *Engaging the Resistant Child Through Computers: A Manual for Social-Emotional Learning* (available through www.nprinc.com), *Building Learning Communities with Character: How to Integrate Academic, Social, and Emotional Learning* (Association for Supervision and Curriculum Development, 2003), and *EQ + IQ = Best Leadership Practices for Caring and Successful Schools* (Corwin Press, 2003), as well as *Bullying, Peer Harassment, and Victimization in the Schools: The Next Generation of Prevention* (Haworth, 2004). Dr. Elias is married and the father of two children.

LINDA BRUENE BUTLER, M.Ed., has worked on the development of school-based programs in social and emotional learning for over two decades. Currently, she is director of the Social Decision Making/Social Problem Solving (SDM/SPS) Program at the Behavioral Research and Training Institute of the University of Medicine and Dentistry of New Jersey, University Behavioral HealthCare's Behavioral Research and Training Institute. She has also served as adjunct faculty for courses in the area of social-emotional learning at the Department of Psychology, Rutgers University; Teachers College, Columbia University; and Department of Psychology, University of Illinois. Ms. Bruene Butler has published and lectured extensively in the area of social-emotional learning and has trained many others to become SDM/SPS consultants and trainers. Her current area of interest is exploring ways that distance learning methods can be used to share and evaluate innovative methods for promoting social-emotional learning.

ERIN M. BRUNO is clinician supervisor at the SDM/SPS Program at the Behavioral Research and Training Institute of the University of Medicine and Dentistry of New Jersey. After receiving her master's degree in drama therapy from New York University in 1997, Ms. Bruno worked as a therapist and school consultant in the area of social and emotional learning. She has extensive experience assisting schools in adopting the SDM/SPS curricula.

MAUREEN REILLY PAPKE is a program development specialist at the SDM/SPS Program at the Behavioral Research and Training Institute of the University of Medicine and Dentistry of New Jersey. In this role since 1989, Ms. Papke has provided training and consultation services to educators at all grade levels as they implement this social and emotional learning program.

TERESA FARLEY SHAPIRO, Ph.D., is a program development specialist and trainer for the SDM/SPS Program at the University of Medicine and Dentistry of New Jersey. Dr. Shapiro is a New Jersey–certified school psychologist. Within the school setting, she has provided a variety of counseling services utilizing SDM/SPS, with both regular and special education populations.